EMBARRASSING SEXUAL MISADVENTURES

D0059125

First published as 1001 *Ridiculous Sexual Misadventures*
in Great Britain in 2009 by Prion
This edition published in 2018 by Prion
an imprint of the
Carlton Publishing Group
20 Mortimer Street
London W1T 3JW

A CIP catalogue for this book is available from the British Library.

ISBN 978-1-91161-016-8

Printed in Great Britain

EMBARRASSING SEXUAL MISADVENTURES

1001 OF THE MOST TRAGICALLY HILARIOUS SEXPLOITS EVER

Gina McKinnon

PRION

INTRODUCTION

There is no worse form of humiliation, nothing more cringe-making, no lower low, than erotic embarrassment. Perhaps you've woken up one morning next to last night's supposed stunner, only to realize as the beer-fog lifted that they more resembled the back of a bus. Maybe you've overheard your current flame telling the world about your lack of sexual prowess. Or perchance your only moment of sexual shame was getting caught with Mrs Palmer and her five lovely daughters in the office loos. Even the couples among us may have blushed with carnal mortification, perhaps being discovered in *flagrante delicto* by the in-laws, getting laid in a lay-by, or being caught out by him or her indoors.

Relax. Your sexploits are nothing compared to the weird and wonderful goings on collected in this ribald little book. In its pages you will find the largest collection ever of hilarious stories chronicling the bizarre, amazing and absurd ways of being caught in the act of mating (with a partner and 'practising' alone, or with a pet). With over 1,001, yes 1,001, factual accounts of bad bonking, fruitless fornication and misplaced masturbation, the books presents a host of cautionary tales about the undignified ways you can be caught getting your rocks off.

From titillating but true tales from Joe and Jane public, star-studded sex scandals and downright deviant tales from across the globe, this is a rollicking roll call of the sexual

across the globe, this is a rollicking roll call of the sexual misadventurers whose private lives have brought them public shame – and unwanted fame. Alongside entertaining records of stupid shaggers and moronic masturbators, *Embarrassing Sexual Misadventures* also includes a series of unique 'top tens' to dish the dirt on the insatiable lust, the overactive libido and the depths of sexual depravity to which humankind stoops on an all too regular basis.

The internet and other media are fair bogged down with such tawdry tales, with local news sources from every corner of the globe to the major broadcasters and newspapers reporting on such sexual slip ups on an almost daily basis. Bad news for the silly shaggers who risk world-wide fame for their amoral antics. With modern technology, the act of public perversion reported on one side of the world is picked up by news agencies from New York to Nepal in a matter of minutes. Good news for websites, the TV news channels, and newspapers. They know which side their bread is buttered, and the old saying 'sex sells' is never truer than when the reported activities involve a sheep, a hoover or a lamp-post.

people like the Scottish man who attempted sex with a bicycle, the Thai student who inserted a compressed air hose in his derrière, or the Polish woman who tried to use an electric food mixer as a sex-toy. Nor do they dig deep and reveal what possessed the British couple to have sex on a Dubai beach, the Dutch lovers who had sex on top of a police car, or the Italian couple whose sexual shenanigans caused a motorway pile-up. The truth is, that the motivation for such activity is by the by. What journalists and broadcasters know is that we, the consumer, will never tire of these true stories of wanton woe. On the one hand we hope they will serve as a warning to all the wannabe flashers, gropers and wankers out there, on the other hand (and if we're being honest) they make for a pumping good read!

So, if you think your sex life is a disaster, think again. And for all the verification you need, kick back, relax, and enjoy all 1,001 online outrages, carnal catastrophes and hilarious cock-ups included in this book. A book which proves once and for all that shady sex stories and hilarity make perfect bedfellows. And that your own sex life... Well, it's a bit on the boring side isn't it, really?

TAKEN FOR A RIDE

When nobody answered the persistent knocks of two female cleaners at one of the rooms in the Aberley House Hostel in Ayr, Scotland, the staff did the usual thing and barged in with their master key. What they came across could hardly be described as usual, however. Naked below the waist, clothed only in a white t-shirt, they found the room's occupant, one Mr James Finlay, 51, engaged in a sexual act with his bicycle.

Obviously a strong defender of bicycle rights, the hostel manager complained to the police. The cleaners went on to explain to prosecutor Helen Cole that they had seen 'the accused... holding the bike and moving his hips back and forth as if to simulate sex.' He was eventually charged with sexual breach of the peace.

The case threw up a whole heap of questions from bloggers on the world-wide web – one of the most common being, 'how on earth does one have sex with a bicycle?' Another common question asked was, "What do you call someone with a passion for pedals and metal?" A bike-sexual, perhaps? Hmm, tricky.

Let's leave the official answer to the Sheriff overseeing the case, Mr Craig Jones, who placed the unfortunate Mr Finlay on the sex offenders' register for three years in October 2007. In his summing up, the Sheriff said, "In almost four decades of the law I thought I had come across every perversion known to mankind, but this is a new one on me. I have never heard of a 'cycle-sexualist.'"

DOUBLE-DECKERED DEBACLE

Persistent kerb-crawlers in England face fines of up to £1,000 and can be disqualified from driving. Not the most sensible thing for a bus-driver to do, then. Agreed? And if you really must be a sad purchaser of sex, then surely an inconspicuous vehicle would be your transportation of choice. Yes?

Well, believe it or not, one Cristoval Guiarro said 'no' to both those questions, choosing in 2003 to kerb crawl in a red double-decker number 57 bus. But wait – it gets worse. The bungling bus-driver didn't even manage to pick up a prostitute. As he drove up to the kerb in his bus and offered a charming young lady £300 for sex, he was promptly arrested by police in Streatham, London, who were carrying out a huge undercover operation to clean up local streets.

THE PROPHET OF THE CONDOM

It is now, one hopes, an irrefutable fact that unprotected sex can lead to AIDS or indeed any other disease of the itchy and scratchy variety. Nothing funny or ridiculous about that you might say. Indeed. It's just that, in certain cases, the safe sex message can be taken a little too far.

I'm thinking here of Mr Gabriele Paolini, a man who so staunchly believes in advocating condom use that it has catapulted him into the *Guinness Book of Records* as the world's most prolific TV prankster. The self-proclaimed Prophylactic Prophet has popped up uninvited over 18,000 times on Italian television to promote his cause, having variously: waved chains of condoms or fake willies during serious TV programmes; hidden a condom in a newspaper which he then presented to Pope John Paul II; and interrupted the state broadcast channel RAI in 2001 during an important transmission. On a more sombre note, for this latter contraceptive-promotion-caper Mr Paolini received a three-month suspended jail sentence early in 2008.

You could say he's no Johnny-Come-Lately when it comes to getting his safe sex message across. Boom, boom.

THE CAR IS THE PLACE MOST ADULTS HAVE HAD SEX OUTSIDE OF THEIR BEDROOM

PUMP IT UP # 1

In 2008, 35 fire-fighters in the Texan state capital got into trouble for viewing pornographic websites on the job. The revelation came only a week after two other fire fighters had been suspended for having sexually explicit material on their work computers.

A RISKY BUSINESS

There are a litany of excuses to avoid sex with the one you love. From the unisex "I've got a headache", to "It's my time of the month," (girls) or 'I've got a sporting injury,' (boys).

It takes a heck of an imagination and one helluva low libido to go to the lengths that one Croatian man did, however. He cheered idiot-lovers the world-wide-web over when he set fire to his own home in order to avoid intercourse with his dear lady wife.

The red-faced reprobate would later regret becoming a fire-starter – a twisted fire-starter – when he got a bill for £15,000 and a two-year prison sentence. Which begs the question: If he no longer fancied her, surely it would have been less onerous to simply ask for a divorce?

SAUCY STICK-UP

Qualified chef Lex O'Connor thought he'd cooked up a brilliant plan when he used a vibrator concealed in a carrier bag to hold up a betting shop in Leicester in 2006. The terrified cashier assumed what was being pointed at her could only be a gun and handed over £613 in cash.

Information from the trial tells us more about the ridiculous robber's character. Over to Tim Palmer for the prosecution. "In fact, what was contained within the carrier bag was the defendant's girlfriend's vibrator." Pah. The stingy git didn't even use his own vibrator to carry out the dastardly deed.

44% OF ADULTS WORLDWIDE HAVE HAD A ONE-NIGHT STAND

Anyway. He'd have saved himself five years in the slammer if he hadn't pretended the vibrator was a firearm, so I'll leave you to ponder this: wouldn't shouting 'Stick-Up' with a second-hand Rampant Rabbit have had the same terrifying effect on the cashier?

'PASSION-PARTY' POOPERS

Texas, USA, 2003. By way of reinforcing the idiocy of this particular misadventure, let's firstly remember that in this state, guns and rifles can be purchased without a licence.

Pity, then, poor Joanne Webb who wasn't selling guns, or any other lethal item*. Rather, Joanne's job was to run 'Passion Parties' selling 'adult novelties' to groups of women at parties – a bit like a Tupperware party, only the plastic items on sale have been moulded into altogether ruder shapes.

In 2003, CNN broke the story that Mrs Webb had been arrested by undercover narcotic agents and had been charged with an obscenity law for selling items "designed or marketed as useful primarily for the stimulation of human genital organs." After huge media coverage, the threat of a one year prison sentence or $4,000 fine never materialised, and in 2008 the Texan law making it a crime to sell or promote sex toys was overturned.

* Disclaimer: I can't guarantee that some idiot or other later in this book won't use a sex toy as a deadly weapon and prove me wrong.

CAN'T BEAT THIS

A French pop star was convicted in 2007 of falsely imprisoning a male escort. The victim, from Scotland, said the musician beat him with a metal chain as he tried to escape from his flat after a naked photo shoot.

SEVEN US PRESIDENTS ARE KNOWN TO HAVE HAD EXTRA-MARITAL AFFAIRS

SNAP!

A 38-year-old man from Essex, England, felt tremendous pain and heard a loud "pop!" while trying to have sex with his wife in 2006. It turned out he had suffered a penile fracture – the lights were out, he missed the target, and banged into her pelvis. Rupert Macintosh's wife Anna told reporters: "We were having sex and he missed and broke his willy." Macintosh didn't get to spare any blushes after the sexcapade, and urologists were able to perform emergency surgery and repair his broken penis.

VIAGRA VICAR VENDETTA SHOCKER!

We'd be excused for thinking that tales of poison-pen letters to mild-mannered country village vicars exist only in Agatha Christie novels, wouldn't we? But a story of a GP and his vengeful undertaker lover will soon have us rethinking our position. In fact you couldn't make up the following plot:

A woman claims to her lover that she's had an affair with the married local vicar. The pair conduct a two-year hate campaign commencing with vile and sexually abusive letters – one of which accuses said vicar of being a 'fatty fuck face'. Pornography is strewn across the victim's car. Gay sex magazines are delivered to his home. Perverted nuisance phone calls are made... alright, you get the picture. The unnamed vicar was not top of Doctor Mick O'Rourke and girlfriend Sally Harrop's Christmas card list.

In 2005, when the pair took the wheel nuts off his car, the vicar decided enough was enough, and police soon arrested the pervy plotters. A list of planned physical assaults was found on O'Rourke's computer, including lacing the vicar's drink with an overdose of Viagra – a list which the couple claimed were the basis for a novel. Which goes once and for all to prove that truth is indeed stranger than fiction. Miss Marple eat your heart out.

THE GLOBAL AVERAGE AGE FOR LOSING YOUR VIRGINITY IS 17.3

HARD TO SWALLOW

After weeks of persistent coughing, phlegm and fevers, 26-year-old Amanda Harmsworth finally visited her GP in Berwick-Upon-Tweed, England. He sent her for an X-ray which quickly revealed the cause of her illness – she had accidentally inhaled a condom during fellatio a few weeks earlier.

IN HOT WATER

Curiosity got the better of Gemma Humphries in her parent's Jacuzzi on September 5, 1999. Directing the air jets toward her sex parts for a thrill left her in hospital with air in her abdomen and acute abdominal pain. The doctor's verdict: "Jacuzzi-jet induced misfortune."

VIAGRA GIVES BRIGHTON MAN THE BLUES

It was *The Sun* newspaper that reported the 2003 story of a man from Brighton, England, who was living his life as a never-ending 'blue movie.' Nope, not a porn addict – we'll come to that sort of person later – but rather an object lesson in not ignoring your GP's advice on limiting the use of Viagra.

For a year, John 'I Admit I Ignored the Advice on the Packet But I Was Having Too Much Fun' Pettigrew had been having trouble maintaining his erection. When the pills his GP prescribed worked wonders for his willy, he thought it sensible to purchase more of the wonder drug from t'interweb. A lot more... Little did he realize that one of the side-effects of the blue pills (there's a clue in the name here) is that they can give the user's vision a blue tint. At the time the report broke, the over-enthusiastic pill-popper had been seeing the world in a blue hue for over a fortnight.

GLOBALLY, 15% OF PEOPLE HAVE HAD SEX AT WORK

CREAM CRACKERS

Imagine the scene. There you are, a lady with a rash of white spots around your anus, which you think is the return of typhoid you'd previously picked up in foreign climes. You go to the doctor and discover that the rash is in fact a hefty and unwelcome dose of the clap. So what do you do – listen to the advice of your doctor and go back to her for treatment, or trust a man who tells you that allowing him to smear a cream on the end of his penis and penetrate you with it anally will cure you of your ills?

I know. It's amazing. But the victim of Britannia Airlines pilot Farrad Massri chose the latter option and further more – it was alleged in Swansea Crown Court – even paid the bogus healer vast sums of cash for the amount the 'expensive cream' purportedly cost. I don't know what's more worrying about this story. Whether it was true rather than an elaborate fabrication, or whether the alleged victim teacher quite literally did not seem to know her anus from her elbow.

DIG IT!

Two gay lovers on a Norfolk, England, farm inventively used the hydraulic shovels on tractors to suspend themselves for masochistic sexual stimulation in 2002. In the carnal calamity that followed, one of the men died from asphyxiation as the chain suspending him from the shovel got trapped around his neck.

SEX JOBS FOR THE GIRLS

Germany. Lovely country: great beer, friendly folk, stunning forests and vibrant cities. What's more, they don't half like getting their kits off. I've been to parks in Berlin, Munich and Hamburg, so I know what I'm talking about. All of these cities have red-light districts that would make an Amsterdam resident blush, too.

So it wasn't a massive shock when English media reported in 2005 that German women, under new employment benefit laws, could be required to work in the sex industry or lose their benefits once they'd been unemployed for a year or more. "How enlightened," the pervs amongst you enthusiastically cry. "How depraved," the feminists!

Calm down there, both sides. The story turned out to have been a poor translation of a German news report, and is thus a misadventure of the journalistic kind.

WHAT A SLAPPER

It's usually women who are given the nomenclature of slapper – although thankfully the sexist term is dying out. But it seems an apt one for the man who lost it over his girlfriend's constant demands for sex. After her nightly nagging became too much and she tried to (a)rouse him from much needed sleep, he slapped her in the face, and ended up in court on charges of assault. The Judge decided that the man had been provoked by his sex-crazed girlfriend and he was not charged for the offence.

AN ARM AND A LEG

Legs have long since been admired as one of the most seductive parts of the human body. A particular leg aficionado is one Charles Cook of Weymouth, England. He was arrested in the 1980s for writhing on the floor pretending to have broken his arm, so he could look up the skirts of any female passers-by who came to his rescue.

COUPLES FROM CHINA ARE THE LEAST LIKELY TO ORGASM DURING SEX

DEATH BY CLINGFILM

Ever considered clingfilm as a lethal weapon? Thought not. Well, think again. On March 24, 2007, graphic designer Stephen Hayes from Chippenham in Wiltshire, England, died from asphyxiation, having wrapped his head in clingfilm, probably after a self-pleasuring sex act went wrong.

Stephen had spent that evening of the 24th at the pub, returning to watch motor-racing on TV with his Dad. Said Dad then found Stephen's body the following day – wearing just one Marigold washing-up glove (with a finger cut off) and the previously mentioned food-wrapping product.

Coroner Peter Hatvany ruled out suicide, noting that Stephen had visited fetishism websites in the previous three days, including a full facial latex website and one for rubber masks. Opting for the cheaper homemade cling-film version led to his untimely demise.

CONCRETE EVIDENCE

You know how the old story goes. Girl meets boy or boy meets boy or boy meets girl and boy. But ever heard the one where boy meets pavement?

In 1993, Craig Tiernan, an electrician from Redditch, England, appeared at Hereford Crown Court charged with five counts of outraging public decency, having been found face down and bare-bottomed in the throes of sexual intercourse with the pavement.

You'd have thought an eighteen month jail sentence would make him see the error of his ways, but no. In 1995, Tiernan repeated his attempts to win the award for 'man with weirdest sexual fetish', reappearing in court for attempted sex with some black plastic bin bags.

We await news of Craig's next carnal adventures with bated breath.

MEXICANS ARE THE NATION MOST LIKELY TO BE SATISFIED BY THEIR ORGASMS

RING-A-RING-A-WASHERS

Ever suffered the mild discomfort of getting a ring stuck on your finger? If yes, a little washing-up liquid and a vat of elbow grease probably did the job to get the bugger off. Now imagine the discomfort, nay, the abject suffering of one Australian man who managed to get sixteen stainless steel washers stuck on his penis.

When ninety minutes of greasing, lubing, and a healthy dose of brute force by Berowa Fire Rescue Officers failed to do the job, the unfortunate experimenter was rushed to nearby Hornsby Hospital. Surgeons used the fire officers' cutting equipment to save the man from the last resort of a penis removal operation. That'll teach him to try to run rings around his manhood.

A MORAL VACUUM # 1

Down under for our next misadventure. No, not another oral sex mishap – this is a tale from our friends in Australia which will leave you humming the theme song to their biggest TV export.

It was 2004 when Brisbane lass Corey Haynes came home to discover her neighbour frolicking in her bathroom with the world's most laughable home-made sex toy* – made from a plank of beech wood, a bottle of washing up liquid and a rubber glove. To make matters worse, the naughty neighbour had also been engaging in an activity that normal folk don't usually associate with a hoover.

Alongside a predictable "it was the drink and drugs wot done it" defence, the perpetrator, one Justin Collymore, denied all wrong doing with the domestic appliance. But Judge Tony Rafer was having none of it, telling the defence lawyer. "I am sure your client didn't hoover the carpets."

Come on, altogether now: "Neighbours, everybody needs..."

* so far in this book... !

COUPLES FROM THE MEDITERRANEAN ARE THE MOST LIKELY TO ORGASM DURING SEX

KNIGHT 'RIDER'

We as a nation are obsessed by the children's TV programmes of our formative years. Depending on how old you are, you'll no doubt fondly remember *Sesame Street*, *Captain Pugwash*, *The A-Team* and *Knight Rider*. One Chris Donald certainly does, particularly the latter programme – and David Hasselhof's camp talking car, KITT. Indeed, Chris remembers KITT so fondly that he publicly blamed the car in Britain's *The Sun* newspaper in 2007 for his adult love of all things related to exhaust pipes, petrol and metal. Chris is one of a growing number of car fetishists who express their sexuality by getting down and dirty with motor vehicles – and for whom 'body work' and 'parts' take on a whole new meaning.

GUYS AND DOLLS

In China, it's not uncommon for Buddhists who have lost loved ones to hold a marriage ceremony between themselves and an object representing the spirit of their dead beloved. But Chang Hsi-hsum raised the stakes – and the comedy value – of the ceremony in 1999, by marrying the spirit of his dead wife in the form of a plastic Barbie doll. The event was observed by well-wishers and family, including Chang's obviously very understanding second wife.

HAZARD OF THE JOB

A woman sought compensation from Florida's Department of Labour and Employment Security for repetitive strain injury in 2007. She had developed the disorder from incessant masturbation while she was a phone sex line operator, had been left crippled with pain in both hands.

SIX OUT OF 10 MEN WOULD RATHER GO TO SLEEP THAN HAVE SEX AT BEDTIME

SEX BOMB

Mild-mannered janitor and concerned citizen Lars Enochsson did the right thing, police said, in calling them in when he discovered a suspect package humming and vibrating in the garage of a block of flats in the Swedish town of Goteborg. Police in turn called bomb disposal experts who were probably relieved, if perplexed, to find the buzzing had died down by the time of their arrival.

Batteries for the ten inch 'Vibro Deluxe Thruster' inside the package had run down as the bomb squad crossed town in busy traffic to the scene of the 'crime.'

(W)HOOVER'S THE DADDY?

When you're bleeding half to death, with the tip of your penis missing, you'd be forgiven for coming up with a lousy excuse for your ridiculous sexual misadventure. But quite how one New Jersey, USA, man thought he'd get away with a story about a random stranger knifing him in the goolies in his own bed is anybody's guess. Needless to say investigators soon got to the bottom of his self-inflicted castration, and discovered his penis had been sliced when he'd attempted to make love to his vacuum cleaner.

AGE DISCRIMINATION

You couldn't make it up. A 70-something playboy from Germany sued a 19-year-old girl for ageism, Bild reported in 2007. Rolf Eden had spent much of his life cavorting with ladies and claimed to have slept with between 2,000 and 3,000 women. When a young lady he was romancing deemed him 'too old' for a sexual encounter, he was forced to take matters into his own hands... and sued.

SEX ON THE JOB TOP TEN

10. Researching this book has shown me that where policemen, doctors, teachers or priests go, a sexual misadventure surely follows. So to Soho, London, in 2004, where two Police Constables were sent out to shoo away ogling onlookers as a porno was filmed outdoors. But instead of stopping the action, the pervy PCs got in on it, and ended up facing another kind of action... of the disciplinary variety.

9. Taxi drivers are known for their money-grabbing natures but one Swedish cabbie took things too far when, in 1989, he charged a passenger with whom he'd been having sex. His bill amounted to over £5,000 to cover cab fare, hotel bills and 'sexual services.' It's not clear if he got a tip.

8. Just when you thought you'd heard the last of Swedish taxi drivers, 14 come along at once – in 2003, caught in a sex sting by a Swedish TV channel. Of 71 men who had been approached by an undercover reporter, believing her to be a lady of the night, 14 were cabbies.

7. A senior transport police officer was cleared of any crime when he had a quickie with a stranger in a public office in 2007 – because he kept his earpiece in. But at an internal hearing in 2008 the officer was sacked, earpiece in or no, and it was noted 'His behaviour was not up to standard.'

6. Earlier in the noughties, a policeman had been sacked by the IPC for engaging in intercourse with a sex worker. He was meant to be investigating a building that was rumoured to be a brothel.

5. A German couple working at a retirement home in Dortmund decided that the further education seminar they'd been sent on wouldn't be any fun. So they told their bosses they'd go and

sneaked off on an S&M holiday for couples instead. The bonkers bondage-lovers both lost their jobs when their plan was rumbled.

4. Here's a modern morality tale of sorts: You live in a sexless marriage so one of you secretly decides to become a prostitute, the other to visit brothels. You can see where this one's going for one Polish couple – one ill-fated and unwelcome chance meeting later, and 14 years of marriage ended in divorce.

3. A naked bathtub sex romp led to three Australian workers being sacked in 2007 after their office Christmas party. Carlie Street had booked a hotel room with two female colleagues to bed down for the night. Instead, she romped with two male colleagues in the bath of the hotel suite, not even pausing for breath when her pal popped in for a pee. She was later reinstated.

2. Doctors and nurses aren't exactly known for their sexual timidity but even for a hospital-based sex scandal, this one is not short on collegial couplings. In 2007, a Sarajevo nurse gave birth to a bouncing baby boy and named up to 20 senior medical men as the possible father. Management at the hospital blew the budget on paternity testing kits, desperate to clear the names of a list of the 20 most influential medical figures in the city.

1. SOMEWHERE OH, OH, OH-VER THE RAINBOW
Sex on the job does not get much weirder than the tales of lust and depravity that emanated from the film set of one of the most well-loved children's movies of all time. While young Dorothy and Toto were filmed skipping down the yellow brick road on the set of The Wizard of Oz, the band of actors playing the charming Munchkins were going at it hammer and tongs in a series of orgies. They apparently were known by workers on the film as "an unholy assembly of pimps, hookers and gamblers." And you thought the Wicked Witch of the West was scary.

KEEP YER PECKER UP

Erectile dysfunction is no laughing matter, affecting men of all ages, races, classes and so on. But I'm willing to bet that any sufferer would have a laugh at the piss-poor technique Zeljko Tupic from Belgrade, Serbia, used to keep his pecker up.

In 2006, it was widely reported that the young man stuck a narrow pencil down his urethra in order to stay erect for a night of passion with a new lover. Newspapers mentioned that his problems began when the pencil shifted during the action, and became lodged in our young hero's bladder. Without wishing to be a pedant, I'd say the problems began when young Mr Tupic decided to take the expression "putting lead in your pencil" just a little too literally.

A GOOD USE OF TAX PAYER'S MONEY?

If you're a money-grubbing moaner who hates to pay their taxes, count yourself lucky you don't live in Norway.

In 1999, the mayor of a remote Norwegian village suggested that holidays should be subsidised for sex-starved bachelors, as the village's population was on the decline. The subsidy would help young men to pay for trips to Asia, Russia and Poland to help them find wives. "For many bachelors, everyday life is tough both socially and emotionally, and we often get contacted by men who want company," Aage Pedersen, the mayor of Kaafjord, told Reuters at the time.

WHAT'S IN A NAME?

Is there room in porn land for two people with the name 'Violet Blue?' Violet Blue, a sex-blogger, author and journalist does not think so. When she discovered that porn actress Ada Mae Johnson had taken on the moniker, she sued for trademark violation and unfair business practice. Until the suit comes to court, Ms Johnson has changed her name to Noname Jane.

WRONGFUL DISMISSAL

A self-medicating sex addict sued his employers when they sacked him from ogling explicit websites on company time and computers. James Pacenza, 58, said he became addicted to online chat rooms after suffering post-traumatic stress disorder from serving in the Vietnam war. His five million dollar wrongful dismissal case with IBM continues.

SOMETHING FISHY

Dolphins are known for their sexual proclivity – recent research has shown they enjoy cavorting with both opposite and same sex partners just for the fun of it. Randy sods.

But 1999 was no fun for an anonymous swimmer off Farsund on the Norwegian coast who had spent a morning frolicking in the sea with a school of the noble beasts. The unlucky chap was mistaken for a fellow dolphin by one of his new-finned friends, and had to scramble back onto his boat when the beast tried to stick its penis between his legs. He relayed the moment of physiological realisation as follows: "At first I thought it was a fin, but dolphins don't have fins on their underbellies."

Perhaps feeling left out, his friend, a diving instructor, claimed that the libidinous mammal had tried to have its wicked way with him too but that his wetsuit had heroically put a stop to the attempted assault.

SPOOKED IN ZANZIBAR

Hold on to your hats, readers, sexual misadventures don't come much more ridiculous than this. A BBC report in 2001 suggested that the beautiful and tranquil Tanzanian isle of Zanzibar was being terrorized by a sex-crazed ghost who had previously haunted the island in 1995 and 2000. Residents claimed that 'Popo Bawa' would appear in a puff of smelly smoke, sodomize his mainly male victims, and threaten to reappear the following night if residents did not warn others of his visit. Witnesses who spoke to the BBC were confused, saying that ordinarily the sexually voracious spirit had only visited during election times. And THIS is why they were confused?

ALIEN SEX FIEND

It's time to turn our attention to the fruitless fornicators who claim to have had interstellar intercourse. Perhaps the most famous tale of alien sex to date is that of Antonio Villas Boas, a now reputable lawyer, who maintains to this day that aliens forced him to have sex with them on his family's Brazilian farm in 1957. After being covered in a strange liquid, he said, he was taken to a human-looking being and made to have sex with her while she growled like a dog. Interviewed later, he said "Before leaving she turned to me, pointed to her belly, and smilingly pointed to the sky."

IN SICKNESS AND IN HEALTH

When you fall into a coma and are sent to a nursing home, you should have a right to a little dignity, yes? It wouldn't be crazy to argue that your husband, when he comes to visit, should be entitled to privacy when he does so. Wellll, yes...

23% OF GERMANS ARE SEXUALLY STIMULATED BY UNDERARM ODOUR

But it's a bizarre set of affairs that sees a court rule that one husband had an expectation to privacy when he had sex with his comatose wife as she lay on her nursing home bed. Tipped off by staff, police had video-taped Leah Johnson's room and later charged her husband with three counts of felony sexual assault, only to find out that a court considered the video-tape evidence illegal.

TOAD-ULLY TAWDRY

The annual 'Toad Watch' scheme in Llandrindod Wells, Wales, sees roads closed to help thousands of lusty toads make their annual pilgrimage to a breeding lake in safety. The scheme started because in previous years, thousands of over-amorous amphibians had been run over as they started out on their mating mission.

SUICIDE BY INSEMINATION

There you are, gadding about, trying to pick up a hot new lady friend, impressing her with your exceptionally long penis, when suddenly she decides to fight you off – and because she's three times your size, she has no problems doing so. Your 10 arms and lengthy penis then get in a fankle, and you manage to inseminate yourself. Oh, and then you die.

Don't worry, this is not a futuristic vision of what will happen if we eat GM crops, but rather the fate of the giant sea squid. Scientists recently discovered several dead males of the species, off the Spanish coast. It did not take long for the geeks in white coats to ascertain that the bonkers beasts had manage to kill themselves, via the novel method of being fatally inseminated by their own sperm.

PULLING YOUR BACK DURING RUMPY-PUMPY HAS AFFECTED 12% OF BRITS

ON THE SNIFF

The questionable expression 'on the sniff' sums up the link between human scent and sexual arousal, denoting that time in a man's life when he may pop out to a drinking hole to seek out a new lady-love. But did you know that male voles – the male meadow vole in particular – gets most turned on when he can smell the sperm of other males? In fact, if he gets a whiff of other males when bedding down for the night with a lady vole he is likely to produce double his usual amount of sperm. This startling news was announced in Nature magazine in 2004.

THE GOSPEL TRUTH

A Dutch gospel church was pipped to the post in a hotly contended contest for a new website domain name launched by the EU. The 'Volle Evangelie Gemeente Rehoboth in Eersel' gospel church had wanted to use the domain name sex.eu to promote sex "The way God wanted it". They lost out, so unfortunately we will never know how the big pixie in the sky intended us to get our rocks off.

EXCUSES, EXCUSES # 1

Let's sail the good ship hypocrisy once more – and where else but to the home of the Roman Catholic Church, Italy. It was here that the Vatican's own Monsignor Tommaso Stenico was caught in a gay sex sting after chatting up an undercover TV reporter on a dating website. The reporter then caught a date that followed on film, shocking viewers with the miscreant Monsignor's chat-up attempts – namely that if he and the reporter screwed it would not be 'sinful.'

1/5 OF THE WORLD'S POPULATION HAVE USED BONDAGE GEAR SUCH AS MASKS

Stenico later said he had been trying to reveal an elaborate plot by Satanists to seduce Catholic priests into gayness. Say what? Yes, instead of holding his hands up to the video evidence, the hypocritical God-botherer only made matters worse, claiming his tryst was part of an underworld conspiracy.

Ironically the Vatican have this to say about homosexuality: "Special concern and pastoral attention should be directed towards those who have this condition, lest they be led to believe that living out this orientation is morally acceptable. It is not."

ROOM, BOARD AND A LITTLE EXTRA

'Drugs and Sex For Sale 24/7' the sign read, outside one Cincinnati landlord's building. But hang on, don't all rush at once. Let's not forget to read the small print: "Please help us, call Cincinnati City Council." In fact this sign had been erected by John Wallen when police repeatedly failed to clear his neighbourhood of dealers and prostitutes, leaving him with only one tenant in a block of six flats. And she was a drug-addled crack whore. Probably.

ACCIDENTAL HONEY-TRAP

A group of five teenage boys got more than they bargained for when they created a virtual lust interest for a love-lorn friend on My Space. After a time they discovered the 15-year-old figment of their imaginations was generating interest from a none too salubrious source. A 48-year-old man had begun sending sexy messages to their fictitious friend. The boys suggested they meet at a local park, called police, and the pervert was promptly arrested.

WOMEN ARE THREE TIMES MORE LIKELY THAN MEN TO HAVE USED A SEX TOY

CARROT AND STICK

It's common for driving instructors to use the carrot and stick approach. Instructor Steve Hall put a novel spin on this when he forced a female learner driver to touch his groin while he had a 12-inch carrot hidden in his pants. It was only when the woman started crying that he removed the pathetic imitation penis from his pocket.

It was not his first and only step over the line with female clients. He told one woman she should run round a car-park with her 'tits out' if she passed her test, another that she would pass if she slept with him, and bullied yet another client into looking at close-up photos of his penis which were hidden in his glove compartment.

He claimed the incidents were jokes, but a judge did not see the funny side and sentenced the instructor to 18 months in jail for the assaults.

BAD CALL

An habitual prank sex caller to fast food outlets was acquitted of any crime in 2006, despite copious evidence that he'd been at the centre of a famous strip-search scam.

He called managers of various well known restaurant chains, claiming to be a policeman and instructing the managers to strip-search female employees.

Andrew T Davies made over 70 calls in 30 different American states, and was eventually charged with impersonating a police officer, soliciting sodomy and sexual abuse. He won his case, but one of his victims managed to sue McDonalds for not properly protecting her during her ordeal. She was awarded five million dollars in punitive damages.

23% OF PEOPLE IN THE WESTERN WORLD HAVE HAD EXTRA-MARITAL RELATIONS

BEYOND A JOKE

In 2003, three Japanese students in China gave the local population the willies when they performed a jokey skit dressed in red knickers and bras, with paper cups for boobs and fake genitals hanging from their wrists. Goodness knows what they were up to, but the national scandal that ensued was beyond a joke – thousands of students at the same university as the pranksters demanded an apology, waving anti-Japanese banners and shouting insults.

'C' U IN COURT

In 2000, British student Andrew Broadbent mistakenly sent a downloaded porno pic to everyone in his college whose name began with the letter C. The head of his college's IT department put it on a disk and called police. The unfortunate keyboard-trigger-happy lad was fined £200 and £80 costs for publishing an indecent image contrary to the Obscene Publications Act.

BEBO BULLYING

Stories of bullying on social networking sites are widespread, but this one deserves a mention for its senselessness and sexual content. In 2007, a 65-year-old grandmother was the victim of a cruel prank on Bebo when someone set up a profile in her name. So far, so ordinary. However, the identity thieves took the smear campaign to ridiculous extremes. They claimed the granny had slept with countless men, had had sex on a pool table in the pool hall where she worked, and even that she'd run over a teenage girl. The culprits were never caught.

THE MOST COMMON PLACE TO USE A VIBRATOR IS... AUSTRALIA

ORAL ERROR

Here's a cautionary tale of what happens when youthful sexual experimentation and modern technology mix. In 2004, a 17-year-old Indian student was at the centre of a diplomatic row when he broke a new law preventing the spread of pornographic material. His crime? He'd filmed himself receiving oral sex from his girlfriend, using his mobile phone, and put the material on the Baazzee.com auction website. Politicians and the media swiftly got themselves in a flap of epic proportions when the lad was arrested after a week-long 'man' hunt.

NO, YOU CALLED ME!

DJs from Australia's 101.9 FOX FM set up a call with two sex line workers to see how long it would take for them to realize that neither one was an actual customer. The breathy conversation that ensued involved a clash of nearly identical scripts, and an embarrassing contest in who was 'relaxing' more. After much confusing to-ing and fro-ing, one girl finally twigged and asked who rang who. With a curt "You rang me, honey", the school-boy prank came to an unclimactic end.

BUYER BEWARE!

We all know that advertisements should be taken with a pinch of salt. So when an ad went on Craigslist in 2006 with a graphic picture of a woman offering herself up for BDSM sex, users should have heeded the mantra 'buyer beware.' Some 178 men didn't and responded with equally graphic pics, unaware that the ad was a hoax, posted by practical joker Jason Fortuny.

Fortuny went on to publish the posted pictures and personal

details of the respondents, many of them married, on the Encyclopedia Dramatica website. He was sued privately by a couple of the men, but the law could not touch him as no crime had been committed.

BENT COPS

In 2000, police in China's eastern province of Jiangsu found a novel way to make a bit of money on the side. They opened a brothel disguised as a restaurant, then arrested the customers and fined them. They made over $700 US from their brainwave – a lot of money at the time, by local standards.

COURTROOM DRAMA

Solemn places, courtrooms – the formal robes, the nervous jury, the at-times-horrific crimes, they all contribute toward a none-too-pleasant working environment. This is never truer than during the case of a murdered child.

So you have to wonder what gave former Creek County District Judge, Jeremiah Jones, the horn when he persistently used a penis pump to masturbate during a particularly horrid child murder trial in 2006. Although the judge denied the sordid self-abuse, the evidence was stacked up against him. Semen was found behind the judge's courtroom chair, a courtroom reporter revealed he had exposed himself to her countless times, and police, on seeing a plastic tube disappear behind his judicial robes, discovered the pump which they claimed the judge had been using regularly over a four-year period.

Unrepentant, the accused whined he had not been using the career-destroying sex-device, but that it had been a 'gag-gift' from a hunting buddy. Tell that one to the judge. Oh.

PORNOGRAPHY IS THE FAVOURED SEXUAL AID FOR 41% OF THE WORLD POPULATION

HOW LOW CAN YOU GO?

You can't get much lower than a married police officer who gives stolen drugs to the hordes of prostitutes he uses. Oh, wait. Yes you can. Former Austin, Texas, police officer Nathan Bayo was using prostitutes that were so drug-addicted, so desperate for cash, that they agreed to accept the officer's wife's clothes as payment for their services. Now, that's what I call scraping the bottom of the barrel.

WHAT A MOOB!

Nope, that's not a typo, but rather a comment on a judgement which said that a man's bare torso does not count as 'private parts.' When Jessie Barlow was jailed for taking secret shots of man-boobs at a swimming pool, a trio of judges in the court of appeal ruled that only women's breasts can be regarded as 'sexual,' in line with the 2003 Sexual Offences Act. Barlow walked away unpunished.

CASTRATION SALVATION

A man was given a protection order from an Australian court when his ex-girlfriend of four years threatened to hunt him down and cut off his testicles. The man was not impressed by laughter which filled the courtroom as his case was heard. "I'm pretty scared," he was quoted as saying.

MILE HIGH MASTURBATOR

Johnny Delgado claimed he was "just adjusting himself" because his jeans were too tight when he was accused of having a filthy fiddle on a flight to Darwin, Australia. He lost his case due to overwhelming evidence from the police who had arrested him when the plane landed, who confirmed that "his jeans were not overly tight."

THE LOST WILLY ROUTINE

Christopher Gates sued celebrity hypnotist Paul McKenna in 1998, claiming he had suffered psychiatric injury after one of McKenna's live shows. In his defence, the hypnotist referred to a letter from a man named Benji who had taken part in McKenna's 'lost-willly' routine on the Howard Stern show. Benji, he claimed, found the experience of being told his manhood was missing to be 'pleasant.' But a judge was pretty clear that, missing willy or not, Mr McKenna had nothing to do with Gate's schizophrenia.

YOU ARE WHAT YOU EAT

If there's one good thing about being pregnant, it's that you can get away with eating whatever you want – coal, bin bags, cakes bigger than your head. One man found it harder to get away with his craving for chocolate penises, when he was twice caught stuffing his pockets with the naughty novelties in the same sex shop in Utrecht, Holland.

TOP TEN SEXUALLY
RELATED DEATHS

10. Suffocation by duvet sounds fairly believable. Strangulation by duvet doesn't. But in 2004, a teenager found her lover hanged from a bannister as he tried to get his sex kicks from a breath-play game gone wrong.

9. We're told from a young age not to play with plastic bags – we should bear this in mind as adults too, considering the death of one Alastair Hunt. Hunt died in 2000 during a solitary sex game while sucking the air out of a plastic bag with a hoover.

8. A 39-year-old Canadian woman kicked the bucket after engaging in 'out of the ordinary' sexual practices using 'very particular' accessories, according to a local policeman. The police would not elaborate on what accessories were used but said they were 'torture devices.'

7. A pair of South African lovers were doing it the wrong side of the tracks when a train ran over them and killed them stone dead. A driver had yelled at them to stop but "they continued with their business," a spokesman sold a Sowetan newspaper.

6. The first known case of death by auto-Erotic asphyxiation was composer Frantisek Kotzwara who asked a prostitute to slice off his goolies with a scarf tied round his neck, while she fastened the other end to a door knob. Unsurprisingly Kotzwara died, but only after he'd had sex.

5. In 1899, French president Félix Francois Faure famously suffered a fatal bought of apoplexy after receiving oral sex from a

Mademoiselle Marguerite Steinheil. Afterwards she received the charming nick-name la pompe funèbre or 'funeral pump.'

4. Police ruled out foul play when a cabbie discovered two naked dead bodies in a street in Columbia, South Carolina. The reason? A search of the area revealed two piles of neatly folded clothes on a nearby roof. The verdict? The two twenty-somethings had fallen off the roof while making love. The question needing to be begged? If they were that careful taking off – and arranging – their clothing, how come their love-making was so passionate they fell off the edge?

3. A Sherlock Holmes scholar left a mystery of his own when he was found strangled by a shoe-lace in 2004, holding a wooden spoon in one hand and laying on a bed surrounded by cuddly toys. At the inquest the coroner said the death could be explained by one of three things: murder, suicide or misadventure during a deviant sexual practice. He recorded an open verdict.

2. As most chefs will tell you, a blunt knife is more dangerous than a sharp one. S&M freak Simon Burley had clearly not heard this top tip when he gave his girlfriend a blunt instrument to cut him down from a noose during a sex game. She played the role of Nazi hangman and was to cut him down when he kicked a chair away. He played the role of prize pervy idiot, dying when the knife she used failed to cut through the rope.

1. HIDEY-HOLE OF HORRORS
Just because you've practised safe auto-erotic sex 100 times, doesn't mean the 101st won't kill you. In a dingy den plastered with S&M images and TV screens showing skin-flicks, a man's body was discovered in 2007. The unfortunate blighter had managed to film his 12-hour death-throes while attempting to make a home-made S&M porn film. His last home movie turned out to be a snuff one.

POT. KETTLE.

A Yorkshire woman lost her case for constructive dismissal and sexual harassment when two ex-employees pointed out that she was the one doing the harassing. A court heard how Alison Faulkes left handcuffs, teddy bears bearing sex slogans, and fake breasts on desks of her male co-workers.

IS IT ART?

A cinema fan sued the Chinese film watchdog in 2007 when they convinced director Ang Lee to cut seven minutes of rude bits from his movie, *Lust, Caution*. "The incomplete structure and fragmented portrayal of the female lead's psyche makes it hard for the audience to appreciate the movie's art," Dong Yanbin said. Nothing at all to do with the seven minutes being cited as the most realistic rumpy-pumpy in cinematic history, then?

SEX ON THE BRAIN

"We want London to be thinking about nothing but sex for three months." So said Marina Wallace from London's Barbican museum, curator of one of the first exhibitions ever devoted to 2,000 years of sex in art. Don't all rush at once though – the exhibition ended in 2007. Still, there's nothing stopping you from thinking about sex for three months all the same.

FOOLISH FELLATIO

It's hardly a match made in heaven – a senior Police Constable and a druggie biker from the notorious Australian 'Finks' gang. But that did not stop Peter Chapman, a Gold Coast policeman, from first allowing Shae Lee Horne to perform oral sex on him, and then giving her information from official police files about a known drug dealer. Hmm. Hardly the romance of the century – so I'd love to tell you that at least they met in a traditionally romantic way, but no. Chapman met Horne when responding to a call she'd made complaining of domestic violence.

DON'T ASK, DON'T GET

One man's tactic for more sex spectacularly backfired according to local Australian paper Perth Now. Fed up with initiating sex, he told his wife he would not put out unless she got things started for a change. Eight years later, and he wishes he'd bitten his tongue – they've not had marital relations since his foolhardy suggestion.

BIG BROTHER'S SMUTTY SIBLING

A Colombian reality TV show for couples has come up with a novel way of voting off contestants. Those who have the dirtiest sex can remain on the show, to be aired on a hardcore pay-per-view channel. Participants on Los Pichones will be expelled by the public if their intercourse is not considered outrageous enough, forcing couples to compete on delights such as group sex, S&M and copulating whilst rolling in animal excrement. At the time of writing, over 800 people have already applied to take part.

ONE IN 10 YOUNGSTERS HAVE HAD SEX AT SCHOOL

THE LAST BARON IN A CAMPUS OF TULIPS

No I haven't lost the plot in using the above title for this particular bout of erotic erroneousness – but we'll come back to it later.

So to Italy, land which is the very epitome of all things romantic and sexy. But there's nothing romantic nor sexy about agriculture and law professor Ezio Capizzano. In 2004, the ageing Lothario was arrested for extortion and corruption when 19 video tapes stolen from his campus study were handed to police. And, yes, you guessed it, they did not contain images of the old goat instructing his female students in crop rotation or legalese. Rather the cassettes were resplendent with graphic scenes of saliva swapping – not to mention exchanges of other bodily fluids.

He was, of course, sacked. Remarkably though, not for his sex-for-grades escapades but for 'misusing public property' – namely the sofa on which the dodgy deals were performed. Even more remarkable is his non-vilification by the media. His countrymen love a randy old sod, it seems, and he was even named by the respectable Corriere della Sera newspaper as "Italy's answer to Sean Connery."

Nonetheless, with unemployment hanging over him, what was a loveable porn prof to do? To answer we must return to the questionable title of this misadventure. Making the most of the fame brought about by the case, he wrote – and has had published – an erotic memoir... and typing its title is something I don't want to do twice!

RAUNCHY RED CAP

Getting your tits out for the lads is all well and good, but not so much if you happen to be said lads' boss – and especially not if you get captured on film doing so. British military policewoman Nicola

Humphreys had been reprimanded for one such moral outrage in 2004. However, not to be 'once bitten, twice shy', she later performed a sex act on her squaddie husband in front of onlookers at an army barracks in Germany. The pair both faced disciplinary action, and were named and shamed in *The Sun* newspaper.

LOAN DECLINED, SEX APPROVED

A German bank manager from the small leafy town of Reutlingen stole over 850,000 Euros to pay for sex with one of his customers after he'd turned down her request for a personal loan. I know, it's a hefty sum for a roll in the hay... But the miscreant told a Tübingen court that he gave 70,000 Euros to the young lady for a number of sexual encounters, and kept just 40,000 for himself. The majority of the loot was used to pay one of the young Italian woman's relatives, who was blackmailing him over the tawdry transaction.

OY OY, SAVELOY

A butcher suspected foul play when a customer who had purchased two giant Schwartenmagen sausages returned to his shop and asked him to keep them chilled until he left for a flight to Dubai. Since the sausages weighed more than when the customer left the shop, the butcher feared the worst – or rather wurst. But instead of finding an explosive device, drugs or jewels stashed away inside the contaminated meat products, he discovered two natural latex dildos. Sex toys are not to be found on general sale in the country where the customer was destined to travel – but ironically, you're not allowed to bring pork products into the country either, so the hapless smuggler was doubly, er, stuffed.

MORE THAN EIGHT IN 10 ITALIANS HAVE HAD SEX IN A CAR

BOSS FROM HELL

Most bosses do like to crack the whip from time to time. Um, that's 'crack the whip', not 'beat with a dildo', Captain Damir Ilyasov of the Russian Army. In 2003 the sordid soldier was stripped of his stripes for beating junior officers with a "black latex baton shaped like a male sex organ", the British *Metro* newspaper reported.

MARINE MEAT

In 2000, pornographic and nude stills from the gay porn website Marine Meat were sent to the top general at the Pentagon with a note suggesting the models were none other than a bunch of gay US marines. The US Marine Corps immediately launched an investigation as to how some of its soldiers ended up on the site. The US military has a 'don't ask, don't tell' policy when it comes to expressing sexual preference. Since the site does not feature 'headshots', it's hard to see what rules were broken, and the men could not be identified.

YOU CANNAE CHANGE THE LAWS OF PHYSICS

I'm no scientist, but I do remember the rule that "every action has an equal and opposite reaction". Dereen Woodward proved this and then some when she spontaneously flashed her boobs at her husband, causing a passing motorist to lose control of his car. In the chaos that ensued the motorist crashed into a dentist's office, a dental nurse freaked out at the noise, her finger slipped during a delicate procedure and a patient bit down on her hand, lacerating two fingers.

PUPPY LOVE BY THE HOUR

Here's a way to lose friends and alienate people: a Russian city councillor – fed up with testosterone- and oestrogen-fuelled teens bonking in public places – suggested that the city pay for 'love motels' where the youngsters could pay for rooms at an hourly rate. Her idea went down like a lead balloon in the prudish ex-communist town she governed.

LITIGIOUS LADIES OF THE NIGHT

Sometimes luck can take an unexpected turn. Imagine the joy of a Brazilian madam who sold the land her brothel sat on for over 500,000 dollars. Then imagine her chagrin when her ex-employees sued her for over half that amount for unpaid holiday pay – as well as bonuses for working the night-shift.

XXX-MAS

In 2000, Carla Perez brought Santa's name into disrepute by posing semi-naked with him in the Brazilian December issue of *Playboy*. To add perverted insult to injury, nudey adverts for the feature were splashed on billboards across the country's capital.

But hang on a sec, how does one bring a mythical figure into disrepute? Over to the professional Santas graduating from Rio De Janeiro's one official Santa academy. This Scrooge-like bunch were so offended by the posters, they threatened to wear black armbands the day they got their professional Santa certificates. They needn't have worried – a judge had already ordered the saucy Santa's bottom to be covered up in case it caused offence.

DIRTY POLITICS

An Australian regional Police Minister was sacked just three days into his tenure after it emerged he'd been prancing about semi-naked at a party three months earlier. To add mortification to embarrassment, he was also accused of gyrating sexually against a colleague, MP Noreen Hays. Ms Hays called the scandal that ensued 'dirty politics.' Elsewhere in the English speaking world we call it 'dirty dancing.'

BONKERS BILL

Professionals who charge by the hour often send bills to those who don't turn up for appointments, so why should prostitutes be any different? In 2002, a San Diego man was sued by one Crystal Glass when he failed to show for their pre-arranged tryst at Raoul's Rose Garden brothel.

MOBILE PHONE MORON

Hell hath no fury like a woman humiliated. Take the case of Lance Sergeant Zoe Grant who sought revenge when her lover Lance Sergeant Rex Buchanan circulated mobile phone sex pictures of her to his mates – who also happened to be her colleagues. After their affair turned sour Buchanan showed the filthy phone flicks around. But the joke was on him when Grant dobbed him in to his wife – he was demoted to the ranks.

COP AN EYEFUL OF THAT!

When one door shuts, another opens, so they say. So it was for Hungarian WPC Livia Kovacs of Zuglo, who was sacked in 2008 when a colleague spotted her in a dominatrix movie – and yes, she was using her police-issue handcuffs and dressed in regulation uniform. Kovacs was unrepentant, claiming she'd had a flurry of film offers since her sacking went public.

NICE... BUT NAUGHTY

Entertainment website Ananova reported that a Belgian woman got into a legal dispute with a local bakery when he displayed rude marzipan figures in his shop window. Baker Van Buggenhout had simply wanted to pep up his valentines display with the filthy figurines but the unnamed woman, who lived next door to his bakery, sued him on grounds of indecency.

WORKED UP IN A LATHER

District Judge Andrew Duvall was a longstanding member of the judiciary in Bedford Pennsylvania, USA, who for many years had with wisdom and solemnity sent many a ne'er do well down to the slammer. It wasn't until he was long into his career that he discovered a different calling entirely...

In 2001, a 21-year-old man appeared in his court on charges of disorderly conduct and public drunkenness. At this moment the Judge's true calling came to light, and he offered to let the young rapscallion off lightly if he would allow him to shampoo his hair. What's more, he said, he could further lessen the charges if the man brought two friends the following day for another impromptu hair-washing session.

Unfortunately for him the accused had friends in low places and the friends he brought along were two state troopers. The Judge's acknowledged hair fetish meant he later had to admit to abusing the power of his office and he was forced to resign.

GREEK PEOPLE HAVE SEX ON AVERAGE 138 TIMES A YEAR

WHAT A BOOB # 1

A Swedish school teacher lost her job and was fined the equivalent of nearly £400 when she flashed her breasts at a male student. The boy had been covering her blackboard in schoolboy dirty doodles when she lost the plot and did the professionally-suicidal deed. She was also made to pay the child compensation.

PUTTING THE BRAKES ON LOVE

Cambridge, England, 1998, and a lesson for all the fellas among you out there looking for love. Police had been disturbed to find a number of attractive young women reporting that the brake cables of their cars had been cut, causing a few near-death experiences. The boys in blue soon caught the perpetrator, Steve Sayer, in a new act of amateur car mechanics. Police psychologists discovered he had a strange sexual fantasy about women crashing their cars, carrying out his crime only on the cars of women he fancied.

His excuse was that with his virginity intact he had "no clue about women." So here's a top tip for Steven and all you other Romeos out there – women rather prefer to keep their limbs intact when you are courting them.

FRUITY!

In a Channel 4 Television documentary in 2004, a number of 'victims' of embarrassing sexual accidents were interviewed. Of the many disastrous ways of getting your rocks off, one of the most chortlesome was the story of a man who harboured saucy sentiments about melons. Nope, not that kind of melon people, the real kind, you know: water, honeydew, canteloupe. But what can possibly go wrong between a man and his melon you may ask yourself? Hardly a carnal catastrophe waiting to happen, is it?

That is, until said gent thought that sticking his melon mistress in the microwave to warm it up would make it feel more authentically like...whatever it was he had a yen for it to feel like. 180° of microwaves later, and the hapless fellow was suffering from second degree burns to his manhood. When questioned over the sanity of his misadventure the foolish fella mumbled: "I used oven gloves to protect my hands but I didn't think about me bobby."

COMPLETELY QUACKERS

We all have our favourite cartoon character, but in 1992 one young lady took her admiration a saucy step too far. She became convinced that Donald Duck was sending her love vibes via her neighbour's satellite dish, and was found frenetically masturbating beneath it, convinced the cartoon water bird was making love to her.

HANKIE-PANKY

Fetishes come in all shapes and sizes as we're discovering throughout this book, but did you ever hear of a sneeze-shaped one? In 2008, ABC news reported on the internet 'Sneeze fetish forum' where sneeze enthusiasts can discuss spluttering, wheezing and honking to their hearts' content. If sneezing doesn't do it for you, don't worry, the site offers an alternative fetish site "for discussion surrounding nose, handkerchief/tissue and nose-blowing fetishes only." Gives new meaning to the expression 'hanky-panky.'

SPEED FREAK

Another notable bout of sexual silliness from Channel Four's film on embarrassing sexual accidents. To Russia this time where one noble amorous adventurer had a grand plan to make the earth move for his lover all night long. Knowing that amphetamines – street name 'speed' – could keep you going all night, he injected the drug directly into his urethra and was, of course, immediately hospitalised. It could have been worse though: some men trying that with cocaine have had to have it amputated afterwards.

WHAT A SPECTACLE!

Witnesses saw quite an, ahem, spectacle when they observed Japanese construction worker Toru Nagasawa use violence to get his mitts on an innocent person's contact lenses in Tokyo in 2005. When police searched the eye-wear fetishists home, they found 154 pairs of glasses and contact lenses.

BARE-FOOTED CHEEK!

Female students, readers and researchers got more than they bargained for in the hot summer of 2008 if they removed their footwear in New Zealand's Wellington public library. Foot fetishist Euegene Peter Kalooi Woodfield spent the summer filming women's sandaled or bare-feet there, in what can only be described as a misadventure in library lewdness. Euegene handed himself in when his fetish got out of hand – or rather foot – and he found himself following one woman through the town, thinking of carrying out a sexual assault on her. Or her feet, maybe.

SANDAL SCANDAL

The parents among you will know young babies often like to have a comforting item in their cots to soothe them to sleep at night – a dummy, a blanket, a soft toy, are all traditional and good options. Omar Abd-el-Gowd's mother rather dimly gave him her sandal as a comfort object in his cot when he was an infant. Well, that's the excuse he gave to Inner London Crown Court, as he admitted eight counts of stealing women's shoes over a one year period. Let's just be thankful she didn't give him her bra or worse...

CAR-BLIMEY!

"Check out the carburettor on that" is not a cry you'll hear very often. Unless, that is, your name is Sandy Wong and you've been arrested not once but twice for getting sexually involved with a motor vehicle. In 2005, Wong was arrested for frotting (rubbing sexually against) a Mini-Cooper, and in 2007 he faced 90 days in jail for pleasuring himself in full public view on the roofs of classic cars at Edmonton's Home and Garden Show in Canada.

OFF THE CUFF THEFTS?

In 2002, the British *Metro* newspaper reported that British Airways staff had been stealing handcuffs meant for passengers who were misbehaving. Safety chief Simon Packer told staff "We have a huge number of fetishists amongst crew. Your exotic practices in the bedroom are your own business, but please stick to the Ann Summers furry handcuffs – replacing ones from the restraint kit is costing BA a fortune."

THE LARGEST CONDOM EVER MADE WAS 67 METRES

TOP TEN MEDICAL EMERGENCIES

10. When a couple were out for a romantic chow down in Washington State, the woman thought it would be romantic to chow down on her partner's penis under the table. She threw an epileptic fit while in the act, bit his penis, and he stabbed her in the head with a fork so she would release him. Both were admitted, blood-stained and blushing, to a local hospital.

9. Remember the old chestnut 'the dog did it'? That's the excuse dreamt up by L.A. attorney Antonio Mendoza when he arrived at the ER with a mobile phone up his rectum. He claimed the dog had dragged the phone into his shower room, he'd slipped, and the phone had gone up his bottom.

8. At least an Oklahoma woman 'fessed up when she went to an emergency room in 2001 with a mobile phone in her backside. She had set the phone to vibrate and her boyfriend was to call it for a bit of randy ring-tone action. In her defence she had practised safe-sex by slipping the phone in a condom first. Unfortunately for her, this foresight had only helped to ease the small Nokia phone further into her rectum.

7. Hugh Heffner is an obvious name to drop in a book about sex – but he's more commonly known for his parties than for misadventure. But in a magazine interview, Heff admitted that in 1977 he had nearly choked to death during a session, only to be rescued by a Playboy bunny.

6. Foreign objects in the rectum are a commonplace occurrence in emergency rooms. This is because the muscles in the bottom tend to pull objects in rather than spit them out, so almost anything can get engulfed if you're not very careful. In 2006, a 29-year-old woman presented herself at the Whittington Hospital, London, with a vibrator stuck where the sun don't shine. The doctor's notes on the case add that he'd previously encountered a whisky

bottle, a light bulb, a magazine and a pair of spectacles in the same anatomical hiding place. Not in the same woman, mind.

5. *Cosmopolitan* Magazine recounts the tawdry tale of a young woman who put her boyfriend's car keys inside her vagina after an argument about car parking. To add to her embarrassment, when she arrived at the ER medical staff could not locate the keys after an internal examination.

4. Cocaine and sex go together like terrorists and Semtex – an obvious, if explosive combination. But not even the daftest druggie would inject the white powder into their urethra... Would they? Sure they would. For one erotic experimenter this meant a three day erection, a flow of blood to other arteries and an eventual amputation of the leg above the knee.

3. Things did not go swimmingly for one man in 1994, when he attempted to mount a swimming pool suction fitting. Robert Cheuvront's black-and-blue penis was eventually rescued by paramedics and an entire vat of lubricant.

2. American Kenneth Pinyan had the honour of being the star of the *Seattle Times* most-read story of 2005. Not much else to with him could be linked to the word honour. Under the moniker of 'Mr Hands', he made sex tapes of himself engaging in what we could euphemistically call horse-play. When he suffered a ruptured colon after frolicking with a particularly well-hung stallion, police were led to his equestrian film collection.

1. GET YOUR ROCKS OFF
You know how it is when you're mixing cement – gets the old pulse racing, doesn't it? Err, thought not. So, who knows what possessed one young man to pour a pound of the stuff up his boyfriend's rectum via a funnel as a form of sexual titillation. As the cement set in, so did the realization that a trip to the emergency room would be in order. We don't know if home-made anus-sculpture is exhibited anywhere, but I for one would love to take a look.

SLUGGING IT OUT

It's like something from a horror movie – two slimy hermaphrodite beasts circle one another ready to mate, their penises up to seven times longer than their bodies. As their colossal copulatory organs jostle for position and become entwined, they are left with but one option to free themselves from one another. One bites the penis off the other at the base, and turns it into a female. Welcome to the messed-up mating rituals of the slug – a case of fruitless fornication so ridiculous that it puts some of our human sexual misadventures to shame!

HOW MUCH IS THAT DOGGY IN THE WINDOW?

A knocking shops for dogs? Yes it really is as daft as it sounds. But one Sao Paulo man has opened the first 'love motel' for pets, ostensibly for owners who are concerned that their pooches aren't getting enough. Over to you, pooch pimp Robson Marinho: "I am absolutely certain this is the first love motel for dogs in the world." Ever wonder why that might be, Mr Marinho?

EGG-STRAORDINARY EVOLUTION

Know the following old joke? Man asks, "How do you like your eggs in the morning?" Sexually responsible woman answers, "Unfertilised, thank you." I know, hilarious. Anyway. The joke's perhaps inspired by the natural world and the ridiculous sexual misadventure of the cichlid fish.

So fearful is the female of this species of egg-eating predators that she sucks her eggs into her mouth before the male has had the chance to fertilize them. Fear not though, chiclid fish lovers, the species won't die out. Scientists have recently discovered that the male, p'd off with being emasculated, has evolved bright red spots on his tummy to resemble the female's eggs. When the female starts her sucking action, he flashes his spots, she opens her gob, and he squirts a stream of semen into her mouth. Et Voila. (And you thought a turkey-baster was daft).

NOT A LAME DUCK

Admit it boys – you've all fantasised about having a willy that's longer than your entire body haven't you? Well, maybe not. Think of the problems – trying to lug the thing around or finding underpants to fit. You've got to feel sorry for the male Argentine Lake Duck, in that case. This hopeless humper has developed a todger so enormous that it's one inch bigger than his entire body length. What's more, his lengthy drake-dick is corkscrew shaped. But the jokes on the girls. So long has his birdy boner become, that he is able to lasso any female he wants if she tries to escape his clutches. Yee and ha.

SO LONG, SCHLONG!

It's a common complaint from women that men can be detached emotionally. Spare a thought, then, for the female paper nautilus, a weird species of octopus, who doesn't get anywhere near her man. Instead, when mating, his penis fills with a super dose of spermatozoa, detaches itself from his body, and darts torpedo-like toward the female genitalia of his choice.

THE OLDEST SEX DRAWING FOUND IS 40,000 YEARS OLD

WILD WOMEN AND SONG

In 2008, *The Guardian* reported that Henry William Allingham was Europe's oldest man, having notched up an incredible 112 years. The world war one veteran lyrically ascribed his longevity to: "cigarettes, whisky and wild, wild women". The best excuse to sow your wild oats, if ever I heard one.

DAMNED IF YOU DO, DAMNED IF YOU DON'T

Never trust politicians, journalists... and authors. In a blatant volte-face, I am now going to tell you about the flip-side of shagging being the route to eternal life. In 2008, Clara Meadmore revealed to the *Sun* that she was a virgin – at the tender age of 105. Still, Mr Allingham's got seven years on her yet, so let's not count our chickens...

THAI ME DOWN

There are many ways to deal with the credit crunch – turn off lights when you leave the room, put on a woolly jumper instead of the heating, cut back on luxuries. But one ex-banking consultant gave a new meaning to the expression 'between a rock and a hard place' when he opened a brothel with his Thai lover in 2007 to try and pay the bills.

Brit Malcolm Love claimed he'd never seen any ill-gotten gains from the house of ill repute, but the presiding judge was not convinced. Love had signed the lease on the parlour, placed ads for it in the national press, and was the signatory for a bulk delivery from the 'Condom Tom' mail order company.

The greedy sod earned £88,000 a year so why he should need to run a brothel is not clear – though he did admit in court to having a wife in Thailand as well as his Thai lover. Greedy sod in more ways than one, then.

BYO

A New York lap-dancing club was closed down when vice cops discovered there was more to the place than meets the eye. At Big Daddy Lou's Hot Lap Dance Club sex was available (at a price – with a porn star it would cost you $5,000), as was cocaine, available from the house dealer, and there were free cold cuts from the buffet. If you wanted alcohol and Viagra though, you had to bring your own. The cheapskates!

LIKE FATHER, LIKE SON

"Farraday was named after his father and he certainly took after him. Fergus must be proud of his wee laddie." Proud? John Farraday and father John Fergus were reunited in Parkhead prison, after a life-time apart. Both were serving sentences for crimes of extreme sexual violence.

VAMPIRE BATTY

A homeless woman was arrested in 2007 after having consensual sex with a man who was letting her kip at his house for a few days. But that's not why she was arrested. After letting Tiffany Sutton tie him up, Brad Naylor was terrified to find her slashing him with a knife, and telling him she wanted to suck his blood. Her reasoning? She was into 'Vampire sex'.

THE AVERAGE WOMAN TAKES EIGHT MINUTES TO ACHIEVE ORGASM

LET'S TALK ABOUT SEX

Parents of five-year-old Harry Ronan were called by social workers after concerned teachers feared he may be suffering abuse at their hands. The call came after Harry had been crying in his classroom, saying that: "Mummy has hurt my willy." Of course, Willy was the name of his comfort blanket, which his Mum had taken away to be washed – the boy's penis was referred to as his winkie.

A REAL TROOPER

When a porn star described only as 'Barbie' was stopped at traffic lights for a minor traffic offence in Nashville, she gave a state Trooper something to write home about when performing a sex act on him behind a bush. The Trooper was put on unpaid leave, and research gives no further clue about his fate. But the main thing this misadventure leaves me wondering is why are porn actresses always 'stars' and never described as playing 'bit parts?' Ah. Yes.

COWABUNGA!

Revenge is a dish best served... with a severed and bloodied cow's head? That can't be right, surely!

According to John Chris Alexander of Westmoreland County, Pennsylvania, it can. When barraging his wife's lover with offensive emails and photos did not put his rival off, Mr Alexander decided to take his revenge to the next level and, in a Mafioso style act of transgression, he sent a beast's frozen head in a box to the man he felt had wronged him.

At least he was contrite in court. His defence lawyer Henry Hilles told the court that his client understood: "that in a civilized society a person cannot send a severed cow's head to anybody."

THE WORLD'S SMALLEST KNOWN PENIS WAS JUST ONE INCH

He was sentenced to probation and 50 hours community service; his wife – with whom he was later reconciled – was sentenced to life with a freak.

RUDE BRITANNIA

In 2008, author Tim Fountain journeyed around Britain to peek behind the curtains of the nation's sex lives for his book Rude Britannia. Fountain uncovered all manner of fetish clubs, including one with a pool-full of urine, and the 'pony-house' where men can dress as horses, as well as interviewing many a sexually depraved saddo. Bet he wished he'd stayed home!

DEAD RUDE

An American State Supreme Court was forced to rule on the blindingly obvious in 2008: sex with dead people is bad and wrong. The Court had to make the judgement when a lower Wisconsin tribunal had ruled that three men who dug up a corpse to have sex with it had done nothing illegal. But it's alright. They remembered to take condoms.

GOOD HEAVENS

Fox News 'Sexpert' Yvonne K. Fulbright investigated the phenomenon of transcendental sex in 2008. Among the experiences she revealed that those reaching higher plains of ecstasy achieved were having paranormal powers, reliving past lives, time travel, and – my personal favourite – seeing the face of God.

THE AVERAGE SEX SESSION, INCLUDING FOREPLAY, LASTS 21 MINUTES

MIDNIGHT SNACK

An English-language newspaper from Sweden, The Local, described a strange event in the spring of 2006. A couple who'd just met in a night club went back to the woman's house for food after sharing a frisson-some evening of drinking and dancing. The next day the man told Stockholm police he'd said no to sex, and yet the woman had performed oral sex on him against his will. Perhaps the cupboards were bare?

DOUBLE STANDARDS # 1

It's a tale as old as time. No, no, not beauty and the beast – although that may be an apt concept in this instance. Rather, the tale of a moral crusader caught red-handed in the act of doing what he's crusading against. The stupid shagger in question on this occasion was Reza Zarei, a Tehran policeman given the task of 'moralizing the city' who was caught in 2008 in a brothel with prostitutes. He wasn't arresting them, either.

NO OFFENCE!

A man who liked to mow the lawn naked got an ASBO banning him from going outdoors in the nod. Yan Price from Pocklington, England, was unrepentant and said he had not meant to cause offence.

WHAT A BOOB # 2

Taking a photo of yourself baring your breasts is one thing, but to do it in your unbuttoned police uniform is another. The Australian female cop who did this in 2007 got a little more than she bargained for when her dim-witted police boyfriend forwarded the image to others in their department. They both came close to losing their jobs.

SOAPY SILLINESS

In 2007, councillors in Goole, England banned a billboard poster for a local car-washing firm. Their censoriousness arose not only from a picture of scantily clad woman giving a pink Cadillac a soap job, but also due to the provocative slogan: "The best hand-job in town."

CHOCOLATE CHUMP

In 1995, a secretary for a London, England, company successfully sued her boss for £4,500 after she was 'forced' to watch him gorge on a novelty chocolate penis over a company Christmas lunch. Profitable, eh?

NO SEX TOYS PLEASE... WE'RE SINGAPOREAN

In 2005, in a bid to increase awareness about sexuality and pep up the country's declining birth rate, officials allowed Singapore's first ever sexhibition. The only problem was that nudity and sex toys that resembled genitals or were considered over-sized, were not allowed. One wonders why they bothered...

ONE IN FOUR MEN FAKE ORGASMS SOME OF THE TIME

FROM STRAIGHT A'S TO STRAIGHT UP LOSER

A straight-A student whose parents described him as a 'good kid' was suspended from his school in Washington and given a citation for sexual harassment for turning up at a neighbouring school dressed in an inflatable penis costume.

WHAT'S UP DOC?

University of Massachusetts Professor Dr Peter Rice was arrested in a sex sting when he offered an undercover policewoman $40 for sex. The professor, who studies gonorrhea in human subjects, claimed he was "information gathering." But nobody believed him – perhaps he should have taken a specimen jar?

STRAIGHT EYE FOR THE QUEER GUY

What do you get if you cross a conservative Republican who has a history of opposing gay rights, and a government computer resplendent with downloads from gay dating sites? Short answer: Jim West, former mayor of Spokane, WA. West was kicked out by two-thirds of local voters when his internet sex infractions came to light. His response to local press was classic – "It's helped me straighten out my personal life." Well, that's one way of putting it.

WHAT A BOOB # 3

A bus driver drove himself to distraction when a female passenger boarded his bus with a more than ample cleavage. The German

A THIRD OF BRITONS LOSE THEIR VIRGINITY BEFORE THE AGE OF CONSENT

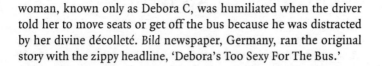

woman, known only as Debora C, was humiliated when the driver told her to move seats or get off the bus because he was distracted by her divine décolleté. *Bild* newspaper, Germany, ran the original story with the zippy headline, 'Debora's Too Sexy For The Bus.'

CALIFORNIA SCHEMING

Scottish businessman Talwar Farooq was caught trying to extort money from a businessman in Paolo Alto, California. Sultan filmed the married man having it off with a prostitute in a hotel room, then attempted to blackmail him for a quarter of a million dollars. The 'victim' went straight to the police, and Farooq was arrested.

KEYSTONE KIDNAPPERS

Flowers, chocolates, love-letters – all good ways to attempt to win back the heart of a young lost love. Paying your mate to dress as a Dalek, hold a knife to your ex's throat and drag her into the woods so you can rescue her? Well, I'll leave you to decide if dim-witted Brit Alex Whooley won his ex-girlfriend back that way.

The details of the Baldrick-esque 'cunning plan' involved a £40 Dalek voice-changing mask from Woolies, and a £20 bribe to friend Peter Burnell to kidnap the poor woman, threaten her at knife point and drag her into the woods. Sadly, details are unclear in the press about how Whooley then planned to rescue the very unmerry maiden.

Doubtless the judge had heard enough and didn't bother asking. He sentenced the rubbish Romeo to 14 months in prison, and his mate to nine.

PORN STORE PALAVER

German F1 racing ace Ralf Schumacher was probably always going to live in the shadow of his car genius older brother Michael. Maybe that's why, in 2004, he gloated that he was going to invest £700,000 in the sex store chain Beate Uhse. Bloody show off. But – like his brother before him – the German public did not take kindly to his exhibitionism, and Schummi 2 reneged on the deal after a TV comic started a smear campaign against him. The callous comedian had t-shirts printed with the slogan 'Hard Cora' as one way of winding Schummi up – the racing driver's wife is named Cora.

SHORT AND SWEET

You know those annoying sex-life surveys which show couples boasting about how often they have sex. Cue example: "Yeah we've been married 15 years but we have sex every morning before breakfast, dinner and lunch. And it's always mind-blowing." If such surveys make you feel inadequate, then take heart from the under-active libido of the porcupine. The unfortunate creature only mates once a year, the male first showering his lover with wee, before having his wicked way with her for the princely duration of two to five minutes.

MAN'S BEST FRIEND?

Whether we keep pets or not we are all familiar with the idea that dog is 'man's best friend.' The saying does not ring true in the case of one Colin Morrel.

In February 2008 it was reported that the lorry driver from Beaumont Leys, England, pleaded guilty to 'allowing' three dogs to

ONE IN FOUR BRITONS THINK THEY ARE VERY GOOD IN BED

have sex with him from 1974 to 2004. He was eventually shopped by his own son, who had discovered a video of his father getting carnal with two canines – a black Labrador and a brown mongrel, to be precise. Mr Morrel admitted to the acts, claiming he had been trying to erase them from his memory ever since, as he knew it was not "quite right."

Motivated by revenge for what the unnamed son called 'slanderous' attacks by his father, he personally handed the debauched video to the police, noting that "it's not as bad as child abuse, but an animal can never speak out however old it gets, so someone has to be their voice. That's another reason why I reported him."

GARDENER GETS TICKING OFF

By the time he'd assaulted his sixteenth victim, Brian P Holt had got his routine down, um, pat. Called in by women for quotes regarding his gardening business, he would tell them they had a tick on their bottoms, and then pat, squeeze and pinch their buttocks to remove the pest. But the real pest was Holt, who was sentenced in a Waukesha, Wisconsin court to three years probation in 2007.

GOING APE

Residents of Bristol, England, were finally able to sleep in peace early in 2008 after weeks of whooping and wailing had been keeping them awake. Locals had complained to a local council, and when officials finally got to the bottom of the racket, they banned two pervy primates at the local zoo from having sex outdoors. I know it's ridiculous, but it's true. Bristol zoo-keepers were dumb-founded when they were ordered to keep the over-sexed apes indoors at least three days a week.

8% OF BRITISH PEOPLE HAVE HAD MORE THAN 21 SEXUAL PARTNERS

TOP TEN PUBLIC MISADVENTURES

10. In 2007, James Barbour and Carol Walters were arrested for going at it full throttle on the central reservation of a main road in Cincinatti. Both were of no fixed abode.

9. British soap actress Gillian Taylforth was a bit of a silly sausage in 1994 when she unsuccessfully sued The Sun for libel after they said she had performed oral sex on her partner in a car on the A1. Part of the evidence against her was a home video, which included Taylforth posing suggestively with a large sausage.

8. How lusty would you have to be to have sex with a near-stranger on a beach in a country where sex outside marriage is a criminal offence? Best ask stupid Britons Vince Acors and Michelle Palmer, who did that very thing in the United Arab Emirate of Dubai in July 2008, after a day-long booze marathon. The newly acquainted couple were banged up for three months each, despite begging for leniency. Palmer made it home to the UK during the Christmas season later in 2008, while Accors remained in jail as there were problems with his Visa.

7. In 2004, British soccer star Stan Collymore was famously stitched up by The Sun, having honey-trapped him to report on his penchant for a spot of dogging.

6. Soccer games and toilets aren't often associated with all things titillating. But in 2006, two fans of Britain's Aston Villa football club were caught in flagrante delicto in a disabled toilet during a match against Wigan. The game was a nil-nil draw.

5. On a cold and frosty morning at Koge train station, Denmark, in 2007, passengers were left to freeze outside as things hotted up in the waiting room for two over-amorous railway passengers.

Keeping their clothes on during their railway rendezvous saved them from a charge of public indecency.

4. Über-pop star George Michael has been caught with his pants down in public on more than one occasion. Famously, when interviewed on TV after being caught by the police whilst giving oral sex to a 50-something trucker he'd just met, Gentleman George said "I've just got one thing to say to him – 'Thank you very much.'" Michael has twice been the hapless victim of sting operations – the other time was by a national newspaper. After the second sting, Michael's long-term partner Kenny Goss was reported as saying, "As far as he's concerned this is what gay men do."

3. In June 2008, an Italian couple were cautioned for obscene acts in public, and disturbing a religious function. Their crime? Oral sex in a confessional box of the Cesena cathedral during mass. And their excuse? "We are atheists, having sex in church is just like having it any other place."

2. It's very bad luck when a roll in the hay leads to being rolled over by a tractor. This is what befell a pair of love-struck youngsters who chose the darkened corner of a field in Brnicko Village in the Czech Republic for an impromptu frolic. The field's owner, who was driving the tractor as a shortcut to a party, was later charged with causing injury to the man's buttocks and the woman's chest.

1. ONCE, TWICE, THREE TIMES A LADY
Kent, UK office-worker Alana May reaches the number one spot for the quantity if not the quality of her sexual misadventure. In 2006, she admitted to outraging public decency for ignoring, not one, not two, but three, warnings from police officers to put it away as she cavorted with a young man in the grounds and against a wall at Selbey Abbey, North Yorkshire.

HOLY COW

Officer Richard Ewing Jr, 38, from Burlington County, New Jersey, US, was charged with carrying out sex acts on cows in 2006. The charges of animal cruelty followed a previous conviction for molesting young girls.

BARNSTORMER

Owners of a barn in Corvallis, Oregon, installed CCTV when they discovered their horse had been sexually assaulted on a number of occasions. Their suspicions bore fruit when they saw footage of a teenager carrying out the attacks. The disturbed youngster was finally caught after the barn owners installed an alarm, and soon the nightmare was over for the mare.

RAWHIDE

Brazilian Getulino Ferreira Paraizo earned five years in jail when he first had sex with and then killed over four hundred cows. Police say the man tortured the beasts, even stabbing them in the eyes, before raping them. Among the clues he left behind at every scene were empty packages of the same brand of cookies.

ALL THE PRESIDENT'S WOMEN

Warren G Harding. Remember him from your history lessons in school? Perhaps not since, by all accounts, the 29th President of the United States was politically cack-handed during his two year reign of power. Indeed his talents seemingly lay in other directions, since he managed not one but two high profile extra-marital affairs during his political career.

The first, with the wife of a friend, one Carrie Phillips, ended up costing his party. They paid for her to take a long, expensive trip to Europe in order not to reveal the jiggery-pokery. She is believed to be the first person to successfully blackmail a political party.

His second mistress, Nan Britton, also managed a first – writing the first known kiss-and-tell book in 1927 entitled *The President's Daughter* about their illegitimate love child, Elizabeth Ann. Although Harding never admitted paternity, he paid a child care allowance for Elizabeth until his death in 1923.

PROTESTING TOO MUCH # 1

An outspoken anti-gay Republican Senator was forced to resign when he reneged on a promise to pay a man for – surprise, surprise – gay sex.

Richard Curtis had contacted police saying that Cody Castagna was trying to extort money from him in a bid to out him as a gay man. But far from trying to blackmail Curtis, Castagna maintained he was only trying to claim the $1,000 that was rightfully his, having carried out an unidentified sex act with the politician.

Curtis's denials fell on deaf ears. Not only did receipts show he had bought two gay pornos before taking the rent boy to a luxury hotel, but witnesses had seen him leaving a changing room in the Hollywood Erotic Boutique wearing, women's long red stockings and a black sequined lingerie top.

Moral of the story: if you're going to fornicate with strangers in a luxury hotel, just be nice and pay up what you owe. Oh, and also, if you're gay, voting against gay rights might just be seen by some as a wee bit stupid, don'tcha think?

57% OF SCOTS HAVE HAD A REGRETTABLE SEXUAL EXPERIENCE AFTER DRINKING ALCOHOL

A MARS A DAY...

A famous urban legend is that British rockers Mick Jagger, Keith Richards and several others had a Mars Bar party with Marianne Faithfull in 1967. This is a delightful event where the chocolate treat is eaten out of an orifice not usually associated with food. Faithfull pooh-poohed the rumour in her autobiography, but the urban legend lives on.

THE INSIDE STORY

Surgery Magazine. I shouldn't imagine this trade journal often raises a laugh. But in 1986, two doctors collated an amusing list of 'apparently self-inserted foreign bodies' that had been removed by colleagues over the years. Of the 182 objects which had been lost in various rectums, the most popular were foodstuffs, bottles and vibrators. The weirdest were a tobacco pouch and a suitcase key.

OFF THE BOIL

The British Journal of Hospital Medicine enlightens us yet further as to the unfailing imaginative resource of the public when it comes to substitute dildos. In 1994, the journal discussed the tactics used by surgeons in Cardiff to remove a microwave egg boiler from a patient's rectum. They resorted to forceps usually used to help ease out babies, if you really want to know...

A POKE IN A PIG

A 72-year-old man chose a farm's quietest pig to sexually attack in 2002. Lynne Bennett, manager of the inner London farm, was not impressed. She said, "If he'd picked on one of the others, he would have been in serious trouble. They would have done him some damage."

BIG IS BEAUTIFUL

Researching this book has led me to all manner of strange sites on the internet, but possibly none weirder than Giantess World. Here men can indulge a sexual disorder known as macrophilia – in other words, a fetish for big women. And by big, I mean gargantuan, humungous, gigantic. Literally. And why? "Seeing a giantess have her way with anything and everything is a combination of a woman being ultimately powerful, sexual and completely dominating all at the same time," the website's founder explained in an interview with salon.com. Well, that explains it!

PLAY WITH FIRE, YOU'LL GET BURNED

Amy Hendry was found masturbating by police in Aberdeen, Scotland's, main shopping centre in July 1999, while near to a number of burning dustbins outside McDonalds. Although at first they did not connect the two crimes, police put two and two together when they found petrol, a lighter and a rag in the woman's bag. She then admitted she suffered from pyrophilia, a sexual disorder causing the sufferer to be turned on by fire.

THE BMW IS THE PREFERRED CAR FOR ONE THIRD OF PEOPLE WHO HAVE CAR SEX

SOMETHING STUPID

When San Francisco paramedics arrived to find a patient doubled up and admitting he'd done something 'really stupid', they probably would never have guessed the doofus deviant had put a frozen fish up his bum. Elaborating on his stupidity, the patient said that after two or three thrusts head-first up his backside, the fish had started to thaw and the dorsal fin had extended, making the entire frozen sex-aid impossible to remove.

SEX FILES

Okay, I admit, it, my love of the pun can sometimes be a tad obvious. But what better way to describe David Duchovny's admission in 2008 that he was being treated for sex addiction? Previously he had denied having the illness.

GHOST-RIDER

Before her tragic and untimely demise, sex-kitten Anna Nicole Smith claimed she'd had sex with a ghost on several occasions. "The ghost would crawl up my leg and have sex with me. I was freaked out at first, but he gave me amazing sex so I had no problem with it," she's reported as saying. What an irony then, that the Daily Star should reveal in 2008 than Anna herself now haunts the Hard Rock And Casino Hotel in Florida where she died. Whether or not she's as free with her sexual favours as she was in her life-time remains to be seen.

THE RECORD FOR THE FARTHEST EJACULATION FOR A MAN COMES IN AT SIX METRES

LOCKING LIPS AND EVERYTHING ELSE

When a Lagos couple died in the throes of passion in 1992, police believed the adulterous pair had been electrocuted by a live wire as they made love on the floor. Superstitious locals thought they knew better – the pair had been under the spell of a curse, they said, that fatally binds unfaithful lovers together forever.

PRIVATE(S) MATTERS

A nurse was reported to the Swedish Medical Responsibility Board when she joked loudly at a party about the size of a fellow guest's wedding tackle. She uttered the words most men would least like to hear: "He had the smallest penis I've ever seen." The man had been having urinary problems, and had been treated by the loud-mouthed nurse for months, he said.

REGURGITATE AND RETURN

The *Times* of London advised us in 2004 about the hopeless humper who demanded his ex-girlfriend give him back all the presents he'd given her during their brief romance. Nikolay Kozlovas asked his ex to return Swiss chocolates, nuts, a kilo of bananas, and an apple, threatening to take his case to the European Court for Human Rights if he lost the case in a local court. But as his ex-lover pointed out, all the 'evidence' had been eaten.

THE FARTHEST A WOMAN HAS BEEN RECORDED TO EJACULATE IS THREE METRES

KISS OF DEATH

In 2005, a Canadian girl was tragically killed after kissing her boyfriend. She suffered from an extreme allergy to peanuts, and died because her boyfriend had eaten a peanut butter sandwich hours before their tryst.

UNHAPPY MEAL

When you hear about a lawsuit demanding three million dollars in damages from a major fast food chain, you'd think it must be to do with sexual harassment, a mouse in someone's burger, or some such thing. But idiotic Stan Majewski was suing the fast food giant after nude images of his wife were uploaded onto the internet when he left his mobile phone in his local restaurant. Next time Stan, try the 'mouse in the burger' option.

ONLY IN JAPAN

The brassiere: an undergarment whose main purpose is to support the breasts, which admittedly can be put to good use as a flirt-aid in the bedroom. But men don't have breasts, do they? No wonder that a heated debate followed when one Japanese online retailer decided it would launch an on-line exclusive, bras for men. Within one week, over 300 bras had been sold to men "looking for their inner woman."

13% OF WOMEN ARE ALLERGIC TO THEIR PARTNER'S SEMEN

LOST IN TRANSLATION

There are certain foreign words which cause no end of mirth to tourists when travelling abroad. The sleepy little alpine town of Fucking, in Austria, for one. Imagine though, if your surname meant a rude word in your own native tongue. It's the sorry tale of Constantin Putica, whose surname – which he shares with 243 other fellow Romanians – has been the bane of his life. "I have got used to people laughing when they hear my name," bemoans the 45-year-old. And why? Putica means "small penis."

NAMED AND SHAMED

One of New Zealand's leading cardiologists lost a battle to keep his name out of the papers, when he was sacked in 2004 for taking photos of his winky and sending them to a female colleague. Dr Harvey White was later reinstated, but suffered public humiliation when a judge ruled his name could not be kept secret.

BOOBY TRAP

Male tourists were warned to watch their backs rather than buxom ladies' fronts when traveling to Uganda in 2008. Fred Enanga of Kampala CID warned that women with chloroform on their boobs were on the prowl. The creative crooks were knocking men unconscious with the fumes, stripping them, and stealing everything bar their underpants before making off into the night.

37% OF AMERICAN WOMEN FANTASISE ABOUT OTHER MEN WHILE IN BED WITH THEIR PARTNER

COCK-A-DOODLE-DON'T

The loss of a sex organ is no laughing matter. Oh alright then, it is when a man cuts off his own penis after mistaking it for a chicken's neck in the dark. This is what befell Romanian Constantin Mocanu when he went after a noisy cock with an axe. "I don't know how I got my penis instead," he said, "but I was so irritated I threw it to the dog. What could I do with a piece of penis?"

FILLIPINA HELL

In 2005, the owner of a British phone sex chat-line was successfully sued when his 'Filipina girls' turned out to be from down the road in Nottingham. The use of vernacular – and one would have thought totally unsexy – phrases like "Cheers, me duck" gave his girls, and the game, away.

PASSING OUT PARADE

A Romanian soldier who fainted while on parade was diagnosed with 'acute sexual frustration' in 2003. An army spokesman said of youngster Adrian Busureanu, "He became feverish, delusional and hysterical – induced by sexual frustration – after being apart from his girlfriend for two months." Aw, diddums.

KEEPING UP APPEARANCES

Journalists are a sordid bunch, make no mistake. Still, media studies students at Damelin College, Johannesburg, were right in thinking that even journalists-turned-lecturer don't talk about sex

53% OF AMERICAN BRIDES ABSTAIN FROM SEX FOR AT LEAST A MONTH BEFORE EXCHANGING VOWS

all the time, or prance about in yellow string vests and G-strings. Unlike their newly appointed tutor. The newsman impersonator was sacked, and found to have more holes in his CV than in his outfit.

PRAGMATIC ABOUT PASSION

For some, sex is the ultimate distraction, an anatomical voyage of discovery to fantasy-land where the worries of the day slip into an explosion of ecstatic squelches. Not for Hollywood actress Jennifer Connelly, who told *Esquire* magazine in 2005: "I do like to read a book while having sex, and talk on the phone. You can get so much done. If the room's dark enough, I like to do some online shopping." Words fail.

MEMORY LAPSE

A court ordered a refund for a customer of a German brothel in 2003, because he could not remember receiving the services rendered, having had a skinful before handing over the cash. The court in Kaarst ruled that for a suspiciously-high £5,400 worth of personal services, the client should have received an itemised bill.

SEWING THE SEEDS OF LOVE

A British farmer complained to police that he could not plough a lonely furrow after doggers in parked cars blocked the gates to his field – particularly at weekends. He told *The Sun* newspaper that public holidays were particularly irksome. "On August bank holiday, 20 cars stopped my tractor getting through to plough."

NO MILITARY 'SERVICE'

When a Cypriot woman's boyfriend kept falling asleep on the job, she did what any frustrated fornicator would do, and complained to her fella's employers. Said employers just happened to be the Ministry of Defence, who had to admit that military service was so exhausting that her solider boyfriend had no energy spare for rumpy pumpy.

OUT OF SIGHT

Wanting a sex change op is no laughing matter. But when you change sex just so you can look like Jennifer Lopez, I think a titter or two is fair game. Michael J Tito, 23, from Chicago, had HRT, a boob job and buttock implants so he could look like the famous songstress in 2003. Which leaves us wondering why he didn't go the whole hog: he changed his name to Jessica.

CASTRATE IN HASTE, REPENT AT LEISURE

Top tip for all you cuckolded husbands out there – ask your wife if she really is having an affair before you slice off your penis with a bread knife. Alfonse Mumbo didn't, and was dumped by his til-then faithful wife when she found out he was now lacking in the trouser department.

ANTS IN YOUR PANTS

Wang Zhendong had a cunning way to give you ants in your pants – breeding the tiny insects to make aphrodisiacs, to be rubbed on to underwear. He was executed in the northeastern province of Liaoning in China after conning investors out of millions of pounds for his ridiculous ruse.

ADMINISTRATIVE ERROR

A middle-aged couple were interviewed in British newspaper *The Guardian* after they received a letter from a firm of London solicitors demanding £503, owed for downloading gay hardcore porn. "We don't do porn" they told the paper, so it's unlikely they viewed the film *Army Fuckers* mentioned in the letter. The paper reported that a mind-boggling 25,000 letters had been sent out by the same firm.

OH, OH, OH MY GOD!

After a long battle, a Swedish court decided that The Madonna of Orgasm Church (Orgasmens Madonnas kyrka) had the right to be registered as a faith community. The church's founder Carlos Bebeacua told the *Skånska Dagbladet* newspaper, "The orgasm is God, the orgasm should be worshiped." How divine!

BRANDED A SPOIL SPORT

It's a risqué request, asking your friend if he'd care to indulge your lusty desire for a foursome. But bolshy Amy Cochran wasn't taking no for an answer when her less cock-sure chum came back with, "not likely, I don't fancy you." She beat him around the head with an iron and knocked her uninterested pal out. Her branding him a spoilsport landed her 14 months in prison.

8% OF WOMEN GET SEXUALLY AROUSED WHEN SPEAKING TO A MEDICAL PROFESSIONAL

TOP TEN VIAGRA-FUELLED COCK-UPS

10. General Sani Abacha, late President of Nigeria, promised to rid his country of corruption and sleaze when he entered office. $1 billion in irregularly withdrawn government funds and one Viagra-fuelled fatal orgy with prostitutes later, and the country finally managed to rid itself of its corrupt and copiously copulating leader.

9. Staying on the world's second largest continent, a café on the island of Sao Tome laughs in the face of the aphrodisiac effects of Viagra. Its 'Pilolo Atomico' cocktail (translation Atomic Penis) is a favourite with regulars who wax lyrical about its sexual potency giving qualities. The downside? The filthy brown liquid apparently tastes revolting, although the impotent imbibers of the drink don't seem to give a toss. Or do they?

8. In 2007, three men were convicted of a huge worldwide scam manufacturing fake Viagra and treatments for male baldness. Double whammy for gullible bald bonkers everywhere then.

7. And you thought our politicians would do anything to win a vote. To Thailand, where Sayan Nopcha, a campaigner for the People's Power Party, claimed a rival had been trying to get round strict new laws on vote-buying by distributing Viagra to elderly men. What a spoilsport! I bet the lucky recipients of the sex potency drug didn't think the vote-buyer was a flop.

6. The Greek Cypriot Government decided in 2005 to add Viagra to their list of everyday items that would be used to measure inflation. Which seems rather appropriate really. You know, inflation? Ahem.

5. 2005 was a good year for Viagra. At that time, a leading Israeli rabbi ruled that the passion-inducing pill could be taken by Jews on Passover, which reversed a prior ban. Rabbi Mordechai Eliahu said the pill could be taken if it was encased in a special kosher casing.

4. There have been several reported cases of Viagra being prescribed for poorly pooches needing a little help with blood flow to the heart. Good news for all you dog lovers out there. In the pet-loving, not bestial, sense that is.

3. What is it with politicians, Viagra and elderly men? The Mayor of La Pardo in Chile felt it his duty to enhance the lives of his 70-plus citizens. Like all good politicians, he made sure his back was covered though. "A doctor will have to certify that they suffer from erectile dysfunction and that their condition would not put them in danger of suffering cardio-respiratory side effects," he told reporters.

2. You know what they say when you're trying to give up one compulsive bad habit – don't replace it with another. Rap on the knuckles then for the British National Health Service in Greater Glasgow where a computer glitch saw smokers who were trying to quit being prescribed our favourite blue pill instead. Still at least those who could not light up would be able to get it up.

1. STIFFIES FOR THE STIFFS?
In the number one spot for Viagra-based silliness is news from China where traditionally relatives have burned paper money to honour their dead. In a bid to modernize the ceremony, younger Chinese are now reported to be burning paper replicas of Viagra so that their dearly beloved stiffs can enjoy posthumous stiffies. Condoms are also being offered to the dead, lest the safe sex message hasn't quite reached the after-life.

SILENCE IS GOLDEN

An Italian couple from the town of Treviso could face jail if they don't keep it down when they're getting it on. When neighbours complained that their raucous romping was keeping them awake, a judge imposed a two week trial period for the loud lovemakers to get their act together – quietly. Back in court for the second time, the male member of the party told the court, "I can only do it if she's shouting." The judge was not impressed and imposed a ban on their antics between the hours of 11pm and 7am.

LEGS ELEVEN

No need to ask Roland Rudman of Torquay, England, whether he's a breast or leg man. Between 2003 and 2006 he secretly filmed the legs and feet of over one hundred unsuspecting female members of the public.

His pervy ploy to get aroused was to lure women into a parked car, which he claimed had broken down. As they sat in the driver's seat and he revved up his metaphorical and literal engine, their legs and feet were filmed in a camera hidden in the footwell. Due to a legal technicality he was spared a jail sentence, but police were able to use civil powers to dish out a 10-year ASBO banning him from approaching any woman nation-wide if he intended to take 'footage' of her.

NOT SO CIVIL SERVANTS

In Germany, civil servants got up in arms – but not up anywhere else – when a new ruling said that they would be denied state help to pay for Viagra. Normally they qualify for state support as they have a special health insurance scheme, but the Federal Administrative Court in Leipzig said excluding the anti-impotency drugs did not contravene German equality laws.

TOO MUCH OF A GOOD THING

"He was a gentleman and a good man and then he started taking the tablets." So said Mrs Tanja Varmejda of Sydney, Australia at the trial of her 80-year-old husband Svetozar for sexual assault and battery. Before her husband had started taking the anti-impotence drug Viagra, she told the court he had been a decent husband and lover, but when his blue pill habit increased to three times a day he turned into a 'sex monster.' In what was described as an unusual case of a spouse suing their ex-husband, Mr Varmejda was made to pay over $200 Australian dollars to his traumatised ex-wife.

HONG KONG FOOLEY

Note to any wannabe Peeping Toms out there. Actually make that two notes. One, what are you, sick?! Two, if you must film up ladies skirts, make sure their boyfriend isn't watching.

Joseph Dunkin, a 51-year-old British man working on a building project in Hong Kong had clearly not read *The Voyeur's Guide to Not Getting Caught*. He was spotted filming a derriere by one victim's boyfriend, who gave chase across the city and then dished out a piece of rough justice.

During the pursuit, Dunkin threw his video camera in a flower bed, where it was promptly peed on by a dog. Once the camera had dried out, police were able to retrieve the evidence and the sneaky-peeker was sentenced to 14 days in prison.

THE AVERAGE BRITISH WOMAN THINKS ABOUT SEX SIX TIMES A DAY

ONE MAN AND HIS DOG

It's not often you hear of a doggy deviant doing the decent thing and taking an animal up the, ah, aisle. But an unnamed Indian man married his dog Selvi in a traditional Hindu ceremony in 1999. Don't fret though. His reasons were entirely legitimate. He'd been told by a soothsayer that he had to marry a canine in order to lift a curse that had been placed on him after he'd earlier stoned two dogs to death. So, that's alright then, eh?

VIVE LE VIAGRA

Goofy gendarmes in Marseille, France, allowed a geriatric male to get away with robbing the same chemist not once, twice or even three times of its entire stash of love-drug Viagra. Four times the randy robber used the same modus operandi, pouncing at closing time wearing a mask and armed with a knife, and forcing the chemist to come up with the goods. No doubt so he could come 'up' with the goods behind closed doors later on...

FEMALE VIAGRA FRENZY

When China Radio International asked for volunteers to test a female version of Viagra, they were deluged with volunteers. Testers at Beijing Universal No 1 Hospital were delighted with the response, having been afraid that the taboo surrounding female sexuality in China could have rendered the study impotent.

OF PEOPLE WHO HAVE HAD SEX OUTDOORS, 6% HAVE HAD SEX IN A BUS-STOP

TELL IT TO THE JUDGE

Judge Robert Kaszubik, chief judge of the US Circuit Court of Appeals, told it to the judge – that is to himself – when he asked for an enquiry into his own trial of smut-maker extraordinaire Ira Isaacs. Among the film oeuvre under scrutiny in the case were the charmingly entitled *Gang Bang Horse Pony Sex Game* and a couple of 'defecation' films. Which was nice.

Contrary to your first thought, the Judge did not suspend the trial because he found the matter too revolting to preside over. Nope, he thought he better had when the *LA Times* found the following deviant delights on his own public website: naked women painted as cows, a slide show of a transsexual strip tease, and a video of a male prancing in a farm with a sexually excited animal.

"Is it prurient? I don't know what to tell you," he told the paper. "I think it's odd and interesting. It's part of life." Sheep shaggers, cow copulaters and those horny for horses everywhere will no doubt hope for Judge Kaszubik to preside over their case, should they ever land in court.

(SEX) GAME OVER

Erotic asphyxiation – breath play – is the surprising practice of restricting oxygen supply so as to heighten orgasm. It usually involves some bondage too. Unsurprisingly, it has proved the tragic demise of many a hopeless humper. Simon Blades regularly played such games with his friend Zoe Chadwick, who warned him repeatedly about the dangers of indulging on his own. Sadly, he did not heed her words of wisdom, and died whilst inhaling chloroform through an old Soviet gas-mask early in 2008.

Of people who have had sex outdoors 7% have had sex in a phone box

BONKERS

A French couple became overnight internet sensations when they were caught on a mobile phone camera having it off in the lobby of a Parisian bank. Footage of their liaison dangereuse was shown for free all over the web, so they were unable to cash in on their bad bank bonking.

ESCORTED FROM THE BUILDING

When a top banking chief resigned over accessing sites of an 'adult nature,' it was clear what news agencies were euphemistically referring to. James Brink, who had the top job with a huge city bank, resigned in 2004, seeing the error of his ways, but maintaining the sites he visited weren't illegal.

NAUGHTY NOVELTIES

"It was a drunken and stupid thing." How many times have we heard that one before? This time, it was the woeful excuse of red-faced reprobate Jose Sandoval who'd been caught on security camera stealing blow-up dolls from the Naughty Novelties store in Winsconsin, USA. Note dolls, plural. Was the $270 'talking luxury model' not enough for you, Jose?

I SPY

Won Jeong-hwa, 34, of North Korea slept with several South Korean military officers in a sensational sex for secrets story revealed in 2008. It's alleged that after some movements of the 'beast with the two backs' variety, Jeong-hwa wheedled information from the military men of the 'troop movement' variety. She faces life imprisonment if convicted.

FIGHT... FOR YOUR RIGHT... TO GOOD SEX

Now for an apparent ridiculous governmental sexual misadventure. News agencies the world over leapt on Ecuadorian minister Maria Soledad Vela's decree that women should have a right to good sex. Male members – of parliament, that is – leapt on the statement, with Assembly member Leonardo Viteri accusing Ms Vela of trying to decree orgasm by law, which, he said, "isn't possible." Sure it is. All you need is a map for every Ecuadorian male member (lewd meaning this time) to find his way to the clitoris.

SPECIAL OFFER

When you receive an email from your kid's nursery headed 'Easter Special', you'd be forgiven for thinking the subject was an Easter event involving bunnies or eggs. Rabbits were indeed involved when parents from the Busy Bee nursery in Strathhaven, Scotland, received such a message, but incredibly they were of the Rampant kind.

Nursery nurse Lindsay Duncan, who moonlights as an Anne Summers rep, shocked mums and dads when she used the nursery mailing list to offer sex toys and bondage gear at discounted rates. The parents were not amused. One mum said, "I feel a bit sick to be honest that someone who works at a kids' playgroup does not see anything wrong in sending me an email offering vibrators and bondage gear."

JAPANESE VACATION SENSATION

In China, a hotel manager and a 'Mami' – a Chinese term for a Madam – faced life in prison after organising a 'sex holiday' for over 200 Japanese businessmen. The randy suits were visiting China on a conference for their construction company, 'Kooki.' In the contract with the conference centre, 'sex services' were listed as a must-have.

RANDY REVEREND

Making himself an internationally stupid shagger of the highest order, Pastor Peter Wirth of the Relevant Church in Ybor City, Florida, made news across the globe when he called for his parishioners to have a 30 day sex marathon to rekindle the spark in their marriages. It was 'ya boo sucks' to singletons though – they were told to take a 30 day vow of celibacy.

LIKE A CHILD IN A SWEET SHOP

In Reims, North-East France, a dozy young man fell asleep while watching a porno in a sex shop. The owner shut up shop and disappeared for the weekend, leaving our sleeping beauty oblivious to his temporary porno prison sentence. Liberation reported that on waking, the ecstatic 25-year-old kept himself busy until most of the next day had passed. However, proving you can have too much of a good thing, he eventually called police and asked to be let out.

IMPECCABLY IMPROPER

Former squaddie, police and prison worker Martin O' Dowd's reputation was ruined quick as a flash(er) when he displayed his penis and then a police badge to an unnamed lady in the loos of the Union Arms pub in Yarm, Yorkshire. His barrister spoke highly of the man, saying, "He is clearly a man of impeccable character who will unquestionably lose his job as well as his good name." Impeccable as far as surprising ladies by flashing your bits at them can be, that is.

SEXSOMNIA

Being able to do something 'in your sleep' is all well and good, but perhaps not when it comes to sex. An Australian couple were unlucky enough to discover this in the late Nineties. The husband suffered from the sleeping disorder 'sexsomnia' and was found by his wife in their back garden, sowing the seeds of love with a total stranger.

SCREAMING ABDABS

When Commissioners from Brooksville County, Florida, opened their inboxes to fetch the agenda for their next permit meeting, they received a bit of a shock. The fourth annual Old School Biker Rodeo, an annual event featuring naked ladies, had posted a link to a website for a 'screaming orgasm' contest. Even though the event raises money for charity and had been held with gratuitous nudity in the past, commissioners turned down the request on grounds of indecency.

45% OF SCOTS HAVE FANTASISED ABOUT HAVING SEX WITH A WORK COLLEAGUE

MARKETING GIMMICK

Sex and death are two subjects that are often lumped together, so we shouldn't be too surprised that an Italian coffin-making company produced a rather impressive naughty calendar with photos of semi-naked women draped over their wares as a marketing gift. Too surprised, no. Amusingly perplexed, yes.

OUR SURVEY SAYS:

— Internationally-respected science journal *The New Scientist* had a piece on a University of New Mexico survey in 2007 which showed that lapdancers in the fertile period of their menstrual cycle earned significantly more in tips than their co-workers. The scientist behind the survey claimed that it showed that the point women are on in their cycle had "a real effect on their earnings."

NOSY NEIGHBOUR

— A vigilante wielding a 39-inch cavalry sword kicked his neighbour's door in when he thought he heard a woman screaming from the next-door flat. Over-imaginative James Van Iveren broke into John Irving's Milwaukee home, insisting he reveal where he had hidden his 'victim.' It turned out the screams were from a Spanish skin-flick called *Casa de Culo* ('House of Ass'). The local DA decided to prosecute Iveren's actions since the noises from the film "were sounds of consensual sex, not rape."

TOILET HUMOUR, NOT FUNNY

"Misogynistic and offensive." This is how politicians and women's groups described urinals shaped like a woman's mouth – complete with lip-sticked lips, teeth and a bright red tongue – in public loos near the opera house in Vienna. The businessman behind the hair-brained toilets promised to remove them within 14 days.

FROM RUSSIA WITH LUST

"Who wants an orgasm?" Oh, put it away, I'm not talking directly to you. It's a question asked by Russian 'faith healer' Boris Zolotov at his traveling mass orgasm seminars, which were popular in the 1990s. When the women attending the event screamed "I do!" Boris would have them gyrating expectantly on a communal bed to Euro trance music, until the shared moment of climax came. A 1993 Reuters report claimed one witness had seen up to 30 women have an orgasm at a session in Zelenograd.

WEDDED BLISS – SO LONG AS YOU'RE UGLY

Good news for the less charming of you men out there. Results from a 2007 study found that married couples are happiest when the man is less good-looking than his dear lady wife. The research, published in the *Journal of Family Psychology*, suggests that, in evolutionary terms, women don't care about men's looks so long as they can give them a sprog. It's in men's evolutionary make-up, however, to bag themselves the best-looking mate they can find. Choosy buggers.

FRENCH MEN, ON AVERAGE, HAVE THE LARGEST PENISES IN THE WORLD AT 15.48 CM

PASSION KILLERS

Doctors in Edinburgh claimed to have cured a woman of her tendency to have frequent uncontrollable orgasms, especially when she was driving. Doctors Robert Will and Paul Reading said the woman did not mind the involuntary sex spasms, until one of them left her unconscious. A drug used for epilepsy eventually cured her.

FAIR MEANS OR FOUL

Animal rights organisations are known for being inventive when it comes to promoting their cause. Take a case in 2007, where inflatable sex dolls were used to protest against fast-food chicken giants KFC. The campaign's motto was 'KFC Blows.'

CREEPY QUACK

Mark Astill was a Chinese massage therapist, supposedly well-liked by his clients, a self-appointed 'miracle worker.' But his 'technique' of using a vibrating massager on women's privates to cure them of their aches and pains proved to be his downfall. He was jailed for eight years for sexual assault.

CARTOON CALAMITY

A cartoonist who drew a scurrilous sex cartoon of the Spanish royal family faced up to two years in jail for insulting them, the BBC reported. The images showed Crown Prince Felipe and his wife

ONE IN THREE NORWEGIANS REGRET HAVING SEX WHILE DRUNK

doing the nasty with the a caption saying sex was the closest he would come to working. The point of the joke was that the Spanish government were to pay $3,500 to couples for each new baby.

LAGER LOUT

As husbands go, Folko Stiebner is pretty crap. The oddball German landed a three-year stint in prison when he forced his wife to have sex with their 60-year-old neighbour in return for crates of beer. This nefarious transaction continued for several weeks until his 32-year-old wife shopped the pair to police. The neighbour received a two-year suspended jail sentence and had to pay over 3,000 Euro to the victim.

GRANNY GROPER

It's not unusual to hear of a sexual misadventure involving a church choir – but ordinarily the added ingredient is a vicar who's none too in touch with his Godly side. It's rather less run-of-the-mill to hear of a groper disguised as a granny feeling up elderly ladies in church pews.

In 2008, at the First United Methodist Church in Ocala, Florida, a 73-year-old choir member was shocked when a fellow parishioner squeezed her breast during choir practice, but was too embarrassed to speak up. When a further mammary molestation incident happened during a bible reading, she and a number of other victims of Robin Forbes, 58, came forward. It was only when police got Mr Forbes to the station they realized the bogus granny was, in fact, a man.

TOP TEN KNICKER-THIEVES

10. When a masked gunman held up a store in East Berlin in the late 1980s, he was told the cash register was bare. He then ordered the store keeper to hand over all items of women's underwear in the shop.

9. We all know about being caught red-handed but what about being caught pink-knickered? This is what befell a nerdy knicker thief who had been stopped by police on suspicion of drug-driving in Australia in 2008. When rummaging for drugs in the car's glove compartment, police found a bag with 81 pairs of women's knickers. The foolhardy thief's "they're my girlfriend's" excuse did not wash when a body search revealed he was wearing a Barbie-pink lady's thong.

8. Not your conventional knicker thief this one, more of a thief with knickers. An old lady looking for a thrill in the fair city of Genoa used the cunning ploy of hiding jewellery from posh shops in a big pair of granny pants – and there was me thinking granny pants a waste of sartorial space.

7. You might recall the turn of the millennium sent a number of people screwy – perhaps even some of you. But I feel sure the ladies among you, if you happened to have been in Osaka at the time, would not have been duped by the pitiful panty-thief who convinced young women to hand over their knickers by claiming there had been an outbreak of the deadly o-157 E. coli bacillus in the city.

6. When sorry seems to be the hardest word, the thing to do is to wait 84 years – in the case of one inhabitant of Barberton, Ohio. The town had suffered the indignity of an underwear scavenger who stole women's panties for 15 years from 1918. Officials received the following signed letter many years thereafter. "I will be 99 years of age. I just want to clear things up. I'm sorry."

5. Lucky he did not fess up in Phuket, where one lingerie-lover was nearly beaten to death when he was happened upon half-inching knickers off a clothing line in plain view of the Thai town's football team.

4. The Isles of Scilly were one of the last bastions of trust, the kind of place where back doors were left open if you popped out to the shops. Stephen Allison put a stop to that in 2005 when his wife's new partner uncovered three bin bags full of women's underwear and sex toys in a loft, items he'd stolen from various neighbours over the years. In court, the victims had to spare their blushes when identifying their belongings. One woman claiming a vibrator among the evidence as her own said, "I know it's mine because... it glows in the dark."

3. Jason Tidy, 39, of Leeds in West Yorkshire, England, did not learn from the mistakes of knicker thefts past. Having been caught in a field by a horsewoman in 1992 in a pair of pants, the pantie perv went on 10 years later to get jiggy with a pair of women's knicks in the changing room of a woman's clothing store. On hearing about the man's hoard of 1,000 pairs of women's knix, the Judge told Tidy his sentence would not be elastic.

2. There you are. Just when you think you're the world's most prolific knicker thief, along comes a Japanese guy who sees your 1,000 knickers and raises you 2,977. Step up Tokyo's Shigeo Kodama who abused his position as a construction worker to climb into ladies' apartments and grab his lingerie loot over a six year period.

1. PANTIE-MONIUM
Think I've made a mistake putting Mr 3,977-pairs-of-knix in the second place spot? Think again. Believe it or not, there is a knicker-thief more ridiculous, more preposterous than he. In 2007, the BBC reported (so it must be true) that an Irish man held up a lingerie store with a knife, dressed as a female elf, which he told Belfast Crown Court had the delightful name of 'Bebo.' I wonder if he pleaded 'elf-defence.'

FORCES SWEETHEART

Australian pop star Tania Zaetta received a crawling apology from the Australian defence ministry in 2008 over claims she had slept with Australian special forces soldiers during an entertainment tour for troops in Afghanistan. Her denials were backed up by her fellow musicians. John Clinton, of 'Wolverines' fame, told a radio programme, "I've heard of quickies mate, but you'd have to be really quick – we didn't have time to do anything." The original claims were made to the ministry of defence in a stupidly titled 'hot issues brief.'

OUT OF THE FRYING PAN

A New York woman underwent a horrifying ordeal in 1994 when she developed car trouble. Taking advantage of her plight, a man held her at gun point, forced her into his own vehicle and drove her to a nearby house. She was then used as a sex slave by Barnaby and Caitlin Calderwell, who were later jailed for the kinky kidnapping. The bound woman eventually managed to free herself using a lighter left by the dim-witted criminals, and fled naked from their burning house.

SAY IT AGAIN

— Research published in the New Scientist magazine suggested that women who are ovulating have sexier voices then their non-egg-releasing peers. Researchers played recordings of women's voices at different points in their menstrual cycle to volunteers of both sexes. Results emphatically showed that those who were at their most fertile had the most dulcet and attractive tones.

OF THE BRITONS WHO HAVE HAD SEX IN THE OFFICE, 11% HAVE HAD IT ON THE BOSS'S DESK

HALF-ARSED STREAKER GETS FULL WRATH OF TEACHERS

Dylan Mangum, a 17-year-old junior from a provincial American high school was suspended when he stripped to his underpants at half-time during a school football game and streaked – well, semi-streaked – across the pitch. Appeals against his suspension were denied as school governors said he'd been "engaging in behaviour that is indecent, overly affectionate or of a sexual nature in the school setting." Blimey, hate to think what would happen if they peeked behind the bike sheds.

AT IT LIKE RABBITS

Joyce Hartley's rabbits were only doing what rabbits do best, but she still landed up in court. Her neighbours Ernest and Frances Haskins were so put out by the pets constant rampant rabbit love-making that Hartley was ordered by a London court to build them a love-shack.

DROP DEAD GORGEOUS

I've heard of some idiotic ways to pull, but playing dead surely takes the biscuit. Oh, sorry. I mean, offering your mate a snack, then playing dead, surely takes the biscuit. The male nursery spider does just this though, when attempting to mate. If he didn't offer the much larger female the tasty treat before he tried it on, she might well have him for lunch.

THE AVERAGE BRITISH MALE FANTASISES ABOUT HAVING SEX 2,555 TIMES A YEAR

THE 'SUBWAY RAT'

As serial offences go, this one takes the cake. On 52 previous occasions, Andy Thomas had been arrested for groping women on the New York subway. So it's hardly surprising that he pushed his tally up to 53 just two weeks after his last release from prison. In April 2008, he boarded a heaving Manhattan subway train and ground his pelvis into a female commuter's bottom. Unluckily for him two plain clothes police officers spotted and recognised him, and he was promptly arrested.

BOTTOM GRABBER GETS THE GO-AHEAD

Repeat derrière rummager Henry Hawthorne has over four decades of experience in launderettes, on trains, at railway stations – you name a place, he's grabbed a woman's bum in it. Yet this, and the fact that one of his victims felt like she'd been 'raped', were not enough to get a High Court Judge to overturn Croydon Crown Court's decision not to ban Hawthorne from the railways. Even his counsel told the court, "It is quite clearly agreed between the parties that Mr Hawthorne is a groper. He reaches for their bottoms." Yet still he is free to roam – literally and with his hands. Female commuters in the area of Thornton Heath, London, be warned!

HACKED

Do people never learn? Sandra Messenger had only just met IT technician Brian Landon in an internet chat room, but decided she trusted him enough to send saucy pics of herself in the nude via email. When their internet entanglement turned sour, Landon emailed the pics to everyone in his ex's email address book. Bet she was 'hacked' off!

TRICK OR TREAT?

$80,000 worth of damage, 100 police officers called out to quell a burgeoning riot, eight of them injured in the ensuing mayhem. You'd think we were describing the aftermath of a mass political demonstration.

But, no, in this instance, Madison, Wisconsin police got heavy-handed with tear gas and the like when the town's annual Halloween Parade got out of hand when several women flashed their bits to the crowd. I say 'bits' as the poor lil' ol' Wisconsin police were too shy and retiring to say if we're talking breasts or bottoms here. Lt. Bill Housley of the force 'explains' that police stepped in when "women flashed, uh, you know, uh, various body parts to the crowd."

FROM THE BOTTOM OF HER HEART

When Jane Dyke convinced herself that husband Dick was doing the dirty on her, she concocted a revenge plan, no doubt from the bottom of her heart. She made up posters with an image of her ex's naked bottom, with the words 'Dicky Dyke: lying, cheating, two-timing arse! Susan Hollinghurst is no better.'

The campaign of vengeance saw her plastering over 200 posters around the man's hometown of Seaford, Durham, England, days after he had emigrated to Cyprus. Both Mr and Mrs Dyke denied any allegations of wrong-doing – she of the street spamming, he of the affair. In fact, both felt like they'd got a bum deal.

41% OF BRITISH PEOPLE HAVE SUFFERED SEVERE CARPET BURNS DURING SEX

TOPLESS PROTEST

The US porn industry is estimated to be worth anywhere between $500 million and $10 billion dollars. So while all manner of sexual misadventures are doubtless going on behind closed doors in the town of Daytona, a city law bans women from going topless in public there.

Deeming the law unconstitutional, Liz Brook regularly protests against the unfair statute which leaves men able to take their shirts off during city events like 'Bike Week.' A city attorney made an exception for Brook at the 2007 event, but said if she went topless she would have to remain hidden behind a six foot awning on the float she was riding. She flouted the agreement and was immediately arrested.

Let's leave the last word to the lady herself. "Big Brother is everywhere," she said, "and it's time to leave little sister alone." Hats – or should that be bras – off to you, Liz!

SOMETHING'S BURNING...
AND I DON'T THINK IT'S LOVE

A warning for all you men who eye up the girl or woman next door. In 1992, Hans-Joachim Kampioni invited his neighbour Heidemarie Siebke over for a few drinks. Things went awry when he got over-familiar and started to badger Siebke for sex, but that was nothing compared to her reaction. The 50-year-old Siebke stunned Kampioni into submission by thwacking him over the head with a chair, severed his penis with a bread-knife, and set fire to his flat to destroy the evidence.

YOU WOULDN'T BET ON IT

Turtle Creek Casino in Traverse City, Michigan is used to drunk and disorderly clientele – it's a casino, after all. Managers for the casino told the police in 2003 that they usually deal with unruly patrons themselves, only calling them in when matters get out of hand. In this case the hand that got out belonged to Bishop Demetrei Khoury Toledo, who oversaw 45 states for the Antiochian Orthodox Christian Church.

Filled with booze and sweary words, the Bishop was captured on the casino's CCTV bothering an attractive middle-aged woman. The footage clearly shows him grabbing her breast when she rejects his advances.

Arresting Officer Trooper Barry Kushner told reporters, "he used some non-bishop type language." That included "a lot of profanity," he added, just in case we needed telling.

VIRTUAL VENGEFULNESS

Modern life. Ain't it grand. Just think in ye olden days when you felt like dumping a lover you had to do so via the boring old method of actually talking to the dumpee in person... or, if you were cowardly, by phone or letter. Nowadays the World Wide Web offers so many opportunities for giving a boyfriend or girlfriend the old heave-ho, some couples don't know where to begin.

I suppose it's hardly surprising that Wikipedia founder Jimmy Wales would choose to announce the end of a relationship on his site, posting the following emotionally cold statement, "I am no longer involved with Rachel Marsden." Not to be outdone in the virtual vengefulness stakes, Rachel put several pieces of Wales' soiled clothing on Ebay, saying: "It was such a classy move that I was inspired to do something equally classy myself."

REVENGE LAID BARE

YouTube has become the stomping ground for revenge-seeking ex-lovers everywhere. But some people really don't get it, do they? Take one woman, billed only as Costacarta, who put a vid on the site of herself stripping with a male gigolo. "Hi John" she says, "It's me, payback time." Erm, aren't you meant to put up an embarrassing vid of your ex, not the other way round? Perhaps that's why the video has now been removed.

TOYING WITH YOUR EX

When an Australian soldier discovered his girlfriend had been making the beast with two backs with one of his colleagues you could say he over-reacted. He persuaded the girl to lure her ex-lover to her home and cuff him to the bed, dressed as a police-woman. The boyfriend then made an appearance, and sodomized the lover with a sex toy. The woman lost her job, but escaped a jail sentence. The vengeful boyfriend eventually killed himself over the sordid affair.

TURKISH BLOOD BATH

In 1993, Zeynep Atici was shocked to hear that her boyfriend Abdullah Kemal Konak was going to leave her for another woman. She reacted immediately, getting him drunk and going at his penis with a bread knife. Doctors managed to reattach the injured appendage, but could not confirm whether sexual function would recover.

AFRICAN AMPUTATION

What is it with jilted ladies and slicing off men's parts? Shanangurai Tinarwo of Zimbabwe clubbed her husband on the head with a log after finding him in bed with another woman and chopped off his womanizing winkie with a knife. He was one of the lucky ones, and his penis was reattached.

TALK SHOW TRANSGRESSION

There's nothing like a good bust up between husband and wife on a day-time TV talk show. In 2002, it was the turn of a couple known only as Steve (43) and Sharon (26) to appear on Britain's *Trisha* show to air their mucky undies in public.

Complaining that his wife's demands for twice-daily sex romps were OTT, Steve went live on air to request that Sharon reign in her insatiable lust and sign a contract limiting their sexual encounters to three times a week. Negotiator extraordinaire Trisha managed to get the couple to meet in the middle and it was agreed they would have sex five times a week, including once in the back garden. And all totally unscripted, of course. UN envoy for sex spats, Trisha?

JUST SAY THE WORD

It's common knowledge that sex can make you go weak at the knees, but one unfortunate woman fainted every time she even heard the word, English newspaper the *Daily Mirror* reported in July 1993. Her illness came to public attention when an acquaintance took advantage of her aversion to the word 'sex' and would utter it so he could molest her when she fell unconscious. In court, lawyers had to use the word 'nookie' to avoid the vertiginous victim falling to the ground.

9.2% OF STRAIGHT AMERICAN WOMEN HAVE BEEN SEXUALLY ATTRACTED TO ANOTHER WOMAN

SHIVA ME TIMBERS

In 2003, New Delhi police arrested a conman who claimed he could help childless women become fertile by fondling their breasts. He excused his bizarre crime saying the Hindu god Shiva had given him his blessing.

CARRY ON DOCTOR?

An American doctor was arrested in 2008 for fondling a patient's breasts. The woman had visited the doctor for a stomach problem, and so knew something was up when he said her problem stemmed from her mammary glands. A case of DON'T Carry On Doctor.

THE LURVE DOCTOR

Call me old-fashioned, but I like my relationship experts to come fully equipped with common sense and high levels of decency. Unlike Kenji Iwatsuki, a leading sociology professor at a Japanese University who also writes books on affairs of the heart. And yet in spite of these qualifications, he was arrested in 2004 for tricking a female student into letting him squeeze her boob. I'm no lurve expert myself, but isn't it preferable to ask your inamorata permission before you feel her up?

CAUGHT DIRTY-HANDED

I'm no criminal mastermind either, but I'd wager if you're going to feel up a pretty young lady, the last thing you want to do is leave behind incriminating evidence. Neither having filthy oily hands from working on his car, nor his victim's cry of "Don't you dare", deterred Harry Strang from squeezing one lady's left breast and then – more forcefully – the right. Her oil soaked yellow vest was used as evidence in court.

Newspapers at the time reported the comparison between the crime and 'The Psychiatrist' episode of classic BritCom *Fawlty Towers* where Basil inadvertently feels up a hotel guest with paint-smeared hands. The comparison's a crude one, of course, since in Basil Fawlty's case the groping was done unwittingly. The only thing unwitting about Mr Strang's molestation was, er, his lack of wit. He even carried out the goofy grope directly outside his own front door.

WHAT A BOOB # 4

The dentist's chair. As if suffering the torture of being poked and prodded in the mouth isn't enough, one woman had to endure the horror of being poked and prodded elsewhere in 2007 in Japan when her dentist touched her up while she was under the spotlight.

MAD PROFESSOR

A-Grades were on offer to Iowa University students – but only if they allowed their professor Arthur Miller to see them topless or if he could fondle or lick their breasts. One arrest and four felony counts of accepting bribes later, and Miller saw the error of his pervy ways. He drove his red BMW to a city park and shot himself dead.

AN ESTIMATED 10.4 BILLION CONDOMS ARE PRODUCED EACH YEAR

EYE CANDY

So you want to be an optician but are you sure you've got the right qualifications? There's a two year apprenticeship in the field, and knowledge of physics, algebra, trigonometry and basic anatomy. Err, yes, let's stick with basic anatomy. Something optometrist Owen Jennings was lacking when he asked women to remove their blouses during eye exams. He was charged when 13 patients came forward stating he did not know his eye from his elbow.

BONE DOCTOR GETS BONER

Just because you've got away with touching up nine of your patients doesn't mean you will get away with it a tenth time. Especially when that tenth patient is an undercover police woman. Time to expose Suffolk, England, osteopath Russell Brooks, who was caught on film rubbing his erection while assaulting the undercover police officer. Film of his ridiculous sexual misadventure, as well as testimony from patients, meant the dirty doctor faced jail in 2007.

DRAG QUEEN DRAMA

In 2007, Catholic traditionalists were far from cock-a-hoop when a San Francisco Archbishop said Mass in a church in the heart of the gay community. In attendance were gay men dressed as nuns, members of the 'Sisters of Perpetual Indulgence.' This group's motto is 'go and sin some more' and describes itself as a 'leading-edge order of queer nuns.'

One outraged, ungenerous Catholic said, "To hand over our Lord and Saviour Jesus Christ to known practicing and promoting sodomites, in the middle of a 'gay-friendly Mass' is beyond the pale." The Vatican are said to be investigating.

THE PORN INDUSTRY IS WORTH £1 BILLION IN THE UK

AMERICAN PASTORAL PICKLE

Opposing same sex marriages is probably to be expected of the president of the National Evangelical Association, which represents 30 million evangelical Christians. Regularly sleeping and taking amphetamines with a gay lover is probably not. No wonder 'Pastor Ted' Haggard had to stand down from his presidency of the association in 2006 when his partner outed him after discovering the true identity of his lover of three years.

A CYBER-STEP IN THE RIGHT DIRECTION

When monks were discovered flirting with girls in on-line chat rooms, Thai officials weren't too impressed. "Instead of using the net to flirt with young girls, monks should find ways to preach Dharma and lead them in the right direction," said Ladda Thangsupachai, head of the Cultural Surveillance Centre.

THE BEST LAID PLANS...

Ambition can sometimes cloud the old judgement. Take Father Petrica Florea, from Costesti in Romania, who convinced a teenager to seduce councillor Constantin Moise, 74, on the altar of his church. His plan was to convince parishioners that the councillor should be ousted from his position, so he could step in and take over. The authorities did not see it that way, and he was done for blackmail.

TOP TEN PEEPING TOMS

10. Legend has it the original Peeping Tom was a Tom who was struck blind for eyeballing Lady Godiva as she rode naked on horseback through the streets of Coventry.

9. A Peeping Tom by definition is a man who leers at women through windows, not someone who falls out of them. Perhaps Tadao Tanaka misunderstood when in 1999 he fell 12 floors from his neighbour's window ledge after climbing on her balcony for a bout of nosey naughtiness. Previous convictions for the same offence convinced police this was how Tanaka met his maker.

8. A randy copper got six months in jail for hiding a camera in a loo roll inside his neighbour's bathroom and spying on her via images beamed to his TV next door. The woman discovered the home-made spying device when redecorating her bathroom, saying "I knew something was up as I usually use peach toilet paper."

7. Wee-weeing women in Singapore could breathe easy for a year in 2001. A Peeping Tom who had been secretly filming unsuspecting ladies on toilets was given a 12 month ban on owning a camera phone, and visiting public lavs.

6. Ever get the feeling Big Brother is watching you? Well, your paranoia might well be justified. In Liverpool, England, Mark Gubbins 38, who worked for the local council, abused his position as a CCTV operator to sneak many a peek into the home of one unlucky lady. Bonking, toilet and other intimate actions were all caught on film for the sexual gratification of the council worker. He got two months in prison.

5. When Sergeant Major David Woodward was found dressed all in black lurking outside the girls' dormitories at Cwrt-y-

Gollen training camp, it soon became clear he was not delivering Milk Tray. Instead he was filming young female recruits as they showered and undressed for bedtime. The course he was running was called 'Look at Life.'

4. It's a fear for every young child – that the bogey-man may be hiding under the bed at night. For one couple, from New York State the fear became reality when they heard rustling noises as they were rustling up a love sesh. Moments later they discovered serial peeper Donei Zabedra-Ilario hiding beneath the bed, hoping to catch a glimpse of flesh.

3. A man who filmed women defecating and urinating as they ran a marathon was unrepentant when his case came to court. "If they are going to do that in public, they should expect people to see them," he whined. Such lack of contrition did not make the court take his 'not guilty' defence seriously, nor did the fact that he was disguised as a giant banana during the crackpot crime.

2. "I just want to see what people do in here." Thus spake Edward Gilmore, an ex-con from Wiltshire, England, during his trial for leering at a nail technician through a gap in the ceiling of a tanning salon. Hmm. Tanning salon. No inkling that there may be a scantily clad or naked woman laying on the tanning bench beneath you, Edward?

1. LOO-NEY LECHER
You remember 'Q', the gadget-meister of the James Bond films – the technical whizz always dreaming up some fantastic new gizmo for Bond to try out? Well this last pervy peeper was nothing like him, though he did rig up an elaborate piece of kit. In 2004, Martin Parson, a technology expert, was jailed for installing two video cameras in each of the loos of his home to film female visitors there. Possession of over 100 videos filmed over a three year period brought him a two year stint behind bars.

ALL THINGS BRIGHT AND BEAUTIFUL!

Religious authorities in Mondragone, Italy, were having 'nun' of it when a local priest tried to organise a beauty pageant for local sisters. "Nuns are – above all – women, and beauty is a gift from God," misguided Father Antonio Rungi told Italy's Corriere della Sera newspaper, shortly before the project got the scrap.

BANNER BANNED

A convent that was to be converted into a hotel by businessman Sean Roche received planning permission in 2007. His plan to use a picture of a naked nun to advertise the hotel did not. The saucy sign showed the woman of the cloth lifting her bodice to reveal a pair of breasts stamped with the words "The Convent."

WHO'S THE DADDY?

Watch an episode of any daytime TV show, and it's clear that questions over paternity are a common problem. You know the shows – the ones where the pregnant woman isn't sure if Dick or Dave is the daddy, the men involved take paternity tests, and the presenter reveals the answer on live TV. Modern life, ain't it marvellous?

Anyway. One German woman upped the ante on this preposterous public palaver in 2008 when she brought a case to a Stuttgart court room to force sex auction website Gesext.de to reveal the real names of all the men she'd been introduced to via the site. Of the forty men who'd won bids to sleep with her, she managed to narrow the possible father of her child down to six lucky winners. Or should that be losers?

The judge ruled in her favour saying the rights of the child outweighed the rights of the men to anonymity. The men involved in the auction sex dates were out of the courtroom and the country quicker than you can say going, going, gone.

MISTAKEN IDENTITY # 1

There's nothing smuttier than watching porn before breakfast, and there's nothing sillier than a man being knifed by his girlfriend because she thinks he is the star of the pre-brekkie porno they're viewing.

The scene for this one is Albuquerque, USA and the stars of the misadventure – but let's be clear, not the porno – are one Louisa Boehmer and her long-suffering boyfriend. When Boehmer became convinced he was a wannabe Dirk Diggler she became so enraged that she stabbed him in the face and bit him in the chest. Her fury did not end there though. She then pursued him down the street, brandishing the weapon, until he finally managed to flag down a cop car.

"She already has battery charges against her. She's not even supposed to be around me," the victim said. So that makes two ridiculous misadventurers in this sorry tale then – whatever was he doing hanging around with her in the first place?

BEWARE OF GREEKS BARING BOTTOMS

In 2007, nine British women, six Greek men and six British men were arrested for holding an 'oral sex' competition on the Greek island of Zakynthos. The men faced charges of encouraging obscene behaviour, and the women of prostitution.

THE SEX INDUSTRY IN THE NETHERLANDS IS WORTH 5% OF GDP

PAPAL PREPOSTEROUSNESS

Masturbation. Doesn't harm anyone, does it? Come on, surely you don't believe those old wives' tales about blindness and hairs on the palms? And no, I can't see a single follicle with my 20-20 vision. Ahem.

So why the Vatican thinks the world needs a moral alternative to masturbation is anybody's guess. According to *The National Catholic Reporter*, the Papacy has sanctioned just such a moral alternative, in the form of a vibrating machine that collects sperm without any 'erotic feelings.' What fun!

CAMERA SHY

When you take part in a world-record-breaking sex marathon, you might cut the organisers some slack if they capture your face on film. Retired teacher Leszek Szwerowski, 61, didn't when his nephew spotted him on the DVD of the World Sex Championships in 2003, gloating about Szwerowski's 15 minutes of fame to the rest of the family. The amateur porn star sued the organisers of the event to the equivalent of £2,500, saying they'd promised to pixellate the faces of participants. Still, 15 minutes isn't bad for a 61-year-old, I'd wager...

WOMAN SHOOTS SELF IN FOOT... AND LOVER IN HEAD

Agata Wisniewksi and lover James Rogers were going at it great guns during a kinky version of cops and robbers when a shot was mistakenly fired, hitting Rogers in the head. He was killed instantly, and Wisniewski was charged with negligent homicide. Officials believed her story that his death was a sex game that had gone tragically wrong, or she would have been charged with the graver charge of homicide.

WHO YOU GONNA CALL?

For every emergency, there's a number you can dial. Cat stuck up the tree? Call the fire brigade. Penis stuck in a vacuum cleaner? The paramedics await your call. Demonic figure living in your fridge? Remember Ghostbusters? They're just the job. But say you're a forty-two-year-old Polish woman and you've not had sex as long as you can remember. Who you gonna call? Bonkbusters? Erm no. Dial-a-hunk. Well you could try...

Hanna Wozniak, 42, of Koszalin in central Poland, did not think to dial any of the huge number of sex chat lines or online sex services the WWW has to offer, however. Instead the damsel-in-distress made over 700 phone calls to local army headquarters and her town council demanding they find her a man for sex. When police finally traced calls to her home, she was arrested and faced a possible year in jail. A police spokesman said: "This kind of behaviour is extremely irresponsible." Horny Hannah said, "I was desperate for sex. It's been so long since I had someone in my bed." Why didn't she just go down the pub like everyone else?

JOANNA'S KITCHEN NIGHTMARE

The kitchen store cupboard offers no end of substitute hard-ons, all of them perfectly legal and above board. I doubt I need to spell it out, but for the vegetable virgins among you, you can't go far wrong with a cucumber or a banana.

Perhaps Pole Joanna Kozlowska found the cupboard bare, when, in 2007, carnal desperation saw her inventing a new kind of kitchen-inspired sex-toy – with a food mixer. All would have been fine (perhaps), and she could have whipped herself into a state of erotic elation, had she not elected to use the make-shift device in the bath. One electric shock and a trip to the emergency room later, Mrs Kozlowska was unabashed, blaming her husband for not tending to her needs.

A BURNING LOVE

In 2007, the German tabloid *Bild* ran a story of two 18-year-olds from the Wismar area in Germany who had met on a beach, fallen in love at first sight, and immediately planned to give their virginity to one another a week later.

Their plan surely did not involve causing 100,000 Euro worth of damage and burning down the attic room and first floor of the girl's uninsured parental home. The place was set on fire by unattended tea-lights the twosome had lit while they bathed in another room to get in the mood for love. The nearly-lovers fled the burning scene that ensued, running naked into the street, their relationship tragically unconsummated.

LINGERIE LITTER LOUT

When police arrested Kazuo Oshitani, a 48-year-old office clerk from Osaka, Japan, for scattering knickers all over his neighbourhood, they could not have known the 'pavement art' would lead them to a bigger crime. Not content on sharing his love of knickers with the world, the panty perv had worn the knix, some of which contained a bodily fluid which we need not identify here. DNA from the knicker-sowing antics linked him inextricably to a 1994 robbery-murder case. Police were able to charge him just before the file for the cold case was closed for good.

NUTS ABOUT SEX

Newspaper reports in 2007 about a Malaysian man who'd been hospitalised with a nut stuck around his penis were baffling. Was it a peanut? A cashew? The mind boggled. The timid Kuala-Lumpur man was planning to get engaged the following week, and had

RON JEREMY IS THE WORLD'S MOST PROLIFIC MALE PORN STAR, HAVING FEATURED IN 1,500 FILMS OVER 20 YEARS

attached the inappropriate appendage in the hope it would lengthen his penis. We have no further clues as to how and why he chose a nut to complete this ambitious task, other than that he was a welder by profession. Oh. That kind of nut.

MISSING PERSON

In 1991, devout mormon Ben Ronson had a single sexual encounter with his new lady love Lola. Both remained clothed during the doubtless earth-non-moving experience. They later married, and their sex life together did not get any nuder. It was only when Lola went missing and he filed a missing person's report that Mr Ronson learned she was actually a male impostor.

THE BLAME GAME

It's a new one on me that a man would blame a nagging wife for his impotency. In 2008, Paulo Rossi from Parma, Italy, sued his wife for £140,000 saying that her whining and moaning had cost him his virility. I hope she counter-sued for lack of sex.

GREEK (UN)ORTHODOX

An Australian woman paid between 500 and 1,000 Australian dollars a session to two men purporting to be from a Greek Orthodox church She handed the wedge over to the men when they claimed they could cure her of a curse that had been placed on her family. Over a five year period, Tony Diamantis, 61, and Antonio Savalas, 38, convinced the woman to attend bogus prayer meetings in hotels and sexually assaulted her. They were both jailed for life.

THE AVERAGE BRITON HAS SEX 2,580 TIMES DURING HIS OR HER LIFETIME

PLEASE JUDGE, CAN I HAVE SOME MORE?

In 2005 newspapers featured the case of the Brazilian bombshell who was taking her boyfriend to court for lack of sex. Her main complaint was that once he'd 'finished,' he left her wanting more. A police officer in the city of Jundiai was reported as saying at the time, "we will treat it as an ordinary complaint and let the judge decide." Like the boyfriend, the media did not finish what they started, and no further news stories are to be found as to the result of the case.

NO BATTERIES INCLUDED

When Charles Veltman, 33, was arrested for possession of tools for the commission of a crime, police also found what the criminal described as a 'home-made vibrator' hanging out his pants. Veltman told Deputy John Tremont that the vibrator was battery operated, and he had planned to rob an electrical store because he had run out of them.

BUCK NAKED

A stripper at an Australian 'Bucks' (or Stag Night) party was arrested in 2008 for molesting the best-man with a vibrator. Fuelled by cocaine and speed, she allegedly forced the sex toy in the party-goer's anus, causing it to rupture. A judge said that despite contradicting evidence from witnesses, Sarah Jones should stand trial.

THE WORLD'S MOST PROLIFIC FEMALE PORN DIRECTOR IS CELESTE, WITH OVER 20 FILMS UNDER HER BELT

TEAM SPIRIT

Ute Winter scored very highly with the players in her husband's football team in Mainz, Germany in 1985. She had, legend has it, slept with all the players in the first team, some of the reserves, and a fistful of the over-40s by the end of the 1985 footie season. At first husband Klaus was forgiving when he discovered her off-the-field action, but enough was enough when he found Ute with the goalie in the backseat of the family car. Why the goalie tipped him over the edge is anybody's guess. I'd have thought he would have been considered a safe pair of hands.

TIT FOR TAT

The Eros Foundation, which represents Australia's adult entertainment businesses, banned French-made adult videos, magazines and sex toys when Jacques Chirac resumed nuclear testing in the South Pacific. They also asked members to ban French-maid outfits, French letters and French knickers.

CAR CRASH CLINCH

Youngsters the world over are forever necking in the privacy of cars away from prying parental eyes. But in Malaysia, where unmarried couples canoodling in public can carry a jail sentence of up to 20 months, such clinches are riskier than for most. It might explain why one young Malaysian couple caused a five-car pile-up after they were chased by police who'd spotted them doing what teenagers do in a supermarket car-park.

LONG ARM OF THE LAW OVERREACHES

It's not unusual for teenagers to experiment sexually, and it should come as no surprise in the days of digital technology that they would take snaps of said natural naughtiness. Bizarrely though, in 2007 two Florida teens were prosecuted under state child porn laws for taking consensual rude snaps of one another.

RANDY RUSSIANS RISK SACK

Tanya Levicheva and Oleg Belonkasvaya fell in love at first flight on a plane flying from Brazil to London. Staff and other passengers were surprised to see the newly acquainted work colleagues pleasuring one another in the back row of the plane. They were arrested as soon as they stepped onto the tarmac at Heathrow.

FERRIS WHEEL FROLICS

Munich's Oktoberfest beer festival usually throws up a few arrests – mostly for drunk and disorderly behaviour. It must have made a change for police then, when they had to detain a German trio in 2006 for attempting to make a porn movie during the busy celebrations. The strange threesome had been attempting to shoot their blue movie on the City's famous big wheel.

MAKING A SPLASH

– When a pair of 20-somethings were spotted waving frenetically off the Belgian coast, it's hardly surprising that lifeguards called in a rescue helicopter and life boats. But the 'rescued' couple claimed they'd not been carried away by waves, but rather were getting carried away in the throes of synchronised sexual swimming.

CATCALLERS GET AN EYEFUL

In 2008, an Israeli tourist was arrested when she stripped after being taunted by workmen's wolf-whistles in Auckland. A police spokesman said, "She was taken to a police-station … and told that was inappropriate (behaviour) in New Zealand." So it's commonplace behaviour in Israel?

PHOTO FURORE

The History of Sex exhibition in the town of Alingsås, Sweden, caused quite a stir for the inclusion of photos showing a man performing oral sex on himself, and a woman clutching a horse's penis. Christian Democrat politicians attempted to have the exhibition closed down, locals bemoaned the low moral tone, and the rest of us simply thought, "who is that guy, and did he have to have a vertebra removed, or is he just really good at yoga?"

A CLASS ACT

British *Strictly Come Dancing* winner Alesha Dixon has often been described as a class turn, but I'd wager she needs to clean her act up a bit. In an interview on pop star Lily Allen's chat show she admitted having sex in a toilet, saying "It was in a really posh club, with plush carpets. Does that make it all right?" Short answer, no.

Mona the Virgin Nymph WAS THE FIRST PORNO TO GO ON GENERAL RELEASE IN THE US IN 1970

TROUBLE AND STRIFE

An Oklahoma police chief was forced to resign in 2006 after complaints when his wife Doris posted lewd photos of herself on adult websites. In the furore that followed, the town's mayor and a councilman said they were stepping down because they were fed up with the public attention. Said the chief himself, "My wife is six foot three and weighs 300 pounds. If there is somebody that thinks they can control her, have at it. I have tried for 11 years and haven't been able to."

SEXY LAGER

In 2007, bottles of Rubbel Sexy Lager were stripped from sale in the UK. Labels on the drink featured a woman in a swimsuit which drinkers could scratch off to reveal her naked torso. An independent complaints panel oddly decided that the name of the drink and the swimsuit meant the beer was being associated with sexual success.

SEX FOR GAS

With gas prices soaring the world over, what's a girl to do? Over to Kelly Cooper of Maricopa County, USA. The 43-year-old woman, desperate to buy petrol, offered to swap sex with a male attendant at a gasoline station in order to pay for her goods. However, the deal turned sour and Cooper assaulted the man with a pair of scissors. On arrest she described the hair-brained scheme as "a sex-for-gas contract gone bad."

DENMARK WAS THE FIRST COUNTRY TO LEGALISE PORNOGRAPHY IN 1968

FIRED UP

In 1997, two American men were charged with setting fire to various motor vehicles. The arsonists, Michael William Smith and Danny Mayes, said they only did it because Tammy Jo Garcia, 27, told them to. Her reason? A San Diego court was told that seeing cars set alight flamed young Tammy Jo's lust.

THE SPERMINATOR

In the 1980s, Cecil Jacobson gained notoriety for impregnating women who visited his fertility clinic with his own sperm. He swiftly became known as 'The Sperminator' and 'The Baby-Maker.' Despite being a Nobel-prize-winning scientist, he claimed that his sperm must have accidentally contaminated the sperm of the husbands he was meant to be helping in the lab. He was banged up for five years for his fertility foolishness.

TOO MUCH OF A GOOD THING

Brit Sarah Carmen suffers from Permanent Sexual Arousal Syndrome (PSAS), a syndrome which increases blood flow to the sex organs and means she can have up to 200 orgasms a day. In 2007 she told the *News of the World*, "Sometimes I have so much sex to try to calm myself down I get bored of it. And men I sleep with don't seem to make as much effort because I climax so easily." Just the strumming sound of a hair- or nail-dryer is enough to get her going. Which can't be much fun for Sarah – she works in a beauty salon. Or can it?

TOP TEN RIDICULOUS MISADVENTURES WITH INANIMATE OBJECTS

10. There have certainly been some mind-boggling news items in recent times concerning those who like to indulge in the improper with inanimate objects. First up, a gentleman from Wiltshire in England who was arrested for simulating a sex act with a lamp-post early in 2008.

9. And so to spring, when thoughts turn to the great outdoors, al fresco dining, and... picnic table molestation. Picnic table molestation?! An absurd activity, which landed Art Prince Jr. in court on charges of indecency, having been captured by his neighbour on video having intercourse with his garden picnic-style table on four separate occasions. The hole where the umbrella goes, before you ask.

8. Cockamamie. Great word – and how better to describe the idiotic antics of the worker who was caught trying to have sex with a Henry Hoover. As for his excuse, that in his native Poland, people are often to be found vacuuming their underpants, two other words spring to mind: "Utter codswallop."

7. A little further from home, the award for the most ridiculous al fresco fiasco with an inanimate object goes to the Hong Kong citizen who had to be cut free from a steel bench after using it as an ersatz vagina.

6. Ah! Paris. Home to all things romantic. Think of its cosy cafés, fine wines, and stunning architecture, and lovers the world over swoon. None more so than Erika La Tour Eiffel – hint: there's a clue in the name as to where this is headed – who is one of 40

women in the world who have declared themselves in love with famous buildings. In 2008 she 'married' the Eiffel tower in front of friends, well-wishers and astonished Parisians, and changed her surname by Deed Poll.

5. Not content to be outdone by pavement and binbag shagger extraordinaire Craig Tiernan, who you may remember from an earlier misadventure, a young Scottish lad was arrested in 2007 for getting in a one-handed press-up position and going in at hammer and tongs on a stretch of tarmac. Show-off.

4. A citizen of Charleswood, USA, was charged for indecent acts after he was twice videotaped sticking his penis through a hole in his neighbor's fence and masturbating.

3. An Edinburgh man who did it with a traffic cone claimed he was simply carrying out a piece of fringe theatre. He was told by a judge never to repeat his amateur dramatics again.

2. What kind of dummy calls the manufacturer to complain after mistaking a shop mannequin for a sex doll? The unnamed man who lodged his complaint after lodging his winky in a 24mm hole meant for a display stand, that's who. A spokesman for the manufacturer of the shop dummy, Displaysense, told reporters, "We will now warn people that our mannequins are for display use only and not for recreational use."

1. GET YOUR MOTOR RUNNING...
Losing your virginity aged 15 is not so unusual. But for Edward Smith, the rite-of-passage took place not with a man, a woman or even with a beast. Rather he had his cherry broken by a motor vehicle. Now aged 57, Smith has managed to have his warped and wicked way with up to 1,000 cars, as explained by a 2008 documentary about so-called 'mecaniphilliacs.'

BOAT PARTY GOES OVERBOARD

In 2004, nearly 100 youngsters were arrested in Cyprus after a boat party descended into an orgy. Police chief Sotiris Haralambous reportedly said the scenes that had been filmed on a mobile phone were "not just graphic, they go beyond every conceivable limit." The majority of teens arrested were British.

COVER UP OR GET BANGED UP

Mexican state capital Villahermosa banned indoor nudity from January 2005. The South-eastern Mexican town was sweltering under a heat-wave when officials decided that they'd had enough of glimpsing naked flesh through the well-ventilated windows and open doors of people's homes.

COSTUME DRAMA

When Louise Whenman's sex shop Pulse & Cocktails was robbed by a bonkers baldy on the rampage, she was able to see the funny side. After seeing footage of the wig-and-knicker-grabbing raid on the internet, Louise quipped, "If only he had come into the shop in the daytime, we could have shown him many more outfits and helped him find the right size."

CALLING THE SHOTS

The Sun announced that a new variety of vibrator would be hitting the British shelves in 2008 – a voice activated one. 'Speed up', 'slow down', 'softer', 'harder', all are commands the electronic sex-slave will respond to. Monique Carty, of onjoy.com, an online retailer of the vibrators told the paper, "Communication is key to a healthy relationship, and there's no relationship healthier than that of a woman and her vibrator."

MOBILE LOWERS TONE

There's a time and place for everything. So, here's a question for you: is a packed courtroom the place for a smutty mobile ring tone which cries out, "Oh yeah... oh yeah.... Do it to me?" Na, course it's not.

Luckily acting magistrate Roger Clark saw the funny side when one man forgot to switch off his mobile in an Ipswich, Australia, court. The idiot might otherwise have ended up with six months in jail for contempt of court. But here's another question for you: Is anywhere a suitable place for such a juvenile ring tone? I'll leave that one to you.

WANKATHON

In 2006, hundreds of wankers gathered at a charity event in central London. Yes, I really mean it – wankers of the masturbatory ilk. Organised by an American 'sex and culture' group, the event offered prizes for the most prolific five-knuckle-shuffler and those who had the most orgasms.

Public broadcaster Channel 4 planned to screen a documentary about the event entitled Wankathon during a week-long series of shows called Wank Week later that year. Sadly censorious killjoys got their way, and the broadcaster was forced to shelve its plans.

ADULT MALES MASTURBATE ON AVERAGE 18–22 TIMES A MONTH

LET'S COME TOGETHER

The EU is forever being accused of spunking tax payer's money. The accusation was never more appropriate than in 2007, when its press unit launched a clip on YouTube to promote European-made films. The clip, entitled Let's Come Together, featured sex scenes from commercial movies like *Amelie* and *Goodbye Lenin*, and showed 18 couples in a variety of sexual poses. "I suppose this film is appropriate," jested Godfrey Bloom, a UKIP MEP. "The EU has been screwing Britain for the past 30 years."

DON'T BANK ON IT

In 2005 there were fears that donors would stop giving to the world's biggest sperm bank when the Danish government decided that donors would have to pay tax on the 40 odd quid they received for their travails. There was an outcry, since most donations came from hard-up (ahem) students. The Government did a U-turn, and the bank did not run (ahem) dry.

DESPERATE TIMES, DESPERATE MEASURES

Where politicians go, the general public surely follow. That's what a Melbourne IVF clinic believed in 2005 anyway, when it asked MPs to become sperm donors in the hope others would be encouraged to follow suit. The clinic's supply of sperm had dried up when a new law was introduced in 1998 which said donors' identities could be revealed when a child produced from their sperm turned 18.

16.7% OF AMERICAN MEN SAY THEY HAVE PAID FOR SEX AT LEAST ONCE IN THEIR LIVES

SENSES WORKING OVERTIME

"I love the smell of Napalm in the morning". One of the world's more peculiar cinematic statements, from Coppola's 1979 *Apocalypse Now*. But how's this for an even weirder olfactory sensation? In 2007 a perfume was launched which had been blended to recreate the smell of blood, sweat, saliva and semen. Maker Etat Libre d'Orange said Sécrétions Magnifiques is an 'olfactory coitus' that is 'subversive' and 'disturbing'. I think a simple 'repulsive' would have done.

JIGGERY-IN-POKEY # 1

It's common knowledge that prisoners – starved of sex, drugs or good old-fashioned fresh air – may try to break out of jail. But here's a twist in that criminal tale – in 2007, a woman was held for trespass when she broke into Standford Hill open prison for an illegal conjugal visit with her husband. He was swiftly moved to a higher security unit.

VIRGIN NON-BIRTH

An Italian couple baffled a fertility clinic when all tests showed they were both fertile but they still did not conceive. When questioned about the sex life of their eight-year marriage, doctors soon uncovered the problem – It seems the deeply religious couple had no clue how to perform the sex act which makes a baby. They were given sex therapy.

DRIVEN CRAZY WITH DESIRE

Drink and drug driving are easily definable crimes. But what should we call driving while having sex? The question becomes important when considering a newly married Italian couple who could not wait for the honeymoon suite. The hasty honeymooners were arrested by traffic police in Bergamo in northern Italy, who'd spotted their car veering dangerously on the road. Inside they found the 70-year-old groom straddled by his 50-year-old bride.

BEWARE WOMEN BARING BREASTS

An ample-bosomed woman distracted staff of clothing stores in Salisbury in 1986 by flashing her breasts, while her accomplice made off with lots of lovely loot. She couldn't have been a distracting double D cup though – they were spotted, and police soon caught up with the pair and their £3,000 sartorial swag-bag.

BITING THE 'BIG ONE'

There you are, minding your own business in the rainforest when, ouch, you are bitten by the venomous and at times deadly Brazilian wandering spider. Provided you survive the bite, just when you thought things couldn't get any worse, you get priapism, suffering the longest and hardest boner of your life. And why? Well a two-year study by scientists has found that the venom of this species of spider contains a toxin, called Tx2-6 which causes erections. So good news for the impotent everywhere – providing they manage to avoid the gangrene of the willy that persistent priapism can cause!

OVER-AMOROUS ARACHNIDS

Promiscuity often leads to a ridiculous sexual misadventure. For the female wasp spider it's no different. True, her partner doesn't mind that she cavorts willy-nilly with a number of sexual partners. But to ensure she doesn't produce any love-children from her extra-marital erotic encounters, her male partner breaks off the tip of his penis while they're doing it and her sexual orifice is blocked. Still, no need for her to spin a web of lies to him indoors about who has fathered her kids....

RISE OF THE MACHINES

Woody Allen would be so proud. In 2003, an American doctor invented a machine which would trigger orgasms in women. He called it the 'Ogasmatron', after the famous device in Allen's movie *Everything You Wanted To Know About Sex (But Were Too Afraid To Ask)*. But his plans for world sex-toy domination fell flat when he could not find any volunteers willing to test to his machine.

POLICE, CAMERA, ACTION!

Police in Gronnigen, Holland, arrested a 25-year-old man and his 33-year-old lover for having sex on the bonnet of a car. Not just any car. Oh no. The pair were so revved up they had sex on the bonnet of a police patrol car, and more strangely still, refused to move on when the police officers ticked them off. The incident was splashed all over the internet, having been caught on a police video camera.

BEETLE-MANIA

Male competitiveness can be a bit of a joke – just watch any drinking game, rugby match or city trading floor, and we'd be forgiven for thinking we'd evolved only little since the Neanderthals. But competitiveness among male seed beetles, desperate to father the most progeny, has become no laughing matter. The cunning beast has developed a super-spiky penis which provides an anchor for his insect sperm, meaning he can be sure to father the most children. Ouch!

CRUTCH ME IF YOU CAN

Unseasonal behaviour saw a woman arrested in Danbury, Connecticut, USA, for fourth degree sexual assault and breach of the peace. Her crime? Sitting on a 65-year-old Santa's lap in a shopping mall's Winter Wonderland and touching him inappropriately. She might have got away with her festive frolics had she not been forced to make her escape on crutches.

BIG APPLE GROPER

You're 67 and have spent your life battling to keep people on the right side of the law, so what do you do just before you retire? Well, you're now in a book about over-libidinous losers, so you step over the wrong side of it, of course. Step up attorney Troy Waller, who was charged in 2008 with forcible touching, third-degree sex abuse and harassment of two female colleagues. His chat-up lines were no less criminal. Sticking his hand down one victim's trousers he leered, "Look what you did to an old man. You made an old man's weekend."

HALF OF ALL BRITISH WOMEN OWN A SEX TOY

TAKING ADVANTAGE

In 2003, Leicester man, Nick Brown pretended to be a first-aider when a young woman collapsed in a local bar. Party-goers in the bar were suspicious when the gormless groper put on a pair of rubber gloves and touched the girl's breasts, ostensibly to find her pulse. He was later arrested when the real paramedics arrived.

PARK LIFE

The number five will resonate in the mind of one Paul Jennings for ooh, about five gazillion years. Five times in one evening, he groped or clutched at an innocent woman while cycling round his local park. Five years was the term of the ASBO given to him by Judge Douglas Field, banning him from talking to any woman he does not already know.

WHAT YOU DON'T KNOW WILL HURT YOU

Finding your lover dead would be enough of a shock. Finding him hanging from an electric wire, dressed up in your bra and panties must be cataclysmic.

Pity then Adelaide Rowe who found her partner and father of three children, Christian Myers, in the throes of dying of auto-erotic asphyxiation in 2007. Her efforts to revive him proved futile. To add to the list of shocks in the tragic event, Ms Rowe told a newspaper, "I never even knew he had any interest in this type of sexual behaviour."

THE MOST POPULAR SEX TOY USED IN GREAT BRITAIN IS A VIBRATOR

PUMP IT UP # 2

In the early 90's there was many an internet report about the bizarre practice of inserting a bicycle pump where the sun don't shine and pumping away for a sexual thrill. It was in ⌐Thailand⌐ where the practice was especially prevalent and where in ⌐1993⌐ youngster Charnchai Puanmuangpak decided to up the ante. He went to his local garage, put the compressed air hose used to inflate tyres up his derriere – and was almost immediately killed.⌐

CASH FOR FLASH

When two giddy teenagers flashed their breasts at a CCTV camera on Worthing beach in England, they got more than they bargained for. They were arrested for outraging public decency and could have been fined up to £5,000. "Everyone thinks it's ridiculous that we've been taken to court. Most people think what we did was funny." Yes, Abbey Linscott and Sarah Burns, that's why you're in this book!

BEE-HAVE!

I've heard of having ants in your pants, but bees? In 2006, an Oslo man stupidly claimed that a bee or indeed a wasp had miraculously buzzed its way into his underpants, after he was accused of flashing. His story went that he had simply opened his fly and tinkered with his todger on public transport to let the crazed insect out. But his story had more holes in it than a honeycomb, and he received a 30-day suspended sentence for indecent exposure.

THE MOST CHILDREN EVER FATHERED BY ONE MAN WAS 1,042 BY A 17TH CENTURY MOROCCAN KING

WHAT A BIND!

For years, Australian Betty Wilson would set off for work leaving her common-law husband tied or bound up as part of an elaborate sex game. On one occasion he freed himself after she had left him bound and gagged for ten hours. But it only took a matter of minutes for him to die when in 2004 she used rope and tape to tie him to a post and gag him, while she nipped indoors for a shower.

When the case came to court the public weren't told if Betty herself could emulate Houdini – but her one year in prison after being convicted of the manslaughter of the bonkers bondage fan will give her ample opportunity to try.

Her conviction came after a jury at Brisbane Supreme Court heard that Ms Wilson opted to use bull dog clips and a slap to revive her lover when she found him dying, tied to the post. Perhaps this – and the following harsh last words to her lover – convinced the jury she had some culpability in the matter, "I told the fucking idiot he wouldn't get out of this one."

BUMP AND GRINDER

Emergency services are used to dealing with all manner of embarrassing medical emergencies, but their vehicles don't always come equipped to deal with them. So paramedics in Manchester, England, had to use their imaginations when they were called out to a man who could not remove a metal ring from his penis. One dose of anaesthetic and a borrowed mini hand-grinder later and the man was left to consider a new meaning for bump and grind.

4.5% OF BRITISH PEOPLE DO NOT LIKE GIVING OR RECEIVING ORAL SEX

SUBTERRANEAN SEX PESTS

In 2003, Japanese officials had to increase the number of women-only carriages on their underground transport network because of the proliferation of male gropers there. In a survey, over a third of young women said they had been touched up by free-fingered commuters.

NOT A CLEVER DICK

It's commonly stated that size doesn't matter – advice two men who visited the consultancy rooms of one Doctor Ravi Chopra's surgery perhaps now wished they'd borne in mind.

Mr Chopra was struck off by the General Medical Council in 2003 for making two cock-ups of the highest order, bungling a pair of penis enlargement operations that left one man disfigured and another with a shorter penis than before.

I'll spare you the gory details but suffice to say the words 'black and blue,' 'tremendous swelling,' 'visibly shorter,' and 'severe pain' all featured in the evidence against the penis-annihilating doctor.

AEROSOL (MIS)ADVENTURE

In the spring of 2008, doctors in the Philippines were the first medics to break patient confidentiality by posting an intimate surgical procedure on YouTube. And not just any intimate surgical procedure – the operation in question was the removal of a six inch aerosol can from a patient's rectum.

This ridiculous misadventure throws up many questions. The most obvious one perhaps is how on earth does a six-inch aerosol can get inside one's rectum? Well, I don't think you need a signpost,

51% OF WOMEN SAY RECEIVING ORAL SEX IS THEIR FAVOURITE SEXUAL ACTIVITY

so let's throw this one over to the patient. The unwitting video-star claimed to press at the time that the colonic calamity was the result of a drunken one-night stand with a man he'd picked up on the street. Bet he wished he'd gone solo for the evening.

THAT OLD BLACK MAGIC

Ah! Frank Sinatra, Ol' Blue Eyes, the original swing star, the crooner with the velvety voice. So what fornicating foray did he get up to then? Err, no, rewind! We're not talking that kind of old black magic, but rather the witchy kind. You know the one – where evil spirits are invoked, body parts are sacrificed, and penis-snatching is a regular occurrence...

Especially in Congo, where Reuters reported in 2008 that police had arrested 13 men suspected of using magic of the not-so-good-for-men's-wobbly-bits variety, to misappropriate their penises, or to make them very, very wee.

"I'm tempted to say it's one huge joke," Kinshasa chief of police Jean-Dieudonne Oleko said. But witnesses assured him otherwise. "It's real. Just yesterday here, there was a man who was a victim. We saw. What was left was tiny."

HIDE AND SEEK

In 2003, *Metro* newspaper reported that German police had launched a massive search for a suspected kidnapping after receiving calls from people who believed they had witnessed a sex crime in action. Turned out that a blindfolded woman being hit with a stick inside a Porsche was consensual sex between two recently acquainted internet lovers. Different strokes for different folks, eh?

ANNE SUMMERS PRODUCE 2.4 MILLION SEX TOYS EACH YEAR

TOP TEN FANCIFUL FETISHES

10. Smelly feet are generally a no-no when it comes to copulation. But for one Israeli computer programmer, odour eaters are the biggest turn off. In 2002, he copied his colleagues' house keys so he could enter their homes, steal their shoes, and have a good old sniff. His fate is easy to sum up – he got the boot.

9. Richard Dotson's mania for shop mannequins has landed him at least six convictions for breaking and entering, and one stint in prison over the past decade. On release from the said prison sentence, the shop dummy fetishist immediately made a smash and grab raid on a cleaning product store, stealing a shop dummy in a French maid's outfit.

8. Though sex and bodily fluids are inextricably linked, sweat isn't generally something that gets peoples' juices, ahem, flowing. Tell that to Torao Fukuda, who was caught stealing American Football uniforms from male locker rooms in 2008, citing his homosexuality and love of sweat as a defence.

7. If mention of that last bodily function had you squirming, then maybe you should look away now. An Ohio man is spending time in jail for consistently collecting urine from public restrooms with the intent of drinking it. As Judge Anne Tyler said when he appeared in her courtroom, the man had: "what can only be described as a urine fetish."

6. Baggage handler Rodney Peterson made the most of his job for Quantas at Sydney airport. Between May 2005 and 2007, he stole the head and pubic hair of 50 different women after rummaging through the bags to which he'd been entrusted.

5. Getting caught not once, not twice, but three times for the same sex crime is a strong indication that you've got some kind of sexual fixation. In the case of James Dowdy from the US, the object of his affections is women's socks – particularly those which have been stolen from their homes.

4. In Singapore, a malodorous miscreant who had a thing for jumping unsuspecting women and sniffing their armpits got 14 years in jail and 18 whips on the butt with a cane.

3. Most fetishists would do anything to avoid being arrested by police – I mean, it's not like your run-of-the-mill fetish can be indulged in the comfort of a prison cell. Not so for one Z-list American celebrity who drunkenly flashed her breasts at coppers though, and was delighted to be arrested: she has an admitted cop fetish.

2. When glamour-puss Marla Maples discovered she was missing more than 40 pairs of her fancy-schmancy shoes in 1992, she installed a video camera in her closet, only to discover her publicist, Chuck Jones, had been helping himself to her footwear. If he'd thought that his shoe theft sneakery would make him a shoo-in for the boss's good books, he had to think again. She reported him to police, and in 1994 he was convicted for the thefts.

1. BOTTOMS UP
An unnamed man from the fair city of Venice landed himself in hot water when he was caught filming ladies' bottoms around the city's famous St Mark's Square. The usual post-arrest trawl of the fetishist's home unearthed film of over 3,000 illegally-perused posteriors. Since police were unable to match faces to bottoms, it's not clear whether the 3,000 bottoms belonged to 3,000 different women, but nonetheless the chap was charged with infringement of privacy.

DON'T GET YOUR MOTOR RUNNING

Romanian footballer Mario Bugeanu scored a spectacular own goal when he and his girlfriend died from carbon monoxide poisoning while having sex in their car in a locked garage in 1999. To keep things decent as they cavorted naked in the vehicle, they closed the garage doors to keep out prying eyes. Their naked bodies were discovered by the garage owner – the player's father – who also discovered that the engine was still running.

PENIS ENVY PAYS OFF

Ever coveted something of a friend's? An item of clothing perhaps, a car, a boy- or girlfriend, even? Maybe. But I bet not many of you have gone so far as to covet your best friend's genitals. Frenchman Henri Cousteau did. His mate Paul Simone was blessed with a nearly-ten inch penis while Cousteau himself was rather more challenged in the manhood department. Not to worry. When Simone was killed in a car crash, Cousteau was delighted to discover he had been bequeathed the gargantuan organ in his friend's will. Over – ahem – come with emotion, Cousteau gushed, "Paul had hundreds of women. I have never had real sex, but now I can have the same success!"

HOLY SEX GAMES BATMAN!

In St Clair, St Louis, USA, an off-duty police officer heard prolonged screaming coming from his new neighbour's home. Not one to shirk his responsibilities, the officer raced to the scene. Oh what a scene he found – lying naked, tied to the bed with a tie, was the source of the screaming, his female neighbour. Lying unconscious on the floor was her husband, clothed in a fancy-dress Batman costume. The wannabe superhero was acting out a role-playing fantasy and had attempted to jump from a wardrobe to 'rescue' his wife – only he missed, hit the deck, and it was he who ended up needing to be rescued.

KEY-ED UP

The pretty Bavarian town of Weiden is surrounded by woodland and areas of outstanding natural beauty. Bavaria – known for its clean cities, its beer... and its lederhosen.

In 2007, a Germany couple in the town were forced to call out the fire brigade when an amateur S&M romp turned bad, and they lost the key to a set of handcuffs they'd used to shackle one another.

So why mention the location of this foolish frolic? When the fire brigade arrived to free the dim-witted duo, not only were they manacled to the bed, but they were dressed in the traditional leathers of their native region.

CAMEL GETS HUMP

There are crap birthday presents and there are crap birthday presents. In the case of one Australian woman, a murderous and sex-crazed camel proved to be the crappiest birthday present ever. A few months after she was gifted the exotic pet – she fed it, gave it a home, treated it as all her other pets – it flung her to the ground, rolled her over and carried out a ridiculous sexual misadventure which would later kill her. The ungrateful beast.

SEXUALLY TRANSMITTED DISEASES AMONG THE OVER 45S HAVE DOUBLED IN A DECADE

ELECTRIC SHOCK-ER

Malcolm Fisher tried to wriggle out of the murder of his wife Kylie in 2004 by saying her death was the result of electric shocks he gave her during sex. They had, he claimed, been practising electric-shock sex and extreme bondage for years. The judge had none of it, and he was charged with homicide.

DOG BITES MAN (HOOD)

A 'man bites dog' story is a term used by journalists to describe an uncommon occurrence – in this case though, the more usual 'dog bites man' story becomes a 'man bites dog' one. Allow me to explain.

In 2001, Andrew Farlow and wife Rosemary were engaged in a long session of sexual silliness when Andy suggested he spread peanut butter on his genitals and encourage their pet pooch to lick them clean. Like you do. In the carnal catastrophe that followed, the dog over-excitedly bit and tore at Farlow's penis, Rosemary threw a perfume bottle at the pooch, enraging it and causing it to bite off part of her husband's anatomy that he doubtless wanted left intact.

Although this story has left its mucky paws all over the internet, I'm not convinced it's true. More of a shaggy dog story then, perhaps?

ANIMAL LOVERS GET BURNED

What's more ridiculous? Inserting your pet gerbil into your boyfriend's rectum via a tube, or lighting a match to see where it has got to when it does not return to daylight? A question that can perhaps only be answered by one of the misplaced miscreants in our next misadventure, a famous urban myth that may have some basis in reality. Spotlight on you, Jim Jones: "In retrospect, lighting the match was my big mistake. But I was only trying to retrieve the gerbil."

Jones ended up in the ER with third degree burns, while his partner Andrew Farnum, sustained first and second degree burns to his anus and lower intestinal tract. Pet lovers look away now – internet reports on this matter do not reveal the fate of the gerbil.

TOO MUCH LOVE

'I love you more.' 'No, I love you more.' You know how that old piece of love-play goes. But things got out of hand in 1994 in Frederick, Maryland, USA, for Manon Fontijn when she gunned down boyfriend Bob Bhamra in argument over who loved who the most. Err. I think that would be Bob... Carmen got 20 years for her protestation of undying love.

A CRUSHING BLOW

Perhaps I need to get out more, but I hadn't even heard of the following variety of sexual foible, never mind imagined that one like it could exist. Wait for it, folks... It's the derivation of sexual pleasure from crushing small mammals to death. But it gets better – or worse, depending on how you look at it.

In 1999, a lady from Okeechobee County, USA, who got her kicks from murderously maiming rabbits and small mice accidentally killed her husband as they made a so-called 'crush' movie of her antics. The woman got away with two years of probation and community service on counts of animal cruelty after it was believed the death of her husband was a sex act that went wrong.

30% OF AMERICANS HAVE FANTASISED ABOUT CHEATING ON THEIR PARTNER

VIAGRA VICTIM

You withdraw your life savings, pawn your wedding ring, purchase a shed load of Viagra and two hookers for the night, and dream of waking up after the raunchiest sex session of your life. Except you don't, do you Georgio Barrsan of Bucharest, Romania? Instead, you awake to a stolen wallet and the realisation that what you've been sold were sleeping pills. Like, duh.

ARMED TO THE TEETH

I've heard of biting the hand that feeds you, but what about biting the penis that f**ks you? In 1994, Sarah Louise Achayok bit her boyfriend's penis in retaliation for suspected infidelity on his part. She was charged with the intent to injure him 'by means of a dangerous instrument.' The local District Attorney saw the funny side, saying, "Alaskan people don't usually consider teeth a dangerous instrument unless they're attached to an 8-foot grizzly bear."

MEMOIRS OF A GEISHA

Erotic asphyxiation features in many of the stories in this book, but perhaps the most bizarre case of all is that of Sada Abe and Kichizo Ishida. The pair became sexually involved through Abe's work as a geisha in Japan in the early 1930's and enjoyed many strange sexual practices together, but none more so than erotic asphyxiation. All was well until 1936 when, fearing Ishida would return to his wife, Abe strangled her lover to death during a sex game. But it gets worse. She then cut off his penis and testicles with a large knife, and carried them round in a handbag until his

THE WORLD'S LONGEST PENIS ON RECORD IS 13.5 INCHES LONG

body was discovered. The case is notorious throughout Japan even now.

DONKEY SCHLONG

If at first you don't succeed, try, try again. Just like Mehmet Esirgen, a 52-year-old Turk who wished to cure his sexual impotence by means of a donkey penis transplant. But finding a surgeon willing to operate on him – using one of three donkey penises he'd lobbed off – proved fruitless. His son became so disgusted with the behaviour of his father that he shot his dad in the leg.

LUBRICANT LUNACY

Sometimes you're just too turned on to nip to the chemists for lube. So, what to do? Well, if you've any sense, you won't follow the example of two San Francisco youngsters who had a rummage in their granny's medicine cabinet for a substitute, slapping nitroglycerin paste on their privates. It increases blood flow to the arteries, and for those with healthy hearts, it can be fatal.

BACK TO BASICS?

The British conservative MP, Stephen Milligan, was a leading light in the then-Tory government's 'Back to Basics' campaign advocating family values. You can see what's coming... In 1994, his dead body was discovered by police, naked save for a pair of stockings and suspenders, electrical flex around his neck, bin liner over his head. His untimely demise was ruled as death by sexual misadventure.

THE WORLD'S SHORTEST PENIS ON RECORD WHEN ERECT IS 4.75 INCHES

HOT DICK-ITTY DOG

It's hardly surprising that those lacking in imagination may make use of a hotdog as a phony phallus. Just try saying the word 'wiener' without thinking of the male member. But here's a bit of simple advice for those simpletons who choose to use the foodstuff as a dildo – don't defrost a frozen one in the microwave before you thwap one off. Otherwise it may break off inside you, and send you on a humiliating trip to the emergency room, as it did to one Indianapolis, USA citizen in 1994.

BOTTLED UP

In 2006, the Urology Clinic at Carl-Thiem-Hospital in Berlin, Germany, had to treat a 49-year-old man who had his willy stuck in a plastic bottle. Try as clinicians might to cut the bottle with a scalpel and glass saw, the penis remained strangled. They eventually resorted to cutting the bottle length-ways with an oscillating saw intended for cutting plaster casts. The penis remained unharmed.

GET A ROOM! # 1

The British seaside holiday resort of Brighton has long since been associated with all things saucy, and boasts over 150 hotels for courting couples headed to the town for a 'dirty weekend.'

What, then, possessed hopeless humpers James Nash and Kimberley Cook to get jiggy with it in a phone box, in full view of passers-by, just outside the city's main police station and court house in the summer of 2008?All was revealed in an 'interview' with The Sun newspaper, the day after images of the fellating female and her gormless guy were splashed across newspapers up and down the country: They'd apparently been humping non-stop since Ben's release from prison following an 18 month jail term for ABH (Actual Bodily Harm). Ah, bless! Their parents must be so proud.

GLASS HALF-FULL?

An article from the *New York Medical Journal* from 1921 entitled 'An Unusual Foreign Body in the Rectum' just goes to show that some people are ever the optimist. In this case, the optimist was the man who inserted a full-size drinking glass (reported as 'four inches high, two and three-eighths inches across the bottom, and two and five-eighths inches across the top') up his backside and thought he'd get away with it. He didn't – although surgeons were able to remove the vessel without any long-term damage.

DOWN HILL ALL THE WAY

Falling in love is a beautiful thing. Falling 150ft over a cliff face as you consummate that love in the back seat of your car is not. Commiserations, then, to Taiwenese duo Lin Gu, 25, and lover Lee Shin, 29, who ended up in hospital after an extra-marital escapade landed them bruised and battered as they toppled down a hill... and no doubt with some explaining to do back home.

CAR CRASH COPULATERS

In the American town of Moscow, Idaho, a carnival worker who crashed into a lamp post blamed his over-excited mates for going at it too hard in the back of his car. He told a court that the car was 'top heavy' anyway and that the bad bonking sent it 'tippy'.

WHAT A CARVE-UP

When getting down to an evening of rough sex, some people really ought to know where to draw the line. Or should I say how to draw the line. In 2007, Catherine McCoubrey from Winnipeg in Canada got carried away with a knife when her boyfriend asked her to carve a heart in his chest after a bout of heavy drinking – very nearly killing him. The unnamed victim was forgiving, though. He had introduced his partner to 'body modification' and the joy of self-inflicted wounds via similar knife carvings.

PINATA PERV

The internet! The computer network that has revolutionised global communication allows citizens of unenlightened countries to access educational tools... and, via YouTube, shows all manner of erudite footage, not least of these being the cautionary clip of a security man having sex with a piñata. You what? A security man having sex with a piñata?

Yes, you read it correctly. Captured on CCTV in the piñata factory he was supposed to be guarding, the stupid shagger par-excellence had sex with a papier-mâché pooch. As if getting down and dirty with a dog-shaped piñata was not lunacy enough, the night watchman claims during the clip that the piñata sex was a conspiracy on the part of his employers. "I think they purposely put the dog in there, lured me in, and added extra wires, and therefore my apparatus still hurts." Err, quite.

THE LAUGHING STOCK OF LONDON

Exhibitionism and theatre go hand-in-hand. Small wonder then that two al-fresco lovers took to the roof of the Great Windmill Theatre

THE WORLD'S LARGEST TESTICLE IS 5CM LONG

to go at it doggy style on a balmy London summer's day in 2007. In this day and age they could hardly have expected their rooftop romp to have gone unrecorded. And it wasn't. Staff from nearby MJZ production company took pictures of the tryst and the couple were promptly catapulted to fame on YouTube to become – as one employee put it – "the laughing stock of London."

PEEP-SHOW

The evidence was stacked against hotelier Edmond Branham of Redcar, England. He had a huge stash of blue movies and sex toys, admitted a 'healthy obsession' with sex, and had hidden a camera trained on the four poster bed in one of his hotel's rooms – with a live link to his bedroom. But at Redcar Crown Court he denied voyeurism, claiming he suspected the couple within of smoking marijuana.

His dumb defence fell on deaf ears, and the Judge sent him down for six months. Meanwhile his victims were deeply upset by the event, saying "lots of intimate activity had gone on that night."

HEAD-BOARD BANGERS

After two years of making sweet, loud music that kept neighbours awake and gave one child nightmares, Adrian Shadwell was banned from his girlfriend Kelly Rottner's home for 21 days by Brighton and Hove City Council in England. Neighbours had been subjected to a barrage of anti-social shagging including headboard banging and loud obscenities, and were even threatened with violence if they asked the pair to pipe down.

But we have to wonder: If they were that lusty seeing each other every day, imagine the raunchy racket when they've been separated for three weeks. Fingers in your ears time, Brighton!

THE NUMBER OF 'DESIGNER VAGINA' OPERATIONS HAS GONE UP 300%
IN THE LAST FIVE YEARS

GOT A ROOM: NOW CLOSE THE CURTAINS!

An overly-libidinous couple worked on their sexual repertoire against a hotel window of the Toronto Skydome hotel in 1997. The hotel overlooks the playing ground for Toronto's Blue Jay baseball team, giving a crowd of over 50,000 a double bill of spectator sports that night. The hotel's two way windows have also given rise – ahem – to one man being arrested for indecent exposure as he masturbated against the glass. Visitors to the hotel now have to agree to pull down the blinds if they plan any naughty action, self-inflicted or otherwise.

OFF THE WALL

What goes up must come down. True, that. So if you are thinking of climbing a 50 foot wall at a beauty spot to engage in amorous activity, do make sure that there is a fig tree around to break your fall, should you take a tumble. Just like the following two British bonkers.
— It was in Magaluf in Majorca in 2007 that Dawn Bowles and Sam Jordan were playing what police called an 'amorous game' when sinning got in the way of sense and they lost their footing, falling the impressive equivalent of six stories through the branches of the tree and finally to the ground. Dawn suffered two broken ankles, but Sam probably didn't give a fig – amazingly he sustained no injuries at all.

LITIGIOUS LOVERS

Instead of thanking the New York Transit Authority for saving their bacon, homeless humpers Darryl Washington and Maria Ramos sued the company when they got hit by a train when making love on the tracks of a New York subway station in the early 1990s.

THE KISS OF LIFE

Paramedics are known for giving the kiss of life, but in general we like them to do so when they have been called to a life-threatening medical emergency. Not so for one senior South African paramedic who got a little way-laid on the way to a remote emergency call one day in 2005. When colleagues became worried about his whereabouts after he'd been missing for two hours, they sent out a search party of three further emergency vehicles. He was found half-way out of town with his kacks round his ankles in the back of the emergency van, giving the 'kiss of life' to someone who was very much alive and kicking. To give the selfish shagger some credit, he did tell colleagues how to get to the remote emergency destination before getting back down to the business at hand.

ON THE BUSES

"Thai Women Should Preserve Old Culture About Sexual Behaviour." Such were the signs in buses that caused an outcry of rights groups protesting to the Bangkok Mass Transit Authority in 2004. Conductors and passengers had been bemoaning the, erm, moaning coming from the back of buses, emanating from students who were indulging in homework of the human anatomy variety. In a spoilsport, if egalitarian, move to end the teenage tawdriness, the bus authority changed the signs to include both sexes.

THERE ARE 38 SLANG WORDS FOR PENIS ON URBANDICTIONARY.COM

TOP TEN RIDICULOUS
REVENGE STORIES

10. A 70-year-old groom who'd been jilted three times by the same woman chucked paint over the house of his 79-year-old fiancé. His act of revenge cost him £4,000 and his relationship. "I still love her but think it's best it ends," he told reporters.

9. A Thai woman's jealousy, um, ballooned, when she discovered her husband was having yet another affair. She severed his penis with a kitchen knife, tied his appendage to a helium balloon and let it drift skyward. Poetry in motion!

8. Lady Sarah Graham Moon's act of retribution was altogether more, well, lady-like. She famously became the patron saint for dumped wives when she cut off one sleeve of each of her philandering husband's Savile Row suits, chucked five litres of paint over his BMW, and gifted a bottle of his vintage claret to each one of their neighbours.

7. The internet has opened up many news windows of opportunity to exact revenge on cheating spouses. In 2008, Bill Rouse put up his 'cheating, lying, adulterous slag of a wife' on auction site ebay for 1p. The joke was on him when his ex protested and he was arrested by police.

6. Bed-and-breakfast owner Errol Charlesworth was shocked to find his wife having a dirty weekend with her bit on the side in their very own rural guest house. He exacted his revenge by throwing all the man's clothes – including several hand-made Italian suits – into a cess pit.

5. Ebay again. An Australian woman tried to put up a pair of knickers on the site, to get her own back on her cheating husband.

The knickers, which she identified as large enough to make 'a nice shawl', were not allowed on the site due to the company's policy of not selling second-hand underwear. And who the hell would buy them anyway?

4. Celtic mythology offers an excessive example of how hell hath no fury like a woman scorned. When her husband Cuchulainn indulged in extra-marital relations with a fairy named Fand, the goddess Emer stormed their secret meeting with 50 armed women. Then, being a soppy fairy, she forgave her hubbie for his liaison dangeureuse.

3. When you live in the public eye you may as well break-up in the public eye. So it shouldn't really have been a surprise when Isabelle Adjani used the cover of *Paris Match* magazine to break-off her engagement to cheating musician boyfriend Jean-Michel Jarre. The cover splash was the first he'd heard of it.

2. Modern-day spurned lovers eat your hearts out. In 1806, a woman put an ad in a Connecticut newspaper warning about a visiting fortune teller, who had tricked her – and four other women before her – into marrying him. Here's an extract for her admonishing ad. "Should he make advances under a feigned name, they may look out for a little, strutting, talkative, meagre, feeble, hatchet-faced fellow, with spindle shanks and a little warped in the back." What a catch!

1. SNAKE IN THE GRASS
It's a hard life being the immortal daughter of a sun god. First, Queen Pasiphae of Greek legend was cursed for some minor offence and made to have it off with the king's bull. Then she discovered that her husband Minos was putting it about. What to do? Well what would any self-respecting vengeful goddess do to a snake in the grass? Why, put a spell on him so he would ejaculate poisoned creatures and so destroy his lovers, of course. Pasiphae herself, being an immortal, was alone in being immune.

NO SMOKING PLEASE – WE'RE BRITISH

A crowded second class compartment on a May bank holiday was treated to a public display of over-affection by two warehouse workers returning to London from a work day out in Margate. Wearing knickers and nothing else, Zoe D'Arcy sat on top of fellow fornicator John Henderson's lap and performed 'full intercourse,' Horseferry magistrates were told. Fellow passengers kept a stiff upper lip during the impromptu sesh, and prosecutor Nazir Afzal revealed that "it was only in their act of lighting up cigarettes that the witnesses came up to them and complained."

NOT SO CIVIL SERVANTS

As sexual fantasies go, this one is pretty lame – the amusing aspect is that one couple found it so arousing they actually carried it out. The fantasy was to have sex outside a mayoral office with civil servants beavering away inside. The reality was a canoodling couple in Bariloche, Argentina, disgusting the mayor of the town and getting themselves arrested for cavorting naked on a bench outside his office.

PARK RANGER GETS NETTLED BY DOGGERS

"When the weather is fine, we find 10 to 15 couples. They are very difficult to catch because they warn each other with mobile phones when they hear us approaching." The wise words of disgruntled park ranger Jos Evers, head ranger of Het Twiske park, near Amsterdam, bemoaning the amount of dogging going down on his turf. Mr Evers has the last laugh though – he has planted nettles and thistles in the area to put obscene outdoor pursuits enthusiasts off.

SHIT HAPPENS WHEN YOU PARTY NAKED

Far away from the rampant smuttiness of Hamburg, Germany's infamous Reeperbahn, lies the sleepy Northern suburb of Kiwitsmoor. Wooden houses nestle on tree-lined roads and all in the world is peaceful and quiet. Small wonder then that two naked party-goers slept through the night and the morn on a random front lawn, only to be rudely awoken by three local policemen, called in by the lawn's prudish owners. Bild newspaper kindly published pictures of the hungover pair in 2007. The walk of shame was a chilly one for both – their clothes were nowhere to be found at the scene.

BEE IN THE BONNET

It's a rite-of-passage for most young lovers to have sex in the back seat of a car. Preferably stationary. But what to do when there's four of you headed to the woods to lose your cherries? How about using your imaginations and have one of the pairs have sex on the bonnet? So far, so good. But doing so in the beautiful English New Forest during a heat wave meant that one foolish foursome got dobbed to the police by one of the many, many walkers in the popular nature area. It's your proud moment, Alex Lepper (16) and Emily Forsythe (17) of Brockenhurst, Hants.

THE WORLD'S OLDEST DILDO OR SCULPTED PHALLUS IS MADE OF STONE AND IS 28,000 YEARS OLD

SCHOOL TRIP

Naughty sexual escapades on school trips are not news of themselves. But when the sexual impropriety is among the teachers, then we're talking! This tale concerns a Swedish school trip to Kenya in the early noughties, where a group of students were disgusted to see their mentors becoming paid-up members of the sex-for-cash gang.

The kids filmed the tawdry teaching staff entering a brothel, but amazingly the head-teacher of their school refused to give them the sack. Outcry swiftly followed when the kids went public with the offending film.

UNHAPPY BIRTHDAY TO YOU

Jilted Sam Raven wanted to give his ex-girlfriend a birthday she wouldn't forget. Fearing she had cheated on him during their three year relationship, he arranged for a friend to hand out business cards at her twenty-first birthday party with links to a web address. Horrified friends and relatives who visited the site were shocked to see lewd pictures of the girl as well as a nasty sex clip. Raven was jailed for three months and all the footage was destroyed – but only after the site had received over 300 hits.

SEX ON THE BEACH

With eight children and seventeen grand-children between them, it should come as no surprise that a Malaysian couple are fond of a spot of jiggery-pokery. But with also over a 100 years of worldly wisdom between them, the Muslim pair might have known that having sex on a public beach would see them charged in a court of

Sharia law – not least as they were not man and wife, but man and sister-in-law.

THE SKY'S NOT THE LIMIT

Not one for the vertiginous... Dumb-founded onlookers called police in 2007 when they spotted a naked pair getting down to business at the top of a construction crane. Police were called, and arrested Justin Dunn and Nicole Hunt who claimed they'd been at the top of the crane taking photos. The police did not press charges, as it turned out the crane was owned by Justin's father.

BOWLED OVER AT TRENT BRIDGE

A pair of sex-crazed cricket fans were caught making love in the cricket ground at Trent Bridge, England, in the late eighties. I say 'caught', but in fact the horny couple had deliberately had sex in full view of spectators during a Test match. They were arrested but not charged.

WHAM BAM, THANK YOU TRAM

A coupled were arrested for making the beast with two backs alongside the tram tracks at Wandle Park Station, Croydon, England. A stunned CCTV operator called police when the couple ignored a tannoy message telling them to stop. Perhaps they were enjoying getting ready for their close up – the station has clear signs posted that travellers are being filmed.

ASIDE SEX TOYS, BOTTLES ARE THE MOST LIKELY OBJECT TO BE USED AS AN ERSATZ PHALLUS

PEEPING TOMS

What do you get when you cross two Peeping Toms and two folk doing the do in a car at a popular make-out spot? Three months in jail for one of the Toms, who in Singapore in October 1997 was sent down for assaulting his voyeur rival. The dim-witted perverts got into a punch up over who should get the best spot to cop an eyeful of the lovers.

ABERDEEN ANGST

A pair in Aberdeen, who were being as one in one of the city's parks, only to discover post-coitally that a thief had pinched their clobber. Worse yet, the naughty nudes' keys went walkies along with their clothes, and they had to call police to get into their home after an embarrassing walk through the city.

MAKING SWEET MUSIC

Tommy Hol Ellingsen 28, and Leona Johansson, 21, were charged 10,000 Norwegian Kroner each for performing a sex-show live on stage during the 2004 Quart music festival. The band that they were 'dancing' for was the charmingly and aptly named 'Cumshots.' The band were also hauled over the coals – but sadly not for the crime of having a really crap name.

LOVER'S LEAP

A lover's leap is a place of great beauty and height generally associated with the suicide of one spurned in an affair of the heart.

AN ESTIMATED 30% OF DVD RENTALS ARE X-RATED

For one young couple however the phrase took on a new meaning when in 2007 their rooftop romp in Columbia, USA, ended in a 50-foot fall to the ground. Reaching the giddy heights of pleasure proved fatal for the pair.

A LIFE SENTENCE

Some funny souls call marriage a life sentence. Yes, very amusing. But in Michigan one of the routes out of marriage – adultery – could also carry a life sentence. In 2007, it was reported that an outdated Michigan law classes marriage as first-degree criminal sexual conduct, the highest sexual felony in that State. How Michigan's attorney general, Mike Cox, took the news is anybody's guess – he had owned up to an extra-marital adventure in 2005.

RESOURCEFUL ROMANIAN

If you want a lesson in safe sex, please ask anyone but Romanian Nicolae Popovici. In 2004, the hopeless humper super-glued a condom to his willy so it would not fall off, as his wife had complained it was too 'roomy'. Even thicker still was the excuse he gave to doctors, that by keeping it stuck on, he could use the contraceptive more than once.

HORSE-PLAY NOT FUN

A Polish animal lover was killed by a sex-crazed horse in 2004. He was trying to calm the beast's overzealous lust for a mare in a neighbouring field when it bit him to death in a frenzied attack. The man was only 24 years old.

THE COST OF LOVING

With mounting student loans and debts, students have to be resourceful to get through university these days. But not everyone would follow the example of 18-year-old lesbian Rosie Reid, who auctioned her virginity on Ebay in 2004. From 2,000 bidders she selected the five highest ones, eventually selling her cherry for £8,400 to a divorced 44-year-old BT engineer and father of two. Reid admitted the experience was 'horrible', but was over with quickly.

A SHOT IN THE DARK

A 27-year-old Sicilian asked his friend to shoot him in the groin with a hunting rifle in the hope it would make his ex-girlfriend rush to his bedside, and they'd be reconciled. Top marks to him for drama and effort. But in the groin? Wouldn't that impair his chances for a sympathy shag somewhat?

A PHANTOM FELONY?

Federal Way is a commuter town in Washington State, USA. I'm telling you this, so you can avoid the place if you're particularly superstitious...

In 2007, a log on the town's police records showed that two women claimed they'd been having nightly visitations by an over-familiar spectre. Or as they put it, that the ghost has been 'having sexual intercourse' with them. One woman claimed the ethereal erotic activity had started at her previous address, the other that the crimes had started recently.

I can find no further clue as to whether the sexually gung-ho ghost was arrested or whether it remains at large. Don't say you haven't been warned!

THERE HAS BEEN A 135% INCREASE IN THE NUMBER OF BOOB JOBS CARRIED OUT IN THE UK IN THE LAST FIVE YEARS

MISTAKEN IDENTITY # 2

When dog-walkers in the central Japanese town of Izu discovered a lifeless form wrapped in plastic, it was all hands on the murder-inquiry deck. The media were in a frenzy to photograph the 'victim's' last resting place, the scene was cordoned off, and the 'body' was sent to the lab. However, it wasn't a corpse that pathologists unravelled from the suspicious green awning, but a life-size sex doll. Mortified police called off the search for a killer, but swore to hunt down the owner of the 'pre-loved' doll.

SOMETHING TO SHOUT ABOUT

In 2006, the *New Scientist* magazine reported that Stuart Brody, a psychologist at the University of Paisley, had discovered that having sex was a good way to prevent stress during public speaking. Of 46 volunteers, those who'd had sex romped through a public speaking test with good performances, while the abstemious were tongue-tied. Only penetrative intercourse was found to work though – oral, self-abuse and other sexual acts did not have any affect at all.

WET DREAM

In 2005, a report revealed that anaesthetic can give people vivid sex dreams. Dr. Steven Barker, head of anaesthesiology at the University Medical Center of Tucson, Arizona, recounted an example for the findings. He had once half-sedated a patient, needing to communicate with her throughout a minor operation. "At one point, I asked her if there was anything I could get for her, and she said, 'Yeah, a man,'" Barker said. "She then proceeded to describe the sexual characteristics of what she wanted, in a pretty direct way." Apparently between 1 and 5% of patients are similarly affected.

THAILAND IS THE MOST POPULAR DESTINATION FOR SEX TOURISTS

MILE HIGH CLUB BY THE HOUR

If you can't get a room, get an aeroplane, says Bob Smith from milehighatlanta.com. In 2006, the media soared into a frenzy with the news that the pilot was offering to take frisky couples out for an hour on his plane, at a cost of nearly two hundred quid. Checking their website today tells me that the company is still in business in Georgia, USA. I also learned that not only do you get a certificate of your sky-high sex session but that you get to keep the sheet you've bonked on "as a souvenir of this special event." Have they never heard of launderettes?

STATING THE UNOBVIOUS

From the outside it looked like an ordinary stone-clad terraced house. But when police raided a home in Durham, England, in 2006, they found members of the sex-slave cult The Koatians, who believe in the practice of domination and submission. But don't worry, ladies. Cult-leader Lee Thompson is all for equality. "Women can be free and they can be dominant, we don't stop that," he says. "But the majority of women in our organisation are obviously slaves because women have a submissive streak in them." Obviously.

WILL WORK FOR SEX

Some people have ingenious methods to get laid if they can't get a girl. In 2007, Lloyd Benterman put an ad on Craig's List which said "Will fix computers for sexual favours." Benterman then claimed to have been inundated with calls from digital damsels in distress, with one woman even giving him a blow job before he'd worked on her computer. Question? If you're that darned irresistible to women, why not just get paid in cash like normal folk?

DON'T TRY THIS AT HOME # 1

One booth at the American sexhibition Erotica LA was particularly busy in 2003. There, Australian Ian Haig, was showing his range of home-made sex toys, made from discarded vacuum cleaners, food processors, and so on. But visitors were disappointed to learn his home-made gadgets were for display purposes only. Try telling that to the misadventurous miscreants featured elsewhere in this book!

FROM RUSSIA WITH BEMUSEMENT

I don't know which is more surprising, that there is an event called the Bubble Baba challenge, where men race each other on sex-doll rafts, or that the event is an annual one in Russia's sporting calendar. In any case, if you fancy your chances in the sport, all you need is an erotic floating device you don't mind losing in wild-water rapids. And your air-fare to St Petersburg, natch.

A GRAVE MATTER

69-times-arrested Gareth Morgan and his nine-times-offending girlfriend Anna Jones pleaded guilty to outraging public decency when he went down on her on a bench in a church graveyard in Ynysforgan, Swansea, Wales, in the summer of 2008.

THE PORN INSPECTOR

A Colorado, USA man is on the run for impersonating a police porn inspector. A what? Yup, you read correctly. An aspiring thief approached the same adult video store three times in nine days asking for free X-Rated DVDs so he could check the performers' ages for the Colarado Police Department's 'underage' unit. Commander Tim Lewis from the local police force in question told the media, "There is no such unit." The vile but inventive criminal was caught on video surveillance but had not yet been nabbed by the boys in blue at the time of writing.

LAWFULLY SILLY

Sometimes the world can seem just a little topsy-turvy. Take sex laws in Singapore: a place where prostitution is legal but oral sex – even between consenting adults – is not. Thus a Singaporean police man faced life imprisonment in 2003 for pleasuring a woman with his tongue.

I, ROBOT... TAKE YOU, HUMAN

An artificial intelligence expert has written a book predicting the future of our love lives in the next 50 years or so. David Levy's book *Love and Sex with Robots* – you can see where this is going – sets out his idea that by 2050 robots will make 'attractive companions' owing to their 'soft skin and touchable hair.' Robots, he goes on to suggest, "don't have to be boring."

ROMPING IN THE AISLES

I've heard of actors having an audience rolling in the aisles, but romping's a new one on me. During the sexually explicit play XXX, London audience members were shocked to see one of the cast giving an audience member oral sex, egged on by the other actors on stage. A Scotland Yard investigation of the amorous dramatics came to nothing in 2003, with the cast claiming that it had all been simulated.

SEX MANUAL TRAUMA

Getting litigious over lesbians proved fruitless for greedy American Adam Constable when his sons – aged 14 and 16 – stumbled over a lesbian sex 'how to' guide in their local library. His demand for $10,000 per child, by way of compensation, was thrown out of court. Disgusted, the unsuccessful cash-in claimant whined that the book had led to "many sleepless nights in our house." I'll bet.

SCARIER THAN DOUBLE MATHS?

A photography class was a real eye opener for Phoenix, Arizona, high school students in 2008. But not in a good way. Their teacher, after handing out projects, switched on his PC and started to view porn clips, thinking nobody could see what he was up to. But the unwitting man had linked his personal computer to a projector screen forgetting that the images – which one student described as 'torture porn' – would be plain for all to see.

SPANKING IS POPULAR WITH 13% OF BRITISH MEN

TOP TEN SEX TAPE SCANDALS

10. Actresses often fake it in the bedroom – it comes with the territory. But in 2007, Iranian actress Zahra Amir Ebrahimi claimed an internet sex tape that was circulating of her was itself a fake. In Iran, being an unmarried woman, she could have been jailed if the tape was proven to be real.

9. A senior police officer resigned in 2002 when lurid sex tapes were found of him with a divorcee. His lover told papers, "He loved to tell me when he was meeting important people and regularly stripped off for me in front of his webcam." The glamour!

8. Soccer player Stan Collymore. Remember him from the public misadventures top ten? Well, many years ago he got into a spot of bother while apparently trying to get a sex-tape of him and a girlfriend released to the public. he failed as the girlfriend made him destroy it.

7. *Frasier* star Kelsey Grammer sued adult web company IEG in 1998, claiming they planned to show a sex tape stolen from his home. The case fell apart when it could not be proved the tape existed. The company later said they had another tape of the actor but that they were "evaluating it." Couldn't have been up to much: It never made it into the virtual world.

6. Socialite Kim Kardashian did not want to follow in her mate Paris Hilton's fornicatin' footsteps, and stopped a porn firm distributing a sex tape featuring her doing her carnal gymnastics with ex-boyfriend Ray J.

5. Malaysian health minister Chua Soi Lek was forced to resign when he became embroiled in not one, but two, sex tape scandals. He used the same hotel and room for a second misadventure, even though the first one had been leaked.

4. Pop stars and salacious sex tapes go together like hard-work and arse-licking for normal folk – both are career-boosters. So why Croatian pop star Severina pissed and moaned when a raucous romp of her with a married man was leaked on the web, God only knows. Maybe it was because she's a devoted Catholic and likes to have a good old preach about abstinence?

3. Ordinarily sex tapes are leaked without the star's approval. Sometimes though, fame-hungry folk make their home-brewed porn public themselves. Take Dustin 'Saved By the Bell' Diamond, who made a tape emetically entitled *Saved by the Smell* in 2006. Diamond's manager suggested at the time that the tape would help the actor's star rise in the future. It didn't.

2. IEG. Remember them from the Kelsey Grammer in non-sex-tape shocker? That same year, 1998, they were in court again for showing a tape of actress Pamela Anderson and husband Tommy Lee's week long sex-marathon honeymoon. The frolicking honeymooners ended up $1.5 million better off after a court awarded them a share of the company's profits. Bet they wished they'd stayed a fortnight.

1. ONE NIGHT IN PARIS
Paris, the city, and Hilton hotels – both things which invoke thoughts of classiness and romance. Funny then, that when you put the two together you end up with the world's most useless heiress. Yes. That Paris Hilton tape. In the number one spot for its success, its graphic nature, the variety of sex acts involved, and the celebrity brought to its 'star.'

MISTAKEN IDENTITY # 3

Having a noisy thirtieth birthday party is bound to make your neighbours complain. So guests at a party in Simmern, Germany, must have been well sozzled when they mistook two police officers who arrived to investigate neighbours' complaints for strippers. After embarrassing 'get your kit off' type clamours, the party-goers eventually saw sense. Nobody was arrested.

ALL ABOARD THE BROTHEL BUS

Mobile homes. Bit geeky aren't they? Mobile brothels, though, that's a different story. Undercover police in Miami discovered such a vehicle after observing men getting in and out of a sleek black stretch limo which was regularly cruising up and down the city's main beach. The police paid 40 dollars each to enter the limo and were offered a veritable smorgasbord of sexual activity from full to oral sex, to anal, to a lap dance. This latter crime led the resourceful rent-a-girls being charged with "violating the public dance hall ordinance." They were not charged with any other crime.

I NEED SEX!

In 2008, British 20-something Laura Michaels had the bare facebooked cheek to use a social networking site to satisfy her sex addiction. Starting a group called 'I need sex', Michaels soon had 35 members, rising to 100 within days. Easy, though, lads. Facebook have since closed the grubby group down.

THE SUBWAY GODDESS

That tube journey to work can be a drag, can't it? Not for Santiago commuters in the sweaty summer of 2008. They were treated to a strange form of protest from Monserrat Morilles, 26. Ms Morilles, railing against strict Chilean morals, spent an entire week riding the subway in her undies and giving spontaneous pole dances to passengers. She was eventually arrested after artfully dodging the cops for seven days.

GIRL ON FILM

A selfish Sicilian shagger secretly filmed his girlfriend while they did the nasty at their home in Palermo, Italy. When they broke up, he sent her tapes of their sexploits, saying, "these are my last thoughts of you." He was sentenced to four months in jail but amazingly his sentence was overturned on appeal since he hadn't shown the offending material to anyone else.

BADGE OF DISHONOUR

A Swedish Association for Sexuality Education was forced to get rid of a badge, known as 'a licence to shag,' which it had handed out to approximately 35,000 of its members. (You know, a bit like a scout or Girl Guide badge, but for carnal knowledge.)

But it was not public outcry that forced them to relinquish the barmy badge. Rather, the Swedish Swimming Federation successfully claimed that the bonking badge was too similar to their own emblem of achievement.

12% OF MEN HAVE MASTURBATED WHILE THEIR PARTNER IS ASLEEP IN THE SAME BED

WE INTERRUPT THIS PROGRAMME...

In 2008, a popular New Zealand rugby show was interrupted with several minutes of hardcore porn. There was a mix-up in the transmissions between the sports and a pay-per-view porn channel. Bet the VT op wasn't the only thing that was discharged that night.

VULGARITY BEGINS AT HOME

Jules Capriati and wife Angela were famed for their notorious suburban swinging parties. Multi-amorous swinging advocates from all around would attend their pervy parties, until the police closed their home sex club, The Cherry Pit.

The 59-year-old (possibly) oldest swinger in his town sued his city council after he'd been banned from holding the sex parties at their Duncanville, Texas home. But the city was adamant that carrying out private acts in a public place is against the law.

WITH FRIENDS LIKE THESE

Popping round to a friend's house for tea can be full of surprises. Perhaps they tell you they're having an affair, or that they're going to be a daddy/mummy. One Egyptian woman got the surprise of her life when visiting a friend: She found herself collapsed in the arms of her best bud's husband. The deviant pair had drugged the woman's tea so that the man could have sex with her, since her friend did not feel up to fulfilling her 'conjugal duties' *Al-Massa* newspaper reported.

NOT CRICKET

British Builder John Matthews was not bowled over when his wife told him she'd been having an affair with cricketing ace Neil Edwards. Having done some building work on the Somerset player's home, Matthews used a key to gain entry and proceeded to reap revenge on the supposed marriage-breaker.

Inside the cricketer's flat he went on the warpath, pouring expandable foam down the loo and bath, sawing his rival's bed in half, and taking a sharp implement to a plasma screen TV.

Edwards denied the affair in court. The couple put on a united front but left £5,000 poorer for the compensation the father-of-three had to pay.

PRETTY STUPID WOMAN

There are plenty of stories nowadays about the revenge tactics of jilted wives – indeed you'll find many in this book. So, in the interests of equality let's turn our attention to one jilted husband and his method of getting his own back.

The twist in this particular tale is that Jonathan Birkett did not take out his wrath on his wife, but rather the man with whom his wife had the affair. Stuart Marten, who at the time was a senior executive at a major telecommunications company, eventually resigned over Birkett's claims on sites like Myspace and Facebook that he had offered his wife half-a-million pounds and a car to leave him. He compared Marten's financial incentive to Mrs Birkett to stay with him to the movie Pretty Woman.

IN THE LINE OF DUTY

Service with a smile. Isn't that the American way? Not for one Beaumont cop, who claimed he had not enjoyed the oral and vaginal intercourse he'd had with two prostitutes – it was just part of his job.

Officer Keith Breiner and colleague Lt. David Kiker were suspended when higher officials discovered they had been cavorting in a brothel, ostensibly so they would have sufficient evidence to close it. Both were suspended indefinitely when the Chief of Police said their claim they'd been given permission to do so was – appropriately enough – "junk."

ST VALENTINES DAY (NEARLY) MASSACRE

When you've been married for over 20 years and your husband has an affair it can come as quite a shock. Yet more shocking is how one woman reacted when her husband Paul Barret was rumoured to be having an affair with local woman, Kim Johnson. Sarah Allen got drunk on February 14, 2007, went to Johnson's house and put lit newspaper through her letter box. Thankfully the paper hit the draught excluder and was extinguished.

KNICKERS TO YOU

All's fair in love, war, and kinky knicker collections. On discovering her husband was a collector of said items, Valerie Thorne hung the offending items from an apple tree in the couple's Lancashire, England, front garden with a brief Dear John note: "Goodbye Wolfram and your Dirty Knicker Collection."

5% OF BRITISH WOMEN ARE INTO RUBBER FETISHISM

REVENGE OVER-COOKED

When Margaret Cook's MP husband, the late Robin Cook, had an affair with his secretary Gaynor she decided enough was enough. She spilled the beans – soya, baked, haricot, runner, butter, the lot – on that and his previous affairs, giving a series of TV interviews, writing a newspaper column and filling two books of sordid detail on the matter.

NOT A THAI BRIDE

In 1994, Brit Mary Coop flew to Thailand for a sun, sea and sex holiday with her partner. She didn't expect the sex would be with someone other than him. When she discovered her partner – who she'd hoped was about to propose – in flagrante delicto with an Aussie waitress, she raised him an antipodean and shagged the Kiwi barman in their luxury hotel. She then cut up his passport, travel, insurance documents and house keys, and dumped them all in the sea. In 2004 she told her story to *The Times*, still dreaming of her Kiwi lover.

KNIGHT RIDER

Daylight robbery is a handy expression which we can use to describe an act of overcharging so blatant that it feels like a robber carried out a crime in broad daylight. So when a man carries out a sex attack on a parked car in broad daylight, what should we call it? Daylight car-shaggery? Whatever. The dilemma arises from the sorry story of a drunken idiot who mounted a Toyota 4x4 while its owner nipped to the shops. Perhaps he thought it was sex-toy(ota).

13% OF BRITISH MEN ARE INTO RUBBER FETISHISM

RANDY RABBI

"When God closes a door, he opens a window." No surprise that this comment should come from a holy man, the Rabbi Fred Neulander, founder of a Jewish Temple in the town of Cherry Hill, New Jersey, USA.

More surprising, although not jaw-droppingly so, is that the words were uttered to his lover, radio presenter Elaine Soncini, a week after his wife had been bludgeoned to death. Soncini and Neulander had begun a highly charged hanky-panky filled affair in 1992, within a month of Neulander giving his soon-to-be mistress grief counselling over the death of her husband. His wife Carol's brutal murder by two hitmen occurred later, in November 1994, six weeks before Soncini's birthday. The randy Rabbi had promised his lover they would be free to be together by the end of that month.

Leonard Jenoff and Paul M. Daniels confessed to the crime in May 2000, alleging Neulander had paid them $30,000 to carry out the deed. In 2002, the Rabbi was convicted – after much legal to-ing and fro-ing – of arranging his wife's murder and was sentenced to 30 years to life at New Jersey State Prison.

MONK-EY BUSINESS

The following incident will have you begging the question of whether the expression 'making a monkey of oneself' should not perhaps be changed to making a monk of oneself.

The pretty Bavarian town of Würzburg, Germany, is home to many impressive historical buildings. Among these is the Maria Laach monastery, home for centuries to a brotherhood of Benedictine monks. In March 2008, the hallowed building made history – not for its architectural magnificence, but for a very wrong reason indeed. It was reported at this time in German newspapers that one of the brothers, ostensibly going into the town on monastery business, took part in an affair most unbecoming for a monk. The unholy shenanigans involved the theft of 150 Euro-worth of gay porn, a Benny-Hill-esque chase through the town, and ultimately capture by police after the brother tried to hoodwink them by throwing the offending material in a bin.

A search of his cell found a hoard of over 200 homoerotic porn films, of which the monk admitted he had stolen 40 from the Würzburg sex shop. How he came upon, or indeed viewed, the other 180 is a mystery. The life of a Benedictine monk not only involves a rigorous routine of silent prayer, sleep and bible reading, but they are not allowed to have any money or possessions.

MUM'S THE WORD # 1

What would be worse – admitting to your mother you are travelling with a penis pump, or telling US immigration officials that you are travelling with a bomb? Ahmed Mustafa chose the latter option when officials found a grenade-like object in his suitcase. The mummy's boy. His story did not go down a bomb, and he was charged with felony disorderly conduct.

PANIC OVER

Mackay regional airport in Queensland, Australia, was shut in a security alert in 2005 when a vibrating sex toy was chucked in a rubbish bin and was mistaken for a bomb. It took over-cautious officials an hour to realize it was more of a 'sex-bomb' than anything else.

WOMEN WITH RED HAIR GET MORE SEX THAN THOSE WITH ANY OTHER HAIR COLOUR

CAREFUL WHAT YOU WISH FOR

A stupid shagger had trouble convincing his girlfriend that a threesome would be a wholesome and fun idea. His girlfriend, being an entrepreneurial type, suggested that if he managed to get five million hits on his business website she would engage in the trilateral tomfoolery. He did, they did, and then guess what happened? He became consumed with jealousy, and she ended up back in bed with the third party. An exotic dancer called Holly, no less. Didn't he remember three's a crowd?

PROPHYLACTIC PILFERING

When thieves in Mexico City made off with over 5,000 condoms from a van used to promote HIV and AIDS awareness, they were good enough to leave behind remote testing equipment for the infection, as well as a giant 23 foot inflatable condom which rode on top of the vehicle.

BOOB ALERT

German tabloid Bild ran the sniggersome headline 'Holiday jet in porno alarm', after an image of a bare-breasted woman kept flickering on the screen of a flight from Munich to Sardinia. Mothers sheltered young children's eyes, Fathers nipped to the lav overcome by all the excitement, and stewards were on call to calm frazzled nerves. The 'porno' turned out to be a moment from the airline's in-flight documentary on beaches in Rimini, which had just happened to have got stuck on the titty shot throughout the flight. Panic over.

AN ESTIMATED 100 PENIS ENLARGEMENTS ARE CARRIED OUT EACH YEAR IN THE UK

WINDOW ON THE WORLD

A pair of over-amorous office workers were given a good ticking off by police community support officers when their public exhibitionism in an office window got out of hand. Co-workers had been cheering the passionate paramours along, but the couple still did not realize they could be seen through the frosted glass windows in Charlotte Street, London, in 2006.

REDUCED PRICE VICE

Delegates at the 2008 Conservative Party Conference were given discount vouchers for a local Birmingham lap dancing club in a booklet distributed with official conference literature. A spokesman for the marketing company who made the brochure said it had been "produced to help maximize the economic impact for local businesses." There's a man who knows his market, then.

THE LATEST FASHION

Ah! Paris. Home to haute-couture and all things à la mode. No surprise then that it's a Frenchman who should have come up with an idea for an accessory for dogs. 'Hotdoll' is a dog-shaped sex-aid with which unloved pooches can enjoy sexcapades without the need for their owners to seek out random pooches in parks. Its inventor Clément Eloy says, "I wondered why there was nothing like a doll already available for dogs. Humans can control their impulses – but dogs just can't do that." Humans can control their impulses? He wants to pick up a copy of this book...

PORN DAMAGE

Men at the Cats all-night video store in Tokyo got a lot more than they bargained for when a disgruntled local set fire to one of the private viewing cubicles there. Fifteen people died and ten were injured when Kazuhiro Ogawa decided he was "fed up with life."

WANT SEX? EAT CAKE*

If you wanted official encouragement to eat more, take heart from a recent study from the University of Hawaii which proved – from a sample group of 7,000 women – that larger ladies get more sex than thin ones. The study found that 92% of the women with a bigger BMI had recently enjoyed some hanky-panky, compared with a puny 87% of thinner girls.

   * But only if you're a girl. In Hawaii.

CARRY ON CAMPUS

The usually po-faced *Independent* newspaper of Britain reported in 2006 about the growing number of American universities whose students are making their own pornographic magazines. From Harvard's failed *H-Bomb* to Boston University's vibrant *Boink*, the mags will be a first-stop shop for those who want to see college students in the nod – without the annoying legal issues. The co-founder of *Boink* said he hoped his mag would help advance "A more 'European' attitude towards sex in America." Lucky them. Puerile titillation all round.

OUT FOR A GOLDEN DUCK

In 2005, a blonde bombshell told Britain's *The Sun* and *Daily Mirror* newspapers that she had kept an Australian cricket player up all night in a game that was definitely not cricket. Australia lost a test match the following day by three wickets, and England took a decisive 2–1 series lead.

DON'T STOP ME NOW...

A Romanian man had a licence to love but not to drive, when police banned him from the roads after he caused a car crash on an A-road. Robert Filip was naked as his girlfriend Andrea Popescu administered oral sex on him while he was behind the wheel. She even continued the foolish fellatio after their car crashed into a stationary vehicle. Said Filip, "I am sorry for what happened but at the time I just could not stop myself."

KEYSTONE CRIMINAL

There are criminal masterminds, and there's Aussie Paul Brady. The bungling thief threatened staff with a baseball bat and stole $200 in cash from a Sydney sex shop, but police soon caught up with him after discovering two schoolboy errors. 1. He leafed through a jazz mag before he exited the store, leaving his fingerprints for the cops. 2. He strolled out nonchalantly after the stick-up, baseball bat in hand, allowing witnesses time to note the registration number of his get-away car parked outside.

THE LARGEST VAGINA ON RECORD WAS 2.5 METRES WIDE

TOP TEN BESTIAL BONKINGS

10. In 2008, a Tasmanian man was caught downloading images of sexual acts with an octopus. He was later found to have a veritable menagerie of 31,000 images and video files involving sexual acts with dogs, ponies, snakes, tigers as well as the afore-mentioned tentacled one. His lawyer said his client's self-esteem was so low he equated himself with a beast.

9. An Afghan soldier was let off when he had sex with a donkey in 2004, when a court believed he'd only shacked up with the beast cause he could not afford a dowry for a human wife.

8. Two British workers were sacked for acting the goat, or rather sheep, in the Algerian oil town Hassi Messaoud, for simulating sex with a herd of sheep. The pervy pranksters could not have been more stupid or disrespectful – the sheep were lined up to be slaughtered for the sacred Muslim festival of Eid.

7. Speaking of goats, Adrian Lowther was convicted of buggery of one in 2002. As if goat-rape was not enough, Lowther had tied his belt round the farm animal's neck, in the first known case of bestial BDSM.

6. About the only sexual thing I can think of about hedgehogs is a crap joke about the word 'prickles.' Not so for Serbian Zoran Nikolovic, 35, who needed emergency surgery after having sex with one, Ananova reported. Don't worry though – he did not do it of his own volition. A witch doctor allegedly told him it would cure his premature ejaculation. Which makes it so much easier to understand, eh?

5. An OAP was spotted having sex with a horse by a driver on a busy dual carriage way in 2006. The man told police he could not

help himself – after spotting the animal in a field he simply had to pull over and satisfy his urges.

4. A pig called Chi-Chi gave new meaning to the word 'porking' when a biker's wife spied it attempting to hump her hubby's beloved Harley–Davidson. The bike was scratched and the seat cover torn in the unprovoked attack, but the bike suffered no lasting damage. The pig/bike owner Walter Wyatt was dismayed then when animal control officers took the beast away and had it castrated.

3. You've got to admire the lawyer who got his client off when he had sex with a dead deer. The clever legal-eagle claimed Paul William Farley did not have sex with an animal – because its lifeless carcass could not be described as such.

2. It was double trouble for police when an investigation into the sexual assault and death of several sheep led them to a pair of identical twins. DNA on a pair of track bottoms found at one of the crime scenes led them to one twin, who blamed his looky-likey brother. Police could not get to the bottom of which twin was the true culprit, and banned both from going near any farm for an 18-month period.

1. DONKEY MAKES ASS OF MAN
When Callum McClellan checked into a hotel with a donkey, signing the register as 'Mr Shrek', the receptionist might have feared the worst. She didn't though, and believed his sorry story that the animal was a family pet. Police were called when the donkey went berserk running through the hotel, and found Mr McClellan handcuffed to the bed. He was arrested and charged with lewd behaviour and animal cruelty. A further charge of damage to a mini-bar was dropped when McClellan claimed the donkey had done it, we are dutifully informed by a newspaper.

THE WRONG WAY TO HAVE LAST RITES

A Taiwanese man paid an erotic dancer to perform at his father's funeral, after promising the old man he'd have a lady strip off for guests if he made it to 100. His dear old dad had been a prolific user of strip clubs in neighbouring towns, as well as a serial shagger – he is survived by 100 descendants.

UNCOOL YULE

Four student nurses were sacked from the Charles Johnson Memorial Hospital in South Africa in 2006 for carousing naked while they were on night duty, a few days before the Christmas holidays. And the ward the randy revellers were found to be huffing and puffing in? The children's ward. Yuk.

HIGH-FLYING PORN

A British newspaper reported that airline companies in America – where else – are having to restrict in-flight wi-fi services because of their punters' propensity for porn. Two of the most popular airline companies in the US were said to be coming over all censorious while their passengers come over... Well, let's just leave it there.

THE PYROTECHNIC PENIS

They say that when you split, you shouldn't try to remain friends, let alone live with one another. One Moscow couple, unable to afford two new homes, broke this golden rule of separation and chose to remain in the same house. This all became too much for the ex-wife in the pair who, in a fit of pique, took a naked flame to her ex's penis while he sat watching telly. The man with the pyrotechnic penis said, "I was burning like a torch. I don't know what I did to deserve this." The unnamed woman chose not to enlighten the press any further.

DON'T DO IT YOURSELF

Another reason not to try DIY penis enlargements. A Cambodian man who doused his penis in hair tonic in an attempt to make it bigger ended up writhing in such agony that he hung himself to relieve the pain. Coroner Vieng Vannarith concluded that the 35-year-old's bonkers brew had not been just the tonic. Officials were then forced to put out a public service announcement warning of the dangers of home-made penis enlargements, since there had been a spate of them leading up the unfortunate man's demise.

OUCH!

You'd be peeved if your penis fell off as a result of a sexual spree gone wrong – if you'd taken part in a particularly disease-infested orgy, for instance. Still, it might have been worth it. But you'd be well pissed off if your penis was lopped off and you'd not even been up to no good. Pity, then, Romanian Nelu Radonescu, whose willy was hacked off by an unhinged surgeon during an intimate operation. Doctors crafted him a new one made out of other skin tissue, and he claimed £100,000 in damages.

NAPPY NUT

Three times, a man from Montgomery County in the USA was arrested for the same crime, trying to satisfy a bizarre sexual fetish. In 1998, 2003 and 2007, the unnamed man had been caught grubbing around in bins to find dirty nappies. He told police he liked to dress in babies' nappies for a sexual thrill and that the dirty nappies gave him "a little extra stimulation" while he got himself off. He was sentenced to three years probation.

NO REST FOR THE WICKED

A man was acquitted of rape in Ontario, Canada in 2008 when a court ruled that an unusual sleeping condition meant he was not responsible for his actions. He suffers from "sexsomnia", where sufferers often attempt intercourse when they are asleep. He had tried to have sex with a woman after a heavy-drinking party.

POTATO WEDGE-Y

A vicar who ended up in A&E with a potato stuck up his bum promised that the alien object had not got there as the result of a sexual misadventure. British paper *The Daily Telegraph* reported that the A&E nurse who took him into surgery to have the potato removed did not question the vicar's story. Well, believe his story and you'll believe anything – like men can walk on water, eh Rev?

ONLY 1% OF WOMEN HAVE HAD 20 OR MORE SEXUAL PARTNERS

CARNIVAL OF FOOLS

If you're going to assault a policeman with a make-shift weapon, you may as well go the whole hog and use a sex toy. One man did just that with a dildo at the 2007 Bathurst motor racing jamboree in England, and was swiftly arrested. Police were then shocked to find another sexual silly wandering round the event wheeling a television set showing porn. He was arrested too. The event is billed as a family affair, so police were less than impressed with the dirty duo.

DESPERATE DAN

"It was the most embarrassing moment of my life. When I got wheeled into a packed A&E on a wheelchair with a hoover attached to my willie, I just wished the ground could swallow me up." Thus spake Captain Dan, The Demon Dwarf who pulls a hoover across the stage with his penis as part of a show in Edinburgh, Scotland. Sadly for him an attempt in 2007 to glue on a loose attachment saw his appendage super-glued to the device instead. A likely story...

INDECOROUS INBOXES

In 2001, 77 employees were suspended and 10 sacked by the Royal and Sun Alliance insurance company. All were being punished for a series of crude and pornographic emails which were zipping around the company's internal email system at breakneck speed. One offending mail showed puppet Kermit the Frog getting jiggy with Fozzie Bear. Staff accused their bosses of over-reaction. And you can see why – the muppets.

THE FIRST ADVERTISEMENT FOR A HOME ELECTRIC VIBRATOR WAS IN 1899

STRIP-TEACH

A German teacher at a school in Zalaegerszeg, Hungary, gave a group of teenagers a lesson they won't forget in a hurry. Joining in with a game of 'dares', footage snapped by a mobile shows the school mistress wiggling her hips provocatively and stripping down to her bra. She was not sacked as her boss claimed she flashed "no more than you would see on a beach."

THE COST OF LUSTING

If you're going to accept a strip-tease in lieu of cash payment for a legal bill, make sure you cough up more than $250. Scott Erwin didn't when he accepted several lap-dances from a client who owed him money. She squealed to his superiors when she saw the paltry reduction to her bill, and the lascivious – and cheapskate – lawyer was suspended for 15 months.

A MORAL VACUUM # 2

Saginaw, Michigan, USA. There's a town you don't hear about very often. And car-wash copulation. An activity that does not pass your ears much, either. But put the two together and what do you get? A 29-year-old man from the strange sounding location, receiving sexual favours from a vacuum at his local car wash. And now the town and the activity are know from here to Timbuctu thanks to the technological gossip-monger that is the world-wide-web!

CALIFORNICATION

Two California prison guards were put in the slammer themselves for having sex with up to nine female prisoners in 2004. Among the criminals involved, one was a murderer and another had kidnapped their own child.

THE WORST BOYFRIEND IN THE WORLD?

A City worker made the headlines when an email he'd sent off to a buddy spread like wildfire around the world-wide-web. Duncan Sinclair, 22, boasted of receiving oral sex while on the telephone to his then-girlfriend, who was 'bored' at an airport. Signing off, "Am I the worst boyfriend in the world?" the West Ham fan clearly delighted in his iniquity. The joke was on him when he lost his job and fiancée.

SPECIAL SAUCE

Chefs everywhere know what goes into their 'special sauce.' I won't spell it out for you, but needless to say, you should never be rude to waiters if you don't want an added ingredient in your own lunch. One Illinois high school student decided to make a special sauce of his own in 2006, adding his 'seed' to a canteen salad dressing. A fellow student dobbed him in, but it was too late – the dubious dressing had already been in use in the school canteen for two days.

TOO GOOD TO BE TRUE

A British school kid could not believe his luck when his teacher allowed him to bring a girl back to his room for sex during a school trip to Portugal. Unbeknown to the pupil, the teacher was filming the holiday romance. When the boy found out he told the school and the teacher was struck off.

AMBASSADOR, YOU ARE NOT SPOILING US

What was an official in Finland's equality ministry thinking when he groped several women's breasts at an official champagne reception? Only Stefan Johannson himself could answer this. What we do know from one witness is that the groping was not "the sort of surreptitious groping that is difficult to define. It was straight-to-the-point blatant groping." At least he was upfront about it.

BUTT BANDIT

A vandal who left greasy imprints of his front and back bottom on the windows of local businesses was dubbed the 'Butt Bandit' by residents of Valentine, Nebraska. The 2,600 residents had two choices: look through their windows at the groin and bottom imprints, or to rub the stains off with petroleum jelly. Having vilely vandalised the town in this way since 2007, the tackle-and-tush terrorist was finally caught in the act late in 2008.

DOWN THE LINE

I don't know who's sillier. The man who called women in the Swedish city of Sundsvall claiming to be a sex researcher, or the women who revealed information about their sex lives to a stranger at the end of the line. The creepy caller not only managed to persuade several women to remove their clothing, but he also gave them lessons in masturbation. Still, bit more interesting than the usual cold calls you get about changing gas suppliers.

NEXT STOP: JAIL!

Passengers on a crowded train were not best pleased when businessman Victor Simons and an unnamed female passenger started going at it like the clappers on the Liverpool to Euston fast train. British Transport police were called, and the duo were arrested when the train pulled into the station.

UNHOLIER THAN THOU # 1

Her bosses described her behaviour as 'scandalous,' her parishioners were gob-smacked, and even Daventry, UK vicar Teresa Davies herself was forced to admit she had hit her 'self-destruct' button. The outrage arose when it came to light she and husband Mick were signed up on several swinging websites, her favourite spot being a secret location in France. Booze hound allegations were the head which finished off the pint of her misfortunes, and Davies was banned from the clergy for 12 years.

INSTRUCTOR LOSES TOUCH

David Austin lost his job as a driving instructor and his partner left him after two young female pupils accused him of touching them inappropriately during lessons. Austin told Judge John Holt he was 'a touchy-feely' person, and physical touching was simply part of his teaching style. He was sentenced to a 12 month supervision order and 80 hours community service.

ORIENTAL ORGY

Never let it be said they don't know how to make merry in Japan. In 2008, a group of 500 Japanese men and women broke the record for the world's biggest orgy. The entire salacious shindig was recorded like some sort of warped Busby Berkley movie. Each position was staged so that all of the couples' sex acts could be performed simultaneously.

HOT HOCKEY MOM

If your abiding memory of the 2008 US Presidential election is how hot the Republican candidate for Vice President was, fear not, your bizarre infatuation can find an outlet – without the need for stalking. On sale now is the "This is NOT Sarah Palin Inflatable Love Doll." With an uncanny Palin lookey-likey on the cover, the box suggests you can "blow her up and show her how you're going to vote" and that the doll "could really satisfy the swing voters."

STIFFED

When transsexual men in Sweden were given the go-ahead to get free prosthetic penises from local health authorities, the public was up in arms. Not because the offer could be deemed a waste of tax-payer's money, but because the fake willies on offer did not get erect.

NO LEG TO STAND ON

A driving instructor got away with fondling and squeezing his female clients' legs for a period of 27 years. In 2005, he was finally arrested and sent down for nine months for the attacks, all on young women aged 17 or 18. Even though Peter Knowles was now of pensionable age, a judge at Preston Crown Court in England felt a jail sentence was in the public interest.

PARK LIFE STRIFE

"We didn't know what he was doing, but we knew it's not right to have your pants down in a park." Top marks for observation to witness Jeff Baumgartner when he came across 55-year old Larry Williamson up to no good in a kids' play park. Police later found Williamson sitting on a picnic table naked, masturbating, with a metal rod protruding from his penis. An inspection of his car found all manner of suspicious objects – binoculars, sex toys, male enhancement drugs, lotions, and a small dog who was desperately in need of walkies.

A KICK IN THE NUTS

In 2007, Canadian police were keen to track down a man who was approaching women and asking them to kick him in the goolies. Although not a crime in itself, police feared the ulterior motives of the masochistic male, and he became a wanted man.

TALK IS NOT CHEAP

A phone technician for a US telecommunications company racked up $220,000 in phone-sex calls by tapping into the land lines of nearly 950 customers. Loquacious Joseph Vaccarelli of Nutley, New Jersey, spent a staggering 15 weeks out of a 40 week period chatting on 900 chat lines, and making roughly 5,000 calls. The randy rapscallion was charged with theft by deception and theft of services.

UP, UP AND AWAY

In 1998, a South African couple caused outrage when they joined the mile-high club on a flight from Johannesberg to London. And why? Because their 'wham bam' shag took place not in the loos, but in the business-class section of the plane. The captain soon curtailed their brazen doings, shouting over a tannoy that the aircraft was not "a shag house." But Reuters reported that by then, most of the "damage had been done."

THE MOST PENISES EVER CLAIMED IN BATTLE WAS 13,320 WHEN EGYPT CONQUERED LIBYA IN 1300 BC

STUD OR DUD?

An impotent old duffer walked out on his lover of ten years to move in with a young woman just four days after a doctor prescribed him with Viagra. Millionaire Frank 'Sonny' Bernado, who had been impotent for four years told his lover. "It's time for me to be a stud again." Roberta Burke sued her ex-partner for $2 million plus damages.

SINNERS OR WINNERS?

The Western Amazons women's rugby team in Australia caused a moral scrum in 1998 when they accepted sponsorship from a local brothel. The Australian Rugby Union stepped in and banned them from accepting the $10,000 on offer. The team had previously caused a mini-scandal when they were sponsored by a scaffolding company and sported a kit with the slogan 'Instant Erections.'

HEX ON AN EX

Imagine the scene. A 46-year-old Hong-Kong woman receives a phone call from a man purporting to be her ex-boyfriend. The man tells her if she pays to have sex with a gigolo, her partner will rush back into her arms. The woman complies three times and has hex-ex-sex, but it doesn't work and she finally cottons on she's been conned. It's a titillating but true tale from 1988 which saw a certain Kwok-hung arrested as both the man behind the phone calls and the gigolo impersonator.

TOP TEN HISTORICAL
SEX SCANDALS

10. Even in the 12th Century, teachers seducing their students was considered immoral. Take the case of Abelard and Héloïse, who conducted a passionate love affair in defiance of the social mores of the time. Even reactionary British newspaper the *Daily Mail* would consider their punishment excessive – he was castrated, and she was forced to become a nun.

9. The Blomberg-Fritsch Affair was a double whammy of a sex scandal which resulted in the Wehrmacht handing over power to Adolf Hitler. And why? Blomberg married a woman who'd posed for rude pictures, and Fritsch was gay.

8. She famously died making love to a horse, a filthy factoid which historians now pooh-pooh. But Catherine the Great also deserves a mention for her love of the toy boy, as well as that rumoured death from horse-play gone wrong.

7. In 1919, Franklin D Roosevelt ordered an investigation into immoral conduct – homosexuality – of the Navy at its Newport base. Scandal ensued after it emerged investigators were told to seduce sexual perverts in a bid to oust them.

6. How sad that a writer as great as Oscar Wilde should have been so cruelly hounded for his voracious love of the rent boy. Well, not for us, as it gives us room to put him in number six spot for the famous series of trials which saw him imprisoned for 'gross indecency' which included blackmailers, cross-dressers and prostitutes as witnesses.

5. In 1810, magistrate Alexander Wood was forced to leave Canada in that country's first known sex scandal. When a rape victim told

him her attacker had scratched his penis, he lined up a host of handsome young men and had them drop their kecks. Claims that he'd fondled boys in the penis identity parade shocked the nation and brought about his deportation.

4. The Marquis de Sade is a prime example of a historical sexual misadventurer. He ended up in prison for torturing and sodomizing prostitutes, and his fictional works recount such lascivious goings on that it would make a modern day smut-merchant blush. His most famous work is 120 *Days of Sodom*, so it's easy to see why he was deemed such a dirty – ahem – bugger.

3. The 'dirty' Duchess of Argyll's 1963 divorce was the most sensational of the time. Why? Lewd pictures came to light of the Duchess meting out a dose of fellatio to an unidentified man. The photo became known as 'the headless man', which is ironic given the activity involved where 'head' was very much part of the action.

2. The Emperor Claudius enjoys a reputation for reigning over one of the most debauched times in Roman history. Lucky blighter. It transpires though, that his wife was no less fruity. She became a sexual celeb when she threw down the gauntlet to the city's most famous prostitute to see who could keep it going longer in a sex marathon. The wanton wife, Melissa, was victorious, going at it for '25 rounds.'

1. LADY RANDY
Winston Churchill's mother, Jennie, is the climax of our golden oldies, and deservedly so. Indeed with more than 200 lovers under her belt – or rather corset – she could be described as the patron saint of the sexual misadventure. Sporting a snake tattoo on her wrist and with beguiling amber eyes, she counted conquests from nobility, the Prince of Wales and countless toy boys among her list of suitors – and had four husbands, to boot.

MORAL DILEMMA

The Guadalajara 'Men's Club.' At first glance, it does not cry out for public funding, does it? But in 1998, Fernando Lopez Hernandez of the Attorney General's Office reopened the strip club after it had been closed due to money laundering activity. The reason? With over 200 workers destined to lose their jobs if the club closed, Lopez felt they had a 'moral duty' to keep it open.

THANKS FOR THE MAMMARIES

A New York strip-club goer sued a topless dancer when she allegedly stuffed her silicone-enhanced breasts in his face, forcing his neck backwards and giving him whiplash. The case was thrown out of a 'People's Court' when a court officer examined the 'Heaven Sent' nightclub dancer's breasts and decreed them not as hard as the plaintiff Paul Davies had testified.

PARKING MAD

You've got to be pretty overcome with lust to have sex in your car. You've got to be pretty overcome with lust and stupidity to have sex in your car in a disabled spot outside a police station. Or like, Roger Duffield, overcome with lust, stupidity and alcohol. When Hampshire police tapped on the window of the randy drinker's car on the evening of August 5, 2003, a breathalyser test showed he was three times over the drink drive limit. He was arrested for both a public display of lewdness and for drinking and driving.

42% OF MEN SAY RECEIVING ORAL SEX IS THEIR FAVOURITE SEXUAL ACTIVITY

WINDOWS ON THE WORLD

In Italy two lovers faced jail when a judge ruled that sex in the back of a car with the windows wound down was an "obscene act" and not the lesser misdemeanour of "indecent public act" that a previous court had ruled. The higher court decreed: "A sexual act that is certainly not obscene in private becomes so if it is done in a public road. Offenders can escape jail only if their car's windows are 'covered' so passers-by cannot see inside."

UNUSUAL FOREPLAY

It's all very well to practice safe sex, but watch out for those pesky condom vending machines. In 1999 in Cadiz, Spain, an amorous couple inserted some coinage in a machine hoping for a quick frolic on the beach. Passion soon turned to mortification when the man's fingers got stuck in the machine after trying to free a trapped package of prophylactics. Passions had cooled – as had the temperature – by the time the fire service arrived to free his fingers.

HOPELESS HUSBANDS

"Our men have turned to vegetables. They leave home early and come back intoxicated. There is nobody to meet the sexual needs of wives." This was the frustrated cry from Kenyan women in the town of Kandara, north of Nairobi, when they barged into a police station in 2000, demanding that officers close illegal drinking dens in the area. The women from 24 church groups claimed that a case of collective brewer's droop was the cause for a decline in the population of the area.

6% OF COUPLES FAVOUR REAR-ENTRY AS THEIR MOST USUAL SEXUAL POSITION

MAN OF CLOTH AVOIDS SACK

When a man from near Venice, Italy, found his wife in bed with their parish priest, the red mist descended and he ratted him out to the local bishop. The middle-aged priest kept his job but was sent to a new parish to be 're-educated', the *Daily Telegraph* reported in September 2008.

EVERY LITTLE DOESN'T HELP

There you are, doing the weekly on-line shop, when, oops, there on your 'favourites' appears a packet of flavoured condoms. But you are on the pill. You can imagine the heated debate that followed between Lynn Newby and boyfriend Andy Allott when doing their online shop early in 2008. One nearly relationship-busting argument later, the pair called the supermarket who admitted their favourites list had been updated in 'error.' Nothing to do with the supermarket trying to get the couple to buy extra stuff, then. Phew. The coupled received a £100 letter and an apology from the company's CEO.

VIRTUALLY UNFAITHFUL

A British couple became the first known to divorce due to a husband's affair in cyberspace. When Amy Pollard's online alter-ego, 'Laura Skye', caught her husband's alter-ego, a medallion-sporting hippy called 'Dave Barmy', having sex with a prostitute she forgave him. But when she later found his character cavorting with another woman, controlled by a real-life American, she'd had enough. Her online character's motto had been "Never give your heart easily."

HAVANA GOOD TIME

A Brighton, England, woman liked a Cuban hotel so much, she got married there. Twice. Four weeks after marrying her childhood sweetheart, Andrea Shepherd flew back to the resort to cop off with the barman who fixed the drinks at her wedding. It had been "love at first sight" when she locked eyes with bartending hunk Jose Miguel, *The Sun* reported.

BAREBACK BUFFOON

"Sex without a condom is the new engagement ring," Endarvis Harshaw of the Youth Radio organization announced in 2008. The unsafe sex advocate argued that it shows more trust and commitment to go bareback than to buy a piece of jewellery "for a marriage that might not pass the test of time." Hmm. Diamond ring or the clap? Know which I'd prefer.

ONE MAN'S MEAT

In 2007 a daily newspaper in New Zealand, *The Press*, had a piece about New Zealand vegans refusing to have sex with meat eaters. Vegan Nichola Kriek told the paper, "I would not want to be intimate with someone whose body is literally made up from the bodies of others who have died for their sustenance."

Trying to find a figure for the number of vegans who might be affected by the limitation proved futile. The website of the New Zealand national vegan society has a note saying, "Veganz is in currently in hiatus due to lack of volunteers." Wonder why?

PROTESTING TOO MUCH # 2

Tomfoolery saw Iain Murtagh of Livingstone, Scotland, charged with public indecency for attempting sex with a car. He was accused of running along a street naked, bending over the vehicle, and simulating sexual intercourse, according to *The Irvine Times*. Murtagh denied the charge. "I was not indecent with that car," he told the paper.

YOU BEAUTY!

In 2006, Miss USA was nearly forced to stand down amid allegations of cocaine snorting, promiscuity, binge drinking and lesbian lurve sessions with Miss Teen USA. Tara Conner retained her crown on the promise she enter rehab, and went on to compete in Miss Universe. Another great role model for youngsters everywhere!

SPOILSPORTS

Tony Curtis and his wife were one of the first passengers to try out Singapore Airline's new double-bedded suite, but were disgruntled to discover the airline would not allow sex in the flash Airbus A380. He told *The Times*, "So they'll sell you a double bed, and give you privacy and endless champagne – and then say you can't do what comes naturally. Seems a bit strange."

ANGLE OF THE DANGLE

In 2000, Film Four got around rules disallowing erect penises and penetrative sex to be shown on telly by showing a 'webcast' on the

THE WORLD'S FIRST SPERM BANKS OPENED IN IOWA CITY AND TOKYO IN 1964

internet of controversial sex scenes from the film *The Idiots*. The channel denied it was a bid to attract viewers with sex.

BACK IN ACTION

In 2005, women in Swaziland set fire to piles of thousands of woollen tassels which symbolize chastity to mark the end of a sex ban imposed by King Mswati III. The 30,000 girls danced and sang, "At last, we can now have sex." The ban was started by the king in 2001 to fight the spread of HIV/AIDS He said that lifting the ban did not give citizens the nod toward promiscuity.

THE FINAL FRONTIER

Human beings' search for new locations for their fornication knows no bounds. NASA put the kibosh on any discussion of astronauts boldly doing it where no man or woman has done it before though, when they banned spacewoman Laura Woodmansee's book *Sex in Space* from their stores. Author Woodmansee was not impressed. "Now is the time to study the sex in space topic seriously and shed our puritanical ignorance," she argued.

BOOBS BANNED

In 2007 a Boise, USA, radio station used a billboard of a buxom woman with the two presenters' faces transplanted on each breast to advertise their show. The ad, proclaiming the duo as 'Two Boobs in the Morning', was swiftly banned.

THE MOST POPULAR SEXUAL POSITION IS THE MISSIONARY POSITION

PLUG IN PLONKER

A 34-year-old teacher was arrested in Cydebank, Scotland, in 2007 for getting himself off with an electric vibrator which was plugged into his vehicle's cigarette lighter. He was parked outside a local high school, and was on his way to work at the time.

DOUBLE WHAMMY

A urologist tried to get away with a flashing conviction by claiming his penis was so small, it would have been impossible for a victim to spot it. A Houston, Texas court upheld his conviction, although it conceded that the man's penis was only 2.8 inches long.

KNOCK OUT

Florida Today reported on a young man who overreacted a tad when his girlfriend refused him sex after a night out on the lash. He took a gun, shot himself in the arm, and knocked himself out stone cold when his head hit the cooker.

RED HOT LOVER

Careful, girls, if your boyfriend's attentions in the bedroom leave you feeling snoozy – in 2008 *The Cincinnati Enquirer* reported that a 46-year-old man got mad when his better half fell asleep while he was 'on the job,' and set fire to her car by way of revenge.

6 IN 10 COUPLES DO NOT SHARE THEIR SEXUAL FANTASIES WITH THEIR PARTNERS

TOP OF THEIR 'GAME'

New Yorker magazine reveals that in the southern India states of Karnataka and Maharashtra, over 250,000 women have been sold by their parents to work as part of an 'elite' sex cult dedicated to the Hindu goddess Yellamma. The states banned the practice in 1982, but some devoutly religious parents are flouting the ancient law.

HELLO DOLLY

Is it against the law to line a Barbie doll collection up on the passenger seat of a car in a public space? It is when the collection nestles in sinister fashion next to a pile of women's undies and a scatter of grot-mags, apparently. Martin Green of Cape May, New Jersey, you're nicked!

WHAT A BLOW!

British joiner Seb Saunders suffered a blow to the head in an industrial accident from which he recovered physically. Two years convalescence were not enough, however, to see him recover from a neurological condition called 'fatuous euphoria' which started after the accident. He became disinhibited sexually and spiralled into a vortex of lust – calling sex lines, ogling porn and visiting prostitutes. When his marriage broke down in 2006 because of the condition, he was awarded £3.1 million in damages by the high court. That's enough to pay for a lot of hookers.

90% OF MEN WHO HAVE PENIS ENLARGEMENTS REPORT A ONE-INCH IMPROVEMENT IN GIRTH

NOISY NEIGHBOURS

Neighbours often lose it during ear-splitting sessions from over-sexuberant neighbours. Christopher Sullivan took things a step too far though, sending his upstairs neighbours threatening packages, including a Polaroid photo of three naked Barbie dolls with their heads cut off, when he could bear their raucous rumpy-pumpy no more.

LORD LOUCHE

A British government minister, Lord Lambton, was dubbed Lord Louche in the 1970s when he was forced to resign in a prostitution scandal. *The News of the World* caught him in a sting, naked in bed with two prostitutes and smoking a funny cigarette. Later, in a BBC interview, Lambton's friend said a row with his father over a title meant he had given up reading and instead had immersed himself in two frenzied activities. One was gardening, the other was debauchery. Should have stuck to the pruning.

TURNING OVER A NEW LEAF

When a randy woman woke her husband wanting some good old-fashioned lovin', she not only got the knock-back, but her husband proclaimed they should give up booze, fags and sex, according to the *Kitsap Sun*. Not newsworthy in itself, perhaps. The woman's reaction to get blind drunk on whisky, attack her hubby and steal his wallet saw her arrested though, and got her featured, albeit unnamed, in her local paper.

THE FIRST VAGINAL TRANSPLANT TOOK PLACE IN SALONICA IN 1973

SEISMIC STUPIDITY

When the editor of *New Travel Weekly* was deciding on the location of a spread featuring scantily-clad young women, he/she was spoilt for choice. The region of Chongqing, China, is home to the Dazu Rock Carving, for instance, which would be the perfect backdrop for semi-naked glamour poses. Instead, models were asked to pose among the rubble at one of the country's recent earthquake sites. The editorial staff were fired and the magazine folded temporarily.

THE DEVIL IS IN THE DETAIL

When British Radio One DJ Kevin Greening died, the tabloids were awash with tawdry detail. *The Sun*, for instance, raved that medics had found "his naked body in a bedroom converted into an S&M dungeon, containing a leather harness, knee-high boots and a scaffolding structure from which hung meat-hooks and chains." The coroner Paul Knapmann was more prosaic however, saying that: "he was found dead having indulged in unorthodox sexual behaviour involving restraint equipment and illegal drugs." Verdict: Misadventure.

WEDDED BLISS RATIONED

In 1980, a Basingstoke, England, man took his wife to court because she was limiting her sexual favours to a once-weekly session. Lord Justice Ormrod, Lord Justice Dunn and Mr Justice Arnold ruled in the UK's Court of Appeal that the woman was not behaving unreasonably, and threw the case out of court.

TAWDRY TESTIMONY

In 2004, Eva Small was acquitted of the manslaughter of Lee Roden, when he was killed in a car she was alleged to be driving. The jury believed that she could not have been at the wheel, as she was giving her boyfriend a blow job from the passenger seat at the time of the fatal crash. A police report showing Lee had been found with his trousers down was a vital piece of evidence for the defence team.

BALANCING THE BOOKS

To Canada in the swinging Sixties, where the Exchequer Court was asked to decide whether business expenses from a brothel were tax deductible. Among the expenses which were disallowed were $2,000 for alcohol and $1,000 paid to "certain men possessed of physical strength and some guile, which they exercised when set to extricate a girl from difficulties." Whatever that means. Footnote: the expenses weren't disallowed because they were deemed too off-the-wall, but only because the madam could not provide receipts.

WHAT'S IN A NAME? # 2

Is a vibrating condom a sex toy or a contraceptive? I can't answer that, but a court in India had to decide on the matter in 2007 when opponents claimed the condoms were illegitimate. The manufacturer claimed the device is a contraceptive and as such good for the public health. Outraged politicians claimed the products were flouting a ban on sex toys in the country. If the manufacturers had wanted to get away with selling it, they might have chosen a more stealthy name than 'Crescendo.'

LOONY LAWSUIT

Some boyfriends really are crap. There you are in a long-term relationship trying out a new position, when snap! Your boyfriend suffers a penile fracture. The last thing you'd expect is that he then takes you to court over his broken boner. But in 2005, a Massachusetts, USA Appeals Court was asked to rule on whether a woman's sudden movement which caused her lover's fracture was reckless, so he could claim compensation. They decided it was merely 'negligent', and dismissed the man's case.

GLASS(ES) HALF-FULL

An optimistic Reno prostitute was arrested when she propositioned a homicide officer for sex. He had been sitting in an unmarked police car when the dozy woman hopped in, and – oblivious to the flashing light on the dash, and the police radio – suggested they get jiggy with it. When asked whether she realized he was a police officer, she replied, "I didn't think police officers wore glasses."

BIG IN JAPAN

The Times brought news of a Japanese invention to the west in 2004 which would have Jordan and the like in raptures. Hideto Tomabechi claimed to have devised a mobile phone ring that increased women's breast size. Over 10,000 women downloaded the 'Rockmelon' tone in a week, with one customer telling a Japanese newspaper: "I listened to the tune for a week expecting all the time that I had been duped. But, incredibly, my 34 inch bust grew to 35 inches. It was awesome."

TOP TEN POLITICAL MISADVENTURES

10. The 75th Prime Minister of Japan was forced to resign in 1989 – not because of his extra-marital affair with a Geisha, which was to be expected, but because he had not bunged her enough hush money.

9. Gary Hart was forced to drop out of the US presidential race in the 80s when he was photographed with a blonde bombshell. Needless to say, she was not his wife. When the fuss died down he entered the race again but was, once again, a flop.

8. English Prime Minister John Major got egg on his face when salmonella-scandal-MP Edwina Currie revealed they'd had an affair in 2002. The affair took place during his government's loathsome Back to Basics campaign which pontificated on family values.

7. Things were hot, hot, hot in Canada's cabinet during the Cold War. Gerda Munsinger, an East German prostitute and Soviet spy managed to sow her wild oats with several cabinet ministers at the time, including the Associate Minister of National Defence, Pierre Sévigny who had signed her application for Canadian citizenship. The scandal became known as 'The Munsinger Affair.'

6. It's like a kind of sexual Tourettes – so often politicians on 'clean up campaigns' turn out to be far dirtier than the public they're meant to be sanitising. Case in point, Eliot Spitzer, New York's Democratic Mayor who resigned in 2008 when he was revealed to have slept with high-class prostitutes via the 'Emperor's Club.'

5. Tapping his foot under a bathroom door proved the downfall for Senator Larry Craig in 2007 – an undercover cop recognized it as a sign that his neighbour was after sex. Craig admitted he was cottaging, but initially refused to resign.

4. Leading British politician David Mellor famously went from 'toe-job to no job' after cringe-worthy details of an affair with actress Antonia de Sanchez were divulged in an UK tabloid. I'd rather forget the whole sorry story, but just in case memory does not serve, the scandal included a football kit and a nauseating lolly-load of toe-sucking. Amazingly he kept his job.

3. Republican Mark Foley resigned from the House of Representatives in 2006 when it transpired he had sent lewd emails and sexually explicit instant messages to teenage boys – boys who had formerly served or were at that time serving as Congressional pages, that is. The investigation continues.

2. At a time when free love blossomed as copiously as flowers in a hippy's hair, you'd have thought John Profumo's month long affair with London showgirl Christine Keller would be but a blot on the political landscape. But lying to the commons about the affair, and Keeler's involvement with a Russian naval officer during the then Cold War, meant the extra-marital fling soon became a national public scandal.

1. BILL'S DRY-CLEANING BILL
Phone calls between a close friend and Monica Lewinsky were the catalyst for the outing of the raunchy romance between the 42nd American President and the Whitehouse intern. The calls paved the way not only for a rare impeachment vote but for a deluge of jokes about dry-cleaners and semen stains.

A CARNIVAL OF CARNALITY

If you want to get pregnant, you could do worse than visiting one of the UK's many seaside resorts. Oh, but only if you're a teenage girl. In 2004 *The Times* cited a report which showed that coastal towns like Blackpool and Brighton have the highest teenage pregnancy rates in the country. Academics who wrote the report said 'carnivalesque excitement' fuelled by seasonal workers, tourists and booze, contribute to sexual risk-taking and the high pregnancy rates. Day out to Brighton, anyone?

PUTTING THE SCREWS ON

A wealthy German heiress was blackmailed by her lover who threatened to make public sex tapes he'd filmed of trysts they'd enjoyed in luxury hotel. The married mother of three had already coughed up six million quid to the blackmailer when he claimed to be receiving death threats from the mafia.

But Susanne Klatten, with her €8 billion fortune, had had enough when he threatened her with the sex tapes. Bizarrely, Helg Sgarbi claimed in his defence he was only doing it to get back at her father, who was an alleged Nazi collaborator.

HUNG OUT TO DRY

Paul James Allen, 36, pleaded guilty to the manslaughter of his lover Toby Warne in 2005 after a sex game Warne had initiated during a drink and drugs session went fatally wrong. Warne suggested Allen put a noose around his neck for kicks, but it was Allen who was hung out to dry in court, when his lover died from asphyxiation.

45% OF BRITISH PEOPLE WOULD LIKE TO HAVE SEX WITH SOMEONE OF A DIFFERENT RACE

SICK IN THE HEAD

Here's some bile-inducing news – a man was arrested in 2007 for giving drain cleaner to women so he could become sexually aroused when they vomited. Stefan Luckham had a previous conviction for forcing a woman to drink bleach, lighter fluid and urine, also for the purposes of sexual stimulation.

A SIGN OF THINGS TO, AHEM, COME

When Diana Ross and the Supremes sang "Stop! In the Name of Love" perhaps they gave serial street-sign shagger Ron Baxter the wrong idea. In 2007, Sioux Falls, South Dakota local paper *The Argus Leader* reported that he was arrested by police when they found him humping a 'stop' sign. A later search of his home revealed a 'large amount' of video showing Dills masturbating to, and having intercourse with, various traffic signs.

MUCH ADO ABOUT NOTHING

In a country where the porn industry is worth billions of dollars, it's hard to understand the public outcry when Ohio state legislator Matthew Barrett made a bit of a risqué slip-up. Meaning to give a group of high school seniors a civics presentation using PowerPoint slides, he mistakenly gave them an anatomy lesson, when the computer he was using displayed the image of a topless woman.

MAKE WAR, NOT LOVE

In 2006, a former female soldier won part of her sexual discrimination case against the Army. One soldier, she told the court, had been shouting her name as he pleasured himself in a tent she shares with him and seven other soldiers. The soldier, Cpl Norbert Taylor, said he was only joking, and acting out a scene from *When Harry Met Sally*.

THE PAIN IN SPAIN

A Hungarian couple were found dead in woods on the 'White Isle' of Ibiza in 2007. Guardia Civil investigators believed the couple died during a ritualistic S&M sex game, finding the woman strangled and her husband hanging from a tree. Police believed that a nearby stash of pornos and magazines about Buddhism and Reincarnation could explain the mystery surrounding the deaths.

A FREUDIAN SLIP?

A psychiatrist attending a men's prison in Nassau County tried a novel approach when dealing with prisoner Damon Bell, a member of the notorious Bloods gang. She put him on a suicide watch, so she could have her wicked way with him away from prison security cameras, and whispered sweet nothings to him under his cell door, believing she could not be heard. She was however, and faced jail in 2008 after lying to the FBI about her involvement with the gangster.

75% OF MEN AND WOMEN FAVOUR THE BEDROOM AS THEIR FAVOURITE PLACE TO HAVE SEX

BLOW UP

A lovelorn youngster opened the natural gas taps in his flat, hoping to end his life after his girlfriend left him for his best-friend. His 15-year-old ex arrived at his flat in Bindlach, Germany to pick up her belongings, and without knowing about the leak, lit a cigarette and ignited the gas, killing one man and injuring 15 other people. The disastrous dumped boyfriend and his ex both survived.

EROTIC EVICTION

The Hilton House Estate in Essex, England, is a posh manor house which offers tours of its farm and park land to children. Hardly the setting for the 'Steam Room', where orgies were filmed starring breasty Janet Time and more than a fistful of men. Unbeknown to the property owner, Time and her partner had been running the 'adult' club in a cottage on the estate for year. When the owner found out, the porno-filming pair were promptly evicted.

VERY WRONG NUMBER

In 2008, a misprint in a New Jersey, USA phonebook saw three numbers in the contact details for the Sussex County Democratic Committee transposed. Swapping the last three digits meant that members of the public trying to call the committee were instead connected to a phone sex line.

18% OF BRITONS HAVE BEEN UNFAITHFUL TO THEIR PARTNER

THREE'S A CROWD

A Swedish priest – who else – was arrested in 2008 for brutally beating his wife. The attack came about because she did not want him to erase photos of an evening spent knocking boots with another man. The pervy pastor from the Stockholm area denied any wrong-doing, but unsurprisingly faced the boot from his parish.

MUSCLE MAN

Police put the kibosh on Fante Kok pestering people with requests to feel their muscles in 2006. He was banned from touching, feeling or measuring muscles or asking people to do squat exercises. Kok has the sexual fetish sthenolagnia, where people get a kick from shows of strength or musculature.

JIGGERY-IN-POKEY # 2

Three copulating coupes were charged with having sex in 2008 – and they weren't even doing it outdoors. Ah, but, the six frisky folk were inmates in an Indiana prison, and had snuck through a hole in the ceiling to get down to their racy jailhouse-rocking.

SEXY SAMOSAS

How much would you pay for a samosa that promised to make the earth move for you and your loved one? A tenner? Yeah, I'd go with that. So, would you believe a pair of frisky Dutch travellers paid over

200 pounds for one of the savoury pastries, which an Indian vendor had promised them was laced with aphrodisiacs? The earth remained static, and the pair hot-footed it to the police who managed to get them back some – but not all – of their cash.

NEED A SCREWDRIVER?

Ex new-Jersey Governor Jim McGreevey's chauffeur claimed to have enjoyed 'hard-core sex orgies' with him and wife Diana Motos, before the couple split up over the Governor's gay affair. Teddy Pedersen told the media, "Me being a part of their sexual relationship enhanced it for them." Motos denied the claims.

WHAT A DUMMY

Another lesson for you here – if you must burgle a department store so you can attempt an orgy with a trio of shop mannequins, it probably makes sense to take your lascivious loot home. Aydin Demir didn't. He was charged with burglary and criminal damage when staff of the newly opened Selfridges store in Birmingham, England, found the fool in bed with three other dummies when they opened for business in 2003.

TONGUE THAI'D

Thai students clamoured for new laws imposing harsher penalties on mobile phone abusers in 2004. At the time, dirty phone-callers and men who snapped under women's skirts would only face a 25 dollar fine.

ONLY 0.8% OF WOMEN HAVE FANTASISED ABOUT HAVING SEX WITH A MILK MAN

SECRET POLICEMAN'S BALL

In 1997, a sex scandal broke concerning some of the highest political leaders in Belgium attending what are known as 'ballets roses,' aka naughty sex parties with young women. The prosecution's case hung on the testimony of police inspector Georges Marnette, who rebuffed claims that he'd been in the buff at the obscene orgies himself. "I wasn't going to hang round wearing my holster while everyone else was either naked or in dressing-gowns." He said. "But if I was in a dressing gown, that didn't mean that I was doing any sexual acrobatics myself." Still, when in Rome eh, Georges?

DEAD RUDE

The death of architect and designer Carlo Mollino shocked Italy when executors found envelopes containing more than 2,000 Polaroid photographs of nude women in an antique cabinet. Although at first treated as a dirty porn collection, the photos were later collected in a coffee-table book in 2002.

SAUCY

In 1996, health officials in Dobbigan, USA, closed down a Mexican restaurant run by the Church of the ABC of Abraham. The closure was not down to the restaurant's scandalously unappetising name (La Cucaracha, 'The Cockroach.') Rather, the principal reason cited by Yuro County Health Department, was that "semen is not a food, and cannot legally be served as a condiment in restaurants in California."

The church group believed that consuming their leader's semen magically linked the 'astral bodies of the group's membership.' Yet the restaurant was not only frequented by church members, but by other folk in the Yuro community as well.

APPLE PIE ANTICS

A teenage boy learnt a lesson he won't forget in a hurry when he tried to emulate the famous apple pie scene in teen-flick *American Pie*. Dendy Heinsbergen was rushed to hospital in Boise, Idaho, with a scalded penis – his teenage hormones raging with racy anticipation, he had not waited for the pie to cool down first...

FUNGAL FREAKERY

An Ohio man called police in 2003 claiming a stranger had broken into his home, forced him to masturbate while he watched, and had even filmed the enforced onanism. The victim told *The Beacon Journal* that before the barmy burglar left, he had fed the man's pet dog dodgy mushrooms, and the dog had died later that day.

THE BEAUTIFUL BLAME GAME

The Chinese football team caused a stir at the 2008 Olympics when they lost 3–0 to Brazil. Hardly surprising, you may say. Brazil – great footballing nation. China – not so much. Their fans were needled to say the least however, when mobile phone footage was discovered of the team canoodling with a group of young women outside the team hotel, before disappearing into it with them, the night before the match. A different kind of pre-match 'build-up,' then?

MEN IN THEIR THIRTIES ARE THE LEAST LIKELY AGE-GROUP TO LOOK AT PORN

PUBLISH AND BE DAMNED

Larry Flynt, the publisher of Hustler magazine, ran an ad in the Washington Post in 2007 offering a one million dollar reward for anyone willing to dish the dirt on their indecorous relations with an elected official. But only if kissers-and-tellers could provide proof. "Can you provide documented evidence of illicit sexual or intimate relations with a congressperson, senator or other prominent officeholder?" asked the ad with unabashed candidness.

CAR TROUBLE

In 2005, Germany was rocked by the news that managers at Volkswagen had bought the support of union officials by inviting them to lewd sex parties and taking them on exotic holidays. Eventually MP Hans-Jürgen Uhl was forced to resign when 21 witnesses came forward saying he'd also taken part in the company's sleaze fests in Barcelona and Seoul in 2001.

JUDGING THE JUDGE

Never let it be said that the Swedes aren't laissez-faire. When Supreme Court Judge Leif Thorsson admitted he'd broken the law by paying for sex with a rent-boy, he was told he could keep his job. Even though he was given a dressing down, he would still be allowed to preside over cases dealing with the same crime he'd committed. Paying for sex is against the law in Sweden, whether with man, woman or whatever.

30% OF BRITONS BELIEVE MONOGAMY IS UNNATURAL

AS GOD INTENDED?

In 2005, the German media went into a frenzy with news that amateur photographer and German youth group leader Stefan Wiest had hit upon a novel approach to make money for – and entice young people into – the church. He staged 12 nude, erotic scenes from the Bible with local youths, and put them together in a calendar. The site selling the dodgy almanac was bombarded with six million hits, and he made over 40,000 Euro for the church.

Bet you think you know where this is going – church youth leader is sacked in a clamour of righteous indignation. Think again. The pastor of the Nuremberg church selling the calendar was creepily supportive. "It's just wonderful when teenagers commit themselves with their hair and their skin to the Bible," he said. Teenagers of Nuremberg, run!

DON'T JUDGE A BOOK BY ITS COVER

Turning tricks is not something one often associates with nuns. But in 1988, a scandal broke which just goes to show that one can often change the habit of a lifetime. Habit. Geddit? Moving on...

The scandal involved a £500,000 prostitution ring, where businessmen and politicians could chose any girl they wanted, whether it be nun, aristocrat or good old-fashioned drug-addled hooker. In terms of nuns, there were more on offer than you could shake a stick at. "If a client wants a nun, we have so many on our books he could even chose which order he would like her to belong to... Carmelite, Benedictine or whatever," a ring-leader of the group said. The ungodly transactions all took place within a mile of the Vatican.

A RISKY BUSINESS # 2

Sydney health officials bemoaned the rising number of sexual misadventures of the STD variety among backpackers to the Australian city in early 2008. As part of a campaign to dilute the spread of sexually transmitted diseases, a shed load of condoms were given out in backpacker hostels. Pub drink coasters were also printed with slogans like "I came for a trip of a lifetime, now I'm leaving with a lifetime infection. Use a condom."

WHAT'S DOC, UP?

In 2008, an Australian doctor from the sunny Gold Coast was charged with professional misconduct for having sex with a patient in his surgery and prescribing her Valium and Endone for kicks. The NSW *Medical Tribunal* did not give out the doctor's name because of his alleged penchant for 'unorthodox' sexual behaviour. The press tantalisingly left out details of what this behaviour might entail, so we can but delve into the dark reaches of our imaginations for an answer.

A WHOLE LOT OF SHAKING GOING ON

If you're a Catholic priest and you're going to have a ridiculous sexual misadventure, it might as well be with a nun. In 2004, a Malawian court convicted a Catholic priest and a nun of disorderly conduct after they were caught engaged in a sexual act in a parked car with tinted windows. Witnesses saw the car shaking in an airport car park –the Earth clearly moved, but we can't say whether heaven did too.

11% OF PEOPLE WORLDWIDE THINK SEX IS THE MOST IMPORTANT
THING IN A RELATIONSHIP

NUN ON THE RUN

Sister Silvia Gomes De Sousa went on the rampage with a machete and threatened to commit arson when she caught Father Carmelo Mantarro in bed with a married woman.

Good for her, you may say, sticking up for what's right and holy. But wait. She didn't go berserk out of duty to Godliness, she lost it in an outburst of jealous transgression. She herself had been humping the holy father for four years, and was not best pleased about the septuagenarian's latest conquest.

CHINESE BELLOWINGS

As sexual misadventures of the rich and famous go, this one has all the right ingredients. Gorgeous movie star and celebrated hip-hop artist involved sexually with a number of his country's top actresses? Check. Obscene images of said encounters posted liberally over the internet? Check. Public brouhaha about the veracity of such images? Check.

These are the ingredients which proved a recipe for disaster for Hong-Kong movie star Edison Chen early in 2008. Chinese bellowings, rather than whispers, could be an appropriate term for the outcry that accompanied his misadventure. But the public need not have bothered, nor should the 25.8 million visitors to The Tianya Bullentin page copping an eyeful at a single discussion thread on whether the images were fake or real. Because a couple of weeks after the web was saturated with pictures of him in various X-rated poses, the star at the centre of the scandal came clean, saying, "I hope that this matter will teach everyone a lesson."

And so it should. In so far as any of us with glittering careers in the film and music industry should not take photos of ourselves having sex with a bevy of beauties, only to leave them on a laptop that's being serviced... So that's an important lesson for about two readers world-wide, in actual fact.

PROFESSIONAL PEOPLE MASTURBATE MORE REGULARLY THAN UNEDUCATED ONES

TOP TEN ROYAL ROMPS

10. Poor old Anne Boleyn. Having witnessed Henry VIII use her sister for sexual favours, she decided she would only let him have a piece of her if they were to marry. But beguiling the horniest King in history ultimately led to her demise. After a brief marriage, she was beheaded on false charges of witchcraft and adultery when he fancied a bit of Jane Seymour instead.

9. The fifth Roman Emperor Caligula is well known for his sexual depravity but here are a few details. He liked to sleep with men's wives and brag about it. He enjoyed incest with his sisters and pimped them out to other men. He even tried to have his horse made a consul and a priest. Okay that last one's not a sexual misadventure, but it's worth a mention for its ridiculousness.

8. In our supposedly enlightened times you'd have thought being a gay royal would not cause much of a to-do. But in 2007, a royal gay blackmail case made the headlines, although in the UK the royal's name was never revealed due to libel laws. All I'll say is that the same laws don't apply in the States or Oz if you care to find out more.

7. In 1354 in Portugal, King Alfonso IV had his son's lover stabbed to death in the woods, for fear their illegitimate children would attempt to take his crown.

6. Henry VI of France was a one, to be sure. During his marriage to Princess Marguerite he managed to get his mistress pregnant. He denied the fact up until the moment the girl went into labour, at which point he asked his wife to help the mistress through the ordeal. Eventually they divorced.

5. Adultery is still somewhat frowned upon in the modern world, but in ye olden days it could even lead to death. In 1568, Eric XIV was imprisoned and poisoned by his half-brother who said he was insane for giving up his wife for his mistress, Karin Mansdotter. She must have been a right minger...

4. In 1820, a right royal scandal blazed entitled 'The Queen Caroline Affair.' The Caroline in question was wife to the Prince of Wales. Both were known for their adulterous natures and sexual profligacy. But Caroline was the fornicator-in-chief in the marriage which earned her the moniker 'The Immoral Queen' and an eventual poisoning to get her off the scene.

3. The British press had a field day in 1992 when Sarah Ferguson was snapped topless having her toe sucked by an American billionaire. The scandal ricocheted around the fact she was still married to Andrew, Duke of York.

2. During the messy break up of Princess Diana and the Prince of Wales, many a sordid revelation was revealed. 'Squidgygate' ranks high in the number two spot for the abject silliness of James Gilbey's pet name for his lover. It doesn't get more nauseating that that, does it?

1. TOO MUCH INFORMATION
But no, how could I forget the transcript of a royal raunch call far more toe-curling and blush-inducing than the above. I refer of course to the call made between Prince Charles and Camilla, where he told his older paramour he would like to live inside her trousers as a tampon. Bleugh.

HOTLINE TO HELL

A homeless man who broke into two churches might have got away with it if he'd tried to steal the alms box. In fact he broke into the Valley Cottage and Elim Alliance churches in New York to call sex lines. He was arrested on burglary and petty larceny charges.

BUSTED!

A German man who was addicted to phone sex was landed with a €7,000 phone bill at a Göttingen hotel after a chatty six night stay. Unable to pay the bill, the libidinously loquacious fella offered to pay in instalments. Police officers weren't fooled though, discovering he was a wanted man for similar offences in nearby Dortmund and Hannover.

CALL OF THE WILD

A phone sex-pest who made nine lewd phone calls to unsuspecting women, moaning, groaning and dirty-talking down the phone, faced jail in Rhyll, Wales, in 2008. Stanley Price told Mold Crown Court that an intruder must have broken in and made the filthy calls. On nine separate occasions? Like, duh!

BAD CALL

Are you naked? What are you wearing? Would you like to have telephone sex with me? Calm down, dears. I don't mean you.

These are the words of Britain's most prolific phone sex pest, Stephen Furlong, 32, who made over four thousand mucky calls to random women over a three month period in 2001. He was caught with the help of a mobile phone company and the use of satellite technology. Judge John Bull passed a 21 month sentence, hoping it would act as a deterrent to other wannabe pervy phone pranksters.

LOOK OUT, THE LODGER'S ABOUT

Spying on your landlord and his girlfriend having sex is one thing, filming it on your mobile phone is another. For Rupert Eley of Medway, Kent, England, it meant nine months in the slammer when his defence that the pair had wanted him to take part in a three-some fell on deaf ears. The prosecutor in the case said her clients were in no way after such a tawdry entanglement and, "that after seeing the film this was very apparent." The mind boggles.

WHEN A STRANGER CALLS

When a stranger comes knocking at your door, you have two options. You could decide he is clearly a murdering, thieving, lunatic come to destroy everything you hold dear, and shut the door in his face. Or you could be a decent human being and let him in.

Householders in Bad Urach, Germany, chose the latter option when a middle-aged man appeared at their doors, asking to use a telephone because his car had broken down. However, one woman's suspicions arose after she'd let him warble on for 15 minutes. "He was red in the face and obviously excited about something. After he bolted, I pressed redial, and someone called Jasmine answered and asked what she could do for me." Locals who let him use their phones would later discover pricey calls to premium rate sex lines had been made by the lying lunatic.

PHOTO OPPORTUNITY

Mobile phones have allowed pervs to find new avenues to explore and a new fetish to indulge in – skirt up-lifting. A keen exponent of the new fetish was a girl's football team manager, caught taking a photo of a female shopper as she bent over to chose a tooth-brush in Boots pharmacist in Britain. He was followed by security guards to his place of work, where police later found 20 similar photos on his mobile phone. Skirting the issue, the offender, Henry Gilchrist, blamed the outrages on stress due to family and work problems.

NOT ASKING FOR IT

"She asked for it." A defence so last-century, so insulting, so misogynistic, I'm surprised the Sheriff at Edinburgh Crown Court did not lock Don 'Pervy' Pertwee up and throw away the key. Instead he jailed him for five months and put him on the sex offender's register when he admitted sending a mobile video of himself engaged in a 'solo sex act' to a young woman in 2008.

PROTESTING TOO MUCH # 3

When condoms, lingerie and sexual images are involved, you'd have thought a burglar would hold their hands up to sex being part of their crime. St. Albans, England, lingerie looter George Lacey denied any sexual motive, despite stealing undies, phoning sex lines in houses he burgled, and leaving dirty doodles and condoms behind at the scenes of his crimes. The judge presiding his case was not convinced, and said that Lacey's "sexual behaviour should not be overlooked," the St Albans and Harpenden Review reported.

40% OF MEN AND WOMEN HAVE FANTASISED ABOUT HAVING SEX WITH A CELEBRITY

SEVEN DAY SEX PEST

A 52-year-old Australian man tried to break the record for making the most sexually explicit phone calls in one week in 2008. Over a seven day period in the spring of 2008, he made over 900 phone calls, starting with heavy breathing, and climaxing with suggestive comments. Police appealed for victims of the warped whisperer to come forward so they could hit him with more than the nine counts on which he'd been charged.

PRESSING THE WRONG BUTTONS

In 1994, a worried mother dialled 999 and sent police to her daughter's home, fearing she was being attacked. The reason? She'd received a call in a voice that she could definitely identify as her daughter's, shouting 'Oh my God!' with a man's harsh tones in the background. Imagine everybody's embarrassment when the police arrived and found the woman's daughter in bed with her boyfriend. They could only assume that someone had pressed the redial button on the phone and hit loudspeaker.

COMPUTER GAME CAPERS

A recreational computer sex-game was discovered in the computer system of New York's City Ambulances in the late 1990s. A computer buff said at the time that the game 'Foreplay' may slow down the computer or stop it working completely. A spokesperson for the hospital said the fact its staff were playing the game had no effect on response time, which had been reduced in recent months.

18% OF BRITONS WOULD DEFINITELY CONSIDER BEING PAID FOR SEX
FOR THE RIGHT AMOUNT OF CASH

FLOORED!

Former Greek culture minister Christos Zachopoulos jumped from a four storey building when his ex-assistant tried to blackmail him with a sex tape in 2007. She demanded $300,000 for the tape not to be leaked. He was floored by the allegations. Snarf.

IT ASDA BE CRIMINAL

ASDA. The low-cost Brit supermarket. Gets your juices flowing, don't it? Hmm. Me neither. One man clearly sees something in the shop we don't. In 2007, Colin Jameson stood at the bus stop outside the Morecambe branch of the store, performed a sex act on himself, and brazenly hopped on the number 5B home.

WRONG NUMBER

"As everyone knows who works with printed materials, mistakes happen." So said a spokesperson for a golfing tournament which saw 100,000 brochures printed with the wrong free phone number for the event. Callers were surprised to hear the following at the end of the line when they tried to book: "You've come to the right place for nasty talk with big-busted girls."

LOVE LETTER STRAIGHT FROM THE HEART

Joseph Dobbie met Kate Winsall at a party in the summer of 2006, where he was awestruck by her beauty – to say the very least. Nicking her email from the original party invite, he cobbled together a smarm-fest of epic proportions on why she should join him for a date at the Tate Modern. After an ordinary opening gambit, he continued. "This is the part where I throw caution to the wind; the part where I listen to my heart and remember that I should live my life as an exultation and revel in the opportunity to try." He then goes on to fawn and creep some more, climaxing with the vomsome, "Your smile is the freshest of my special memories."

Candid and sweet as he might be, he perhaps gives himself away with his parting words. "One last thing, I promise that it is enormously rare for me to stray as far from sobriety as I managed on Saturday night." And when you were typing the now famous love note, Joseph, and entered the ridiculous email hall of fame, how far had you strayed then? Answers by email to....

HITTING ROCK BOTTOM

A man's love of big-bottomed ladies cost him his life in 2007. Car mechanic Pablo Ortega bribed plus-sized ladies in order to snap shots of their clothed bottoms for a cheap sexual thrill. But when Mica Gutierrez went for her close-up, she took along Henry Voigt, who attempted to rob the mechanic's store whilst the posterior Polaroid was being taken. Ortega caught him in the act, and was killed in the struggle that ensued.

MISTAKEN IDENTITY # 4

Baronet Sir Benjamin Slade put in a bill to his insurers, Lloyds of London, when a male peacock sexually attacked an employee's car at Maunsel House, his 1,300-acre estate in Somerset. The 'peacock blue' Lexus was scratched and dented by the sexually charged and confused bird.

F**K YOU VERY MUCH

During the thank-you speech at a 2001 wedding in Southend, Essex, England, a groom took great care to thank his new bride's family for paying for the lavish 300-plus-guested event. He then handed a manilla envelope to each guest and awaited their reaction to the contents. Inside was a candid and sexually explicit shot of his bride and his best-man. With a 'fuck you' to the best-man, the groom then left the party. The marriage was annulled shortly afterwards.

BOOT-Y CALL

Florian Neuz and his mistress Steffi Klose had nowhere to go, so they decided to enjoy the first flushes of their extra-marital relations in the boot of Neuz's car, parked on the hard-shoulder of the A7 autobahn. They saw the funny side when the boot slammed shut on them before they got down to brass tacks, and they were forced to call police. Luckily Klose had kept her mobile phone with her, in case her husband rang asking what she wanted for supper.

KING OF THE SWINGERS?

Trying to impress his new wife with his athleticism proved a nightmare for Italian Marco Zagni of Milan. He swung through their honeymoon suite window on a rope à la Tarzan King of the Jungle, but hit a wall and knocked himself out cold. His bride was less than impressed. "How could I marry somebody so stupid?" she asked reporters.

HAIR-BRAINED

A Christchurch, New Zealand hairdresser called the cops when her client started making an up and down pumping motion under the hairdresser's cape he was wearing. Finding herself terrified and alone in her salon after-hours, she beat him over the head with a hairdryer, rendering him temporarily unconscious. When the police arrived, they found the man had been up to nothing more than wiping his spectacles clean.

THE LONG AND SHORT OF IT

Joe Newman was a jazz trumpeter, known for his eye for the ladies. In 1989 he had a penile implant to increase the girth of his love trumpet. The surgery went badly wrong, and the musician ended up suffering from internal bleeding. He died from the post-operative damage in 1992.

UNDRESS FOR SUCCESS # 1

Former TV journalist and Tapei City councilwoman Chu Mei-feng's 47-minute secretly filmed sex tryst became one of the most viewed sex tapes on the web in the early noughties. Just google it and you'll soon see why. Anyway. Although the tape cost Mei-feng her job, she later wrote a best-selling book and brought out a hugely popular pop record. Meanwhile, the white thong knickers she wore in the tape became extremely popular, and Taiwanese lingerie manufacturers sold a shed load of them on the back of the vulgar vid.

SUCKERED

There are several cases of the Thai prostitute 'nipple scam.' A recent one involved a Manila lady-boy covering his nipple in a tranquiliser and asking a British tourist to suck it off. The Manchester teacher woke from a drug-induced sleep short of one Rolex and the equivalent of 500 pounds in cash.

PAGE 3 WANNABE

Nurses at Northampton General Hospital, England, were banned from social networking sites when one of their number appeared topless on Facebook. The naughty nurse had posted a photo of herself flashing her boobs, and was caught out because a patient could clearly be seen in the background.

BREAST IS STILL BEST

Residents of Costa Blanca, Spain, collected a petition with over 10,000 signatures in an attempt to ban topless bathing from their beaches in 2007. The town's mayor found this an itsy-bitsy, teeny-weeny bit prudish, and tourists have been given the green light to strip off for the foreseeable.

WHAT GOES UP MUST COME DOWN

A 52-year-old man was admitted to hospital with priapism after taking ecstasy and marijuana at a New York disco. Medics failed to relieve his drug-binge-induced two-day boner with medication, and were forced to use 'needle aspiration' to get rid of the erection. Ouch.

FANNYING ABOUT

Aussie Scott Davidson was charged with committing an indecent act at Brisbane Crown Court in 2005. How else could judges have described the act of fondling a giant latex vagina while accosting terrified women in a busy shopping mall? A ridiculous sexual misadventure, perhaps?

DOCTOR OH NO !

A leading gynaecologist at a clinic in Chiba, Japan, was arrested when a patient caught him snapping her naked body during an intimate examination. When police raided his home they found 15,000 photos, including nine photos of patients taken at the clinic. Hideo Nakagawa said, "I took the photos for medical research."

O-NO-7!

In 2006, Lee Tamahori, director of the James Bond film *Die Another Day* was arrested for offering to 'orally copulate' an undercover police officer for money... while dressed as a woman. The director once told an interviewer: "Sex should not be in the movies, and it should be in the home."

DOUBLE TROUBLE

Police easily tracked down a double-penised man who had forced a woman to perform fellatio on him in Malaga, Spain, in 1992. For some reason they found it less easy to charge him, and the two-dicked attacker got off scot free.

FIGHT FOR YOUR RIGHT TO FILM YOURSELF SHAGGING

Women's groups in the West would probably consider sex tapes and women's rights chalk and cheese. But when a Korean songstress had her songs pulled from radio stations and TV after a sex tape was leaked on the internet, she became a voice for the movement in her country. She denied knowing her former manager had a camera poised on her when they were getting coitally acquainted, and denounced those who criticised her. Anything men can do, women can do too, she said.

FROM HERE TO NOWHERE

In 2006, computers crashed at stock markets in Brazil as employees tried to upload a much publicised sex tape. Brazilian TV beauty Daniela Cicarelli had been caught romping with her boyfriend Renato 'Tato' Malzoni on a beach by a paparazzo in a scene reminiscent of the 50's sex shocker *From Here to Eternity*. When the popular clip was deleted from YouTube, viral voyeurs crashed the network looking for it on other websites and file sharing networks.

GROUPIE SEX

A 2005 sex tape of Limp Bizkit head honcho Fred Durst caused him much redness in the face – it involved him in the throes of passion with a groupie.

COSTUME DRAMA

When ice-skating champ Tonya Harding and husband Jeff Gillooly's 'honeymoon' sex tape found success after being leaked on the net, they decided to release it as a film. Turns out the *Wedding Night* tape was a sham – the bride's gown was actually a fancy-dress outfit.

A FIRST TIME FOR EVERYTHING

Jayne Kennedy has many firsts to her name: She was the first African American Miss Ohio, the first female NFL reporter, the first black *Playboy* cover girl. But the first for which she appears in this book is her appearance in the first known celebrity sex tape. Her ex-husband Leon Kennedy made the tape public when the pair split up.

OVER-EXPOSED

Vietnamese star Huang Thuy Lin was sacked from her hit TV series after a nude sex tape was leaked on the internet. *The New York Post* said "the exposure has ruined her career," which is a funny choice of words in this situation...

ANNA SWAN (1846–88) USED TO BE THE PROUD OWNER OF THE LONGEST VAGINA IN THE WORLD - 2 METERS 30CM

TOP TEN SONGS BANNED
FOR SEXUAL CONTENT

10. In the 21st century musical arena of hos, bitches and bump 'n grind, the lyrics to the Rolling Stones' "Let's Spend The Night Together" seem a tad limp. But allusions to one-night-stands were too much for the 1967 audience, and radio stations opted to play the B-Side, "Ruby Tuesday".

9. Heavy breathing, orgasmic moans and its title, "French Kiss", were enough to see the BBC banning Lil Louis' seminal house music track in 1989.

8. George Michael had a song banned way before everyone knew about his love of swordsmanship with random strangers. In 1987 his "I Want Your Sex" was banned by the BBC – but only before the 9 pm watershed.

7. How touchy were censorious types in the 1970s? To answer this question we need only consider that country chanteuse Loretta Lynn's celebration of birth control, "The Pill", was vetoed on radio stations across the entire US of A. Cripes. The song doesn't even mention sex.

6. The Dead Kennedys' "Too Drunk to Fuck" is a bit more like it! The direct approach of the song, which empathises with sufferers of brewers droop, was given the thumbs down by Britain's Radio One and, of course, stick-in-the-mud Aunty Beeb.

5. Those of you with a sensitive disposition, look away now, this one's a real shocker. For its musical vileness, I mean. As to its moral reprehensibility I'll leave it to you to judge whether George

Formby's "When I'm Cleaning Windows" can be deemed the 'smut' it was labelled when released in the 1940s.

4. Only born-again-virgin pop sensation Cliff Richard could call for his own song to be banned. In 1973 he released the song "Honky Tonk Angels" believing it to be about the Salvation Army. Where's he been living? On a bus with fellow squeaky clean teens oblivious to his own sexuality? Oh. Honky-tonk angels are prostitutes of course, and when Cliff found out he barred anyone from playing his unintentionally deviant ditty.

3. Had to include this one. Not only does it appeal to my puerile side, but it does exactly what it says on the tin when it comes to sexual misadventures of the vinyl variety. We're talking here about Ivor Biggun's first foray into tuneless tawdriness, and his 1979 hit, "The Winker's Song".

2. Frankie said Relax. The BBC didn't follow their imperative command, and Brit DJ Mike Read decided not to play the record on air, having finally worked out what the lyrics to the song were three months after its release. In case you were born after 1984, the risqué "relax, don't do it, when you want to suck to it, relax, don't do it, when you want to come," were the immortal lines that saw the song banned.

1. A LOT OF GAUL!
The self-proclaimed 'cabbage-headed' man Serge Gainsbourg sure did have a way with the ladies. He also had a way with words. Especially indecorous ones. The filthy Frenchman hits the number one spot pop-pickers. Firstly, for the banned "Je T'Aime, Moi Non Plus", with its 'going in and out between your kidneys' line. But more so, for the 1971 concept album, *The History of Melody Nelson*, which tells the tale of his doomed Lolita-esque relationship with a 14-year-old English girl. Nice.

PAGE 3 GIRL IN SEX-TAPE SHOCKA!

British glamour model Keeley Rebecca Hazell is used to getting her kit off, being a topless model for tabloid newspapers like the *Daily Star*, The Sun and so on. She came over all coy, however, when a sex tape of her and ex-boyfriend Lloyd Miller found its way onto the internet. She obtained an injunction to stop the video from being shown, though doubtless the intrepid sex-tape investigator would find it if they looked hard enough.

LOWE POINT

80s pin-up Rob Lowe's reputation famously took a knock when he became embroiled in one of the first celebrity sex tape scandals. The tape was controversial as one of the two young women in it was underage, a fact Lowe claimed he did not know. He was later treated for sex addiction and his career bounced back.

INBOX IGNOMINY

A bonking banker got more than she bargained for when opening her email inbox in 2007. There in the flesh, engaged in the sins of the flesh, she saw her own bouncing booty staring back at her. Nobody could say how the intimate photos taken with her ex-boyfriend had made it to her email account, or to her boss's... or to her many colleagues... but needless to say all eyes were on the ex. (After they'd been taken off said booty of course.) An investigation was launched after the unnamed woman was reportedly very distressed by the event.

KID ROCK GETS HIS ROCKS OFF

In 2006, a sex tape featuring Kid Rock, singer Scott Stapp and a bunch of groupies did the rounds on the net. When Robert Ritchie (a.k.a. Kid Rock) found out, he took out an injunction to stop the film being shown. Top marks for not looking to boost your career with lewdness. Bottom marks for exploiting your female fan base.

UNDRESS FOR SUCCESS # 2

Mix together scandal-magnet John Leslie, Brit babe Abi Titmuss, an unidentified woman, and a bagful of sex-toys and what do you get? A 2002 sex tape which ruined Titmuss's career as a family chat show presenter, but proved the catalyst for a new one as a presenter on pornographic channel, Television X. A home away from home, then!

THE GRANDDADDY OF BLUE MOVIES

A priapic pensioner with an impressive appurtenance mistakenly took part in an audition for a blue movie, and was immediately talent-spotted by the movie's director. David Bozdoganov was an instant hit in films such as *The Old Neighbour* and *The Handyman at Work*. He wasn't such a hit with his female co-stars though. Says director Alexander Plahov, "David believes in the beneficial power of garlic, and insists on rubbing it on his erection before a scene, and it's rather smelly."

MOBILE MUPPET

If you make a homemade sex video on your mobile, you'd think you'd try not to lose the offending article. A 17-year-old Singaporean student was mortified when she did just that, and the sex session with her 21-year-old boyfriend made it onto the net and later onto DVD. The cheeky cheerleader later claimed she had not sought fame by deliberately having the vid made public.

WHAT THE BLAZES?

A fire crew who shone powerful lights on a group having it off in a hedgerow got their just desserts when they were fined and disciplined for their behaviour. The group of men, who were dogging at the time, complained when the Avon firemen put the spotlight on their illegal activity. The fire service could not give any explanation why their crew were in the area at the time.

CAUGHT RED HANDED

A stalker got his comeuppance when he made a dirty phone call to his victim while she was in a police station complaining about his behaviour.

Sandy Krolic of Corio, Australia, had been calling the victim non-stop over a seven day period with increasingly sexually explicit calls. When he filmed himself masturbating on his camera phone, the woman had had enough. As she sat in the station making her complaint, he rang once again, and police were able to trace his call and promptly arrest the offensive onanist.

A FREUDIAN SLIP

A top psychiatrist to the stars was accused of abusing his position in 2003 when he had an illicit affair with a patient. The shady head-shrinker apparently did little for his patient's mental health when he phoned her at 3.30am and asked her to masturbate with him over the phone, one of many dirty phone calls he made. Because the woman waited so long to come forward, lawyers were able to stop the case coming to court.

PLEASURE SEEKER GETS IN OVER HIS HEAD

In 2007, Gary Ashbrook inflated a condom with laughing gas and put it over his head for a sexual thrill. It was no laughing matter, though, when he suffocated and came to a sticky end from his solo sex session.

JIGGERY-IN-POKEY # 3

In 1997, Amy Lou Stoat, 19, was arrested on a lawn outside a prison in Great Falls, Montana, USA, for getting her (jailhouse) rocks off. Complying with her prisoner husband's request, she undressed, sprawled on the grass and had a good old flick of the pea. It was not clear whether her hubbie or any of the other inmates got a glimpse of the 'show', but Stoat was nonetheless charged with indecent exposure and unlawful communications with an inmate.

UNDERWEAR AS OUTERWEAR

A man clothed head to toe in women's undies, his head covered in a pair of hot pink panties, exposed himself to the bikini-clad baristas at the Java Girls coffee shop in 2008. Disgusted, the half-dressed women retaliated and threw boiling coffee in the flasher's face. Bet he'll wear his knickers under his trousers from now on.

THE ARGENTINE FIRE CRACKER

U.S. Congressman and presidential candidate Wilbur Mills was caught driving into the Tidal basin in the 1970's, intoxicated, with stripper Fanne Fox in tow. Despite the scandal he was re-elected to Congress with a nice 60% share of the vote. When he later appeared on the stage of a burlesque show, drunk again, with the same stripper, he had to admit to Congress he was a drunk. She was now known as the Argentine Fire Cracker. He was simply fired.

STEAMY WINDOWS

A Hong Kong television reporter who was arrested for masturbating on a bus said he was only trying to 'ease his stress' when he flouted himself full-frontal in the window of the top deck. The act of public indecency lost him his job, and he was put on a one-year good behaviour bond.

CAUGHT SINGLE-HANDED

You've got to admire the guts of the 25-year-old Australian man who indulged in a round of hand-to-gland combat in front of a police station in 2005. He was spotted by security cameras and officers

50% OF WOMEN HAVE HAD ANAL SEX

managed to arrest him before a police cruiser received the spoils of his one man wank-war.

IN-FLIGHT 'ENTERTAINMENT'

You've been asleep on a boring flight, and wake to find someone has come and sat next to you. How nice, you think. A bit of company.

Not for the passenger who found her newly arrived companion in a neighbouring seat masturbating. In nervous embarrassment the woman turned away and ran her fingers through her hair, only to notice "a substantial amount of an extremely sticky substance." She later unsuccessfully sued the airline.

TOILET TROUBLE

An FBI worker was arrested on suspicion of three misdemeanours in 2007 – public sexual indecency, criminal trespass and indecent exposure. His crime? He was in the women's loos on a university campus when a cleaner caught him playing with Mrs Palm and her five lovely daughters. In line with FBI policy, it was not confirmed if he was a secret agent, or just a secret wanker.

PRISONER GETS OFF – BUT NOT OUT

In 2007, a Florida man gave new meaning to the expression 'doing hard time' when he was sentenced to 60 days in prison for masturbating in his prison cell. He had been spotted by a female guard – who was watching the cells on CCTV – and found guilty of behaving in a vulgar or indecent manner. The sentence was added to 10 years he was already doing for a more meaningful crime.

30% OF WOMEN WHO HAVE HAD ANAL SEX FOUND IT A PLEASURABLE EXPERIENCE

JOG ON!

Being caught spanking the monkey in front of two joggers is not that unusual a crime. You've got to feel slightly sorry for British wanker Mick Hollinghurst then, when a court ordered he should parade around the scene of his crime, wearing a sign reading, 'I was convicted of committing an indecent act in High Park.' A higher court overturned the order on appeal and the man was told to get psychiatric help. As well, thankfully, as avoiding public parks for 18 months.

POLICEMAN HAS A SOLO BALL

The night shift can be well boring. Especially if you're a copper in a maximum security police station in Spain. Well, I can't think of any other reason why Police Inspector Jorge Mendoza headed to a cell there to indulge in spot of companionless coitus with his love truncheon. So over-libidinous was he though, that he forgot everything in the jail is filmed by CCTV.

It was his rotten luck that – months later – human rights inspectors viewing random footage of the station happened to randomly pick a video of the night the inspector had abused himself. Still, at least he wasn't abusing one of the prisoners...

SMILE! YOU'RE ON CANDID CAMERA

Serial New York subway masturbator Daniel Hoyt inspired one of his victims to start the website Hollabacknyc.com, where women who've been flashed or frotted can post mobile pics of their aggressors in a bid to out them.

Hoyt himself, despite being the catalyst for the site, was

unrepentant when *The New York Post* interviewed him about it. "I've met women who enjoy it," he said, "I've had a woman tell me, 'You know, that sounds exciting to me'." There is but one word for him. Tosser.

STONE ME!

In 2006, a Russian blogger claimed that a British spy had filmed himself up to no good on an electronic device disguised as a stone. Seems that instead of doing the usual spy work in the combat arena, the official was engaged in activity of the hand-to-gland variety. The device had supposedly then been seized by Russian counter-spies, and the claims were made on the web shortly thereafter. Sounds like a load of Bol-sheviks to me!

DON'T TRY THIS AT HOME # 2

If you've got a sexual peccadillo, it's probably best to try it out behind closed doors, ideally in the privacy of your own home. The alternative is landing a stint behind the kind of closed doors for which you don't have the key. But would you believe a Canadian man was banged up for four months in 2004 simply for masturbating in his own living room?

When neighbours spotted Jim Benjamin choking the chicken on a dark autumn night, they alerted police, fearing he was 'masturbating to their children'. The case went to the Canadian Supreme Court which rejected the notion that people's private living spaces can be turned into public places just because someone can see inside. Benjamin had all his lights on and the curtains were open at the time of his ridiculous solo misadventure.

DON'T READ THE SMALL PRINT

Who said that newspapers were old hat? Not one serial masturbator, at least. In 2007, Todd Carthy was identified from CCTV footage as the man who had been persistently self-stimulating on Seattle buses, using a copy of the *Seattle Times* to cover up his penis. He told that same paper that he'd taken up masturbating in the hope of increasing his genital size. "I was trying to get this huge thing to make me a tough guy," he whined. "I have this compulsive disorder; I can't stop."

A BUMPY RIDE

When you're arrested for masturbation in a public place, you'd think you'd behave on the journey to the police cells. Not so one Swedish man, who continued his pumping action during a 40 minute ride in the meat wagon. Police, suspecting his compulsive wanking to be a bigger problem, discovered the man was known to them already for having his way with himself in churches across the Lund region.

UNHOLIER THAN THOU # 2

Careful now. I'm about to mention something that could get you really hot under the collar. Paper Museums. What? That's not got you going? Well it may then surprise you to hear that a Buddhist monk was arrested in 2008 for thwacking one off while having a tour round an exhibition on the history of paper. Maybe he was just bored rigid...

THREE THWACKS IN A FOUNTAIN

When newspapers reported that a British man was arrested on his stag night for cavorting naked in a Bratislava fountain in 2007, sympathies were with the naughty nude and papers urged his timely release. I wonder if we'd have been as magnanimous had we known what Slovakian papers widely reported – that the man was really done for a display of public lewdness, having thwacked a few off in the City's famous fountain?

PULLING A FAST ONE

What's more foolish? Filming yourself speeding at more than 100mph while masturbating at the wheel of a car laden with drugs and a gun, or telling the police who stopped you that you planned to use the gun to shoot kangaroos? Only one man can answer this, and that's kangaroo-killing-car-chicken-chokin' Brandon Danvers. Although Danvers was given a prison sentence for the madcap misdemeanour, Aussie police granted him bail so he could first marry his girlfriend. Nice.

MAD, BAD AND DANGEROUS TO KNOW

Long before we had Russell Brand, another wavy-locked hero of lasciviousness reigned supreme. Time to remember the 18th century's Lord Byron, the poet who fell in and out of love as often as he put curl papers in his hair – that's every night, by the way – and left a trail of destroyed women in his wake. It was via his most public affair with Lady Caroline Lamb that he earned the title 'mad, bad and dangerous to know.' Well, he was for her, anyway. When he dumped her, she tried to stab herself.

PEANUT BUTTER NUTTER

I don't know which is freakier – reports that a man cleared his custard into a jar of peanut butter, or that he believed he saw the face of computer game character Supermario in the jar. The man was found by his 11-year-old daughter chuntering on about the 'Mushroom Kingdom,' which is a feature of the games, while he masturbated. The deviant dude was of course arrested.

PERSONAL SERVICES

When Jerry Springer interviews hopeless humpers on his much loved chat show, it must be a bit like looking in a mirror. And one of those steamy above-the-bed ones too.

Did you know that before he became a television celebrity, Springer was a politician? And one of those sex scandal type politicians, I mean. It was during his campaign for the position of State Governor that a raid on a brothel revealed he had written a cheque for a prostitute's services. Despite admitting his insatiable lust, he was re-elected in 1975 and later elected mayor in 1979. He then left politics to be more at one with the people. But not in that way. On his talk-show, I mean.

A SCORE IN THE TOILET

State Representative Bob Allen was arrested in 2007 for soliciting oral sex from a male undercover policeman. His defence – the cop was a 'stocky black guy' and he gave him $20 cause that frightened him... Twerp!

WOMEN WHO READ ROMANCE NOVELS HAVE SEX TWICE AS OFTEN AS THOSE WHO DON'T

THERE AIN'T NOTHING GOING ON BUT THE RENT (BOY)

British Liberal Democrat MP Mark Oaten quit frontline politics in 2006 when the *News of the World* published a 'scoop' that he had been having a six month long affair with a rent boy. Married with two children, Oaten resigned his position, but remained a member of parliament.

Tales of his sordid affair have swished around the media like excrement in a sewer. Revelations and rumour which abounded included reports in *Private Eye* and *The Daily Telegraph* that coprophilia was a feature of his sex sessions. And his excuse for this stupid shagging escapade? The pressures of public life and the fact that we was going bald.

DO AS I SAY, NOT AS I DO

During the much publicised moral crusade 'Back to Basics' campaign by the British Tory government in 1993, a tabloid exposé revealed that Environment Minister Tim Yeo was father to an illegitimate child with Conservative councillor Julia Stent. I don't think you need reminding that the campaign waxed lyrical about the wonders of parenting within the sanctity of marriage.

THREATENED WITH EXPOSURE

A sex tape was offered for sale in 2008 featuring porn queen Sky Lopez and the actor who played David Hasselhoff's son in *Baywatch*. In a twist to the usual sorry sex tape tales, the actor, Jeremy Jackson, claimed he was forced to hand over the tape by a gang of hoodlums in Lopez's pay.

4 OUT OF 5 SUN READERS THINK PORNOGRAPHY HAS A POSITIVE EFFECT ON THEIR LIVES

TOP TEN SILLIEST SEX SCENES ON FILM

10. Bit of a cheat at number ten. I mean, surely there's no way David Cronenbourg meant James Spader having his wicked way with a wound in Rosanna Arquette's leg to be considered 'sexy?' And that's not to mention the other manhood-meets-metal shots in the film. *Crash*. Sexy? No. Silly? Indubitably.

9. More foolish foreplay scene this than fully-blown sex, but I could not resist a mention of *Armageddon*. As Ben Affleck and Liv Tyler discuss the merits of animal crackers, our hero takes a gazelle-shaped savoury biscuit and moves it up and down semi-naked Tyler's body. He goes on to spew a ludicrous description of the cracker's journey. "He could head north, to the mountainous peaks above." (Liv laughs) Ben: "Or go south." Most. Embarrassing. Love. Scene. Ever.

8. Ooh, Ben, you may be a Hollywood heart-throb but you don't half come across all amateur dramatics in your sex scenes. So to *Gigli*, where I'll let Jennifer Lopez's invitation to Affleck to perform cunnilingus speak for itself. "It's turkey time ... gobble gobble..." It's enough to put you off Christmas AND oral sex in one fowl swoop.

7. Affleck and Lopez had recently split at the time of filming the above, so there may be some excuse for lacking on screen fireworks in *Gigli*. Nicole Kidman and Tom Cruise have no excuse for their unconvincing conjugal coitus in Stanley Kubrick's *Eyes Wide Shut* – they were married at the time in real life. Whatever that proves.

6. Nicholas Roeg's *The Man Who Fell to Earth* should be shelved for crimes against cinema sex scenes. First, for the sex scene where aliens from David Bowie's planet get off by being sprayed with milk while jumping on trampoline-like equipment. Second, for possibly giving hideous goth band Alien Sex Fiend the inspiration to form. Unforgivable.

5. What is it with pop royalty and absurd soft-core in mainstream films? So to Prince's *Purple Rain* where he flounces with his co-star Apollonia in a love scene that will have you feeling about as hot under the collar as the freezer cabinet in Iceland.

4. And before you think I'm singling out pop Kings and Princes, let's not forget that her Madgesty, Madonna, had her own moment of silly celluloid salaciousness with Willem Defoe in *Body of Evidence*. Word to the Wise, Ms Ciccone. Pouring hot wax and tying up your man doth not an S&M scene make.

3. Matt Dillon. Phwoar. Denise Richards. Phwoar. Neve Campbell. Not so much. Still, two of Hollywood's hottest stars in a swimming pool can't be bad can it? And yet they, and Neve, acting out a threesome in the nonetheless thrill-tastic *Wild Things* is somehow as erotic as a bowl of cold porridge.

2. *Poison Ivy* is a classic example where forbidden fruit can simply look rotten. Especially when underage sex is made to seem okay in a mainstream Hollywood movie with the child star from ET!

1. SEXUAL GYMNASTICS
If only the expression 'sexual gymnastics' had not been around for donkey's years, we could assign its invention to the film *Damage*. The 1992 film where Jeremy Irons and Juliette Binoche struggle like demented sumo wrestlers practising backwards rolls is the very epitome of the concept. Though there ain't much that looks sexual about it.

A PRINCE AMONG PROSTITUTES

The grandson of Italy's last King, Vittorio Emanuele, was arrested in 2006 for his role in a 'high-class' prostitution and illegal gambling ring. He was released after spending some time under house arrest. It wasn't the first time he'd got into a spot of bother with the law. He'd been accused of manslaughter linked to a shooting in Corsica in the 1970s, but was acquitted in 1991.

EXCUSES, EXCUSES # 2

What is it with politicians and their bizarre excuses for their sexual indiscretions? When Ron Davies, the former Welsh Secretary, was caught in a known gay cruising spot, he claimed he'd been looking for badgers. He stood down, which came as no surprise to those who recalled he'd resigned once already over a similar misadventure in 1998.

DON'T TRY THIS AT HOME # 3

Pelvic pain is not something usually suffered by men, so when an unnamed 22-year-old from Brighton, England, turned up to Royal Sussex County's A&E, doctors in charge thought an x-ray was in order. Further bafflement followed when the x-ray showed several small balls lodged in the patient's bladder. As the pain worsened, the man had to fess up. He had been sliding a small necklace in and out of his urethra for sexual kicks when the thread had snapped, and the balls had disappeared from sight. Doctors saw no alternative but to pick each bead out individually with tweezers. Ow!

BALL-BREAKER

Dr Gavin P Matthews Jr made an edifying contribution to the *Medical Aspects of Human Sexuality Journal* in July 1991. Edifying, that is, for those who self-pleasure with factory machinery. Earlier that year he had treated a patient who had come into his hospital, claiming to be suffering from "men's problems." The patient only needed to drop his kecks for an explanation. Swollen, covered in zig-zag lacerations and pus, was the place where the man's left testicle ought to have been.

After surgery to fix the wound, the man recounted his sorry tale to the doctor. Being unmarried and a bit of a loner he had begun the regular practice of masturbating against the canvas drive belt of a piece of running machinery in the factory where he worked. One day, in a lapse of concentration, he caught his scrotum between the pulley-wheel and the drive belt, and was thrown in the air and knocked out cold. On regaining consciousness he did not realize he was one ball-bag short of a full wedding tackle, and closed the gaping wound he found in his nether regions with a staple gun. Doctor Matthews finishes his report on the scrotum self-repairer wryly, thus: "I can only assume he abandoned this method of self-gratification." The location of the missing testis remains a mystery.

VARIETY IS THE SPICE OF LIFE

Lord Lambton, a defence minister in Ted Heath's 1970s British government, resigned in 1973 when the *News of The World* exposed him as a brothel habitué and marijuana user. After Lambton retired, he said that he had purchased the services of prostitutes because, "People sometimes like variety. It's as simple as that." That's right. Lovers. Bit like your morning breakfast cereal? Sheesh.

OPEN HOUSE

In 2008, a British Conservative cabinet member quit his job when he was investigated over claims he was using his house for paid group sex. David Bourne and wife Carol were both also Wolverhampton City Council members. Resigning from his position he was less than sorry. "People are free to criticize me," he said arrogantly. "I don't care."

TWO SHAGS

A politician having an affair with his secretary is one thing. Having to endure the sordid details is another. It's your 15 minutes of shame, former British Labour Party Deputy Leader John Prescott. His ex-lover Tracy Temple dished the dirty details on the fling to the *Mail on Sunday* in 2006, giving the newspaper many salacious details. Later revelations from Temple's diaries published in *The Sun* went in to even more embarassing detail.

CABIN FEVER

Paul Crouch was a founding member of the American Christian TV station Trinity Broadcasting Network. In 1998 he paid an ex-employee Enoch Lonnie Ford $425,000 to end a lawsuit he'd filed for sexual harassment. Ford had maintained that he'd been threatened with job loss if he didn't get jiggy with Crouch in a log cabin in 1995. Crouch said he only paid the money so that a lengthy lawsuit could be avoided. The revelations came to light via the *Los Angeles Times* in September 2004.

A PICTURE OF HEALTH?

A Scottish ambulance worker committed sexual breach of the peace in 2008 when he snapped a mobile phone picture of an unconscious patient's privates. Peter Maynard, 30, was put in jail for four months for his amateur glamour photography efforts.

COP-ING AN EYEFUL

Dutch prostitutes complained that police were spying on them in the northern Dutch town of Groningen in 2005. Prostitutes from a working girls foundation De Straatmadelief penned a letter to the city's mayor to dob in the pervy policemen, reporting that as many as 12 police cars at a time would park near specially assigned 'sex zones' to ogle them while they were 'on the job.' "Instead of focused inspections, they are coming and watching like monkeys," the girls said in their letter.

THE PETTICOAT AFFAIR

In 1831, a sex scandal erupted over the involvement of British Secretary of War John Henry Eaton and a widowed lady. Unbelievably, the simple fact that Eaton's lover Margaret "Peggy" O'Neale had been married before led to the resignation of much of the cabinet.

BRIEF ENCOUNTER

British Labour MP Chris Bryant caused uproar in 2003 when he posted pictures of himself in a pair of Y fronts on the Gaydar website in a gay-sex quest. Well, knickers to those who laughed at the openly gay single man, I say. Don't politicians have a right to a love life too?

THE FIRST FRENCH KISS IN MAINSTREAM CINEMA WAS IN *Splendor in the Grass* IN 1961

HOOKED ON HOOKERS

With prostitution being legal in Holland, you'd have thought Dutch Labour party politician Rob Oudkerk would have got away with saying he'd been paying for sex. However, he suffered a vote of no confidence when it transpired the hookers he'd been seeing were drug-addled illegal ones from the dodgy Tippelzones in Amsterdam.

PORN AGAIN CHRISTIAN

In 1988, Jimmy Swaggart resigned after he'd been photographed cavorting with prostitutes. At the time he was the USA's leading TV evangelist. His confessed 'moral failure' was all the more notable since he'd once called a rival Reverend caught in similar circumstances "a cancer in the body of Christ."

However, when the prostitute photographed at the centre of the scandal came forward, she said though Swaggart had been a regular client, they hadn't gone the whole hog sexually, and that he usually just asked her to do a strip-tease. We have to wonder what this rather less titillating moral failure makes Swaggart, then. Influenza in the body of Christ perhaps?

DOCTORS STUMPED

At the turn of the last millennium doctors were mystified when a patient arrived with severe swelling around the anus and a raging fever. Ron Guptey's health swiftly deteriorated and the following day he was dead. An autopsy revealed that a black widow spider had laid its eggs in Ron's intestine. And how? Closer examination revealed splinters of bark from a tree up the patient's jacksy. He'd been experimenting in tree-stump-love when the eggs found their way into his rectum.

55% OF MEN HAVE FANTASISED ABOUT HAVING A THREESOME

BOTTLED-UP

Fizzy cola bottles are iconic symbols of America. Maybe that's why there's a plethora of stories about their use as masturbatory tools on the internet – with the embarrassed bottle abuser usually winding up in casualty. One particular such cautionary tale deserves a mention.

In 1975, a young lady from Wichita, Kansas, was rushed to hospital with a fizzy pop bottle in her vagina. Rather than admitting she had used the item for sexual gratification, she bizarrely told doctors she had used the bottle for 'personal hygiene' after sex. A hole was drilled in the bottom of the bottle to free the vacuum which had caused the make-shift cleansing tool to become stuck in the first place.

A TICKET NOT TO 'RIDE'

A female motorist was given a ticket in Israel in 2007 for having sex in her car – in the middle of the road. A police spokesman said the female driver and her male passenger ceded to their lust without pulling over to the side of the road, causing other drivers to swerve to dodge their stationary vehicle.

JUST CAN'T GET ENOUGH

Police in Stuttgart in Germany had trouble separating a drunken sex lout from his 'lover' in a public shopping centre in 2006. He had somehow become stuck in an anatomically correct inflatable sex doll, to whom he was clinging for dear life.

31% OF WOMEN HAVE FANTASISED ABOUT HAVING A THREESOME

HELLO DOLLY (AGAIN)

Craig McCullough really needs to find himself a significant other. In 2004, he was arrested for stealing a bridal mannequin and making off with her down an alleyway. A later misdemeanour might give us some clue as to what he intended to do with his bridal booty – in 2007 he was arrested again after being found in a public restroom lying next to a blow up doll with his pants around his ankles.

MISADVENTURE ON THE SILVER SCREEN

"It's supposed to be the best sex in the world but, as Berkley thrashes around in the water, it looks more like the first ten minutes of *Jaws*." So said a spokesman for *Empire* magazine when awarding Paul Verhoeven's *Show Girls* the number one spot in their search for the worst sex scene in cinematic history.

The Berkley in question was Elizabeth Berkley, who joined actor Kyle MacLachlan for a 20-minute breast-bouncing, arm-flailing, vocally energetic romp in a swimming pool, which many have commented is better suited to the Olympics than to the cinema screen.

The misadventure has not done MacLachlan's career any harm, and he's even got his kit off again on screen on more than one occasion. As for Berkley, the cinematic misadventure is said to have put the brakes on her acting career for a time. She has now bounced back and enjoys success in TV Shows such as *CSI Miami*, but her breasts have remained firmly ensconced in her brassiere ever since.

ROSES HAVE THORNS

What do you call the male equivalent of an English Rose? You know, someone who resonates English-ness, has charm, wit and boyish good looks to boot? Well, it ain't Hugh Grant, that's for sure. Prior to his 1995 encounter with prostitute Divine Brown on Hollywood

Boulevard, Grant might well have been the male equivalent of an English Rose – an English Oak, perhaps. But details of his oral-sex-for-cash scandal would soon put paid to any claims he may have in that department.

Grant's career did not suffer though, perhaps since he made no bones about the wrongness of the deed. On Jay Leno's show, just after the incident, he said wisely, "I think you know in life what's a good thing to do and what's a bad thing, and I did a bad thing. And there you have it." Indeed. Next!

COULD IT BE MAGIC?

The 1992 sex scandal which saw the world looking at Woody Allen in a new light could have been a career-wrecker. You remember the one? He shacked up with Mia Farrow's adoptive daughter Soon-Yi, 35 years his junior. Farrow only found out after discovering nude Polaroids of her daughter on the living room mantelpiece. In a 2005 interview with *Vanity Fair*, Allen said the relationship had a 'paternal feeling to it' but that it worked 'like magic.' Amazingly he said he felt the romance had helped further his career. Ms Farrow called the relationship 'a tragedy.'

VERY PERSONAL TRAINER

Mike Jones, American personal trainer and 'masseur' surely gets the 'Exposing the Most Public Figures as Hypocrites by Having Gay Sex With Them' award. Not only was he at the centre of the Ted Haggard sex scandal – outing the evangelical church leader, who opposed gay marriage, for his hypocrisy – but he also claimed that anti-gay politician Senator Larry Craig had paid him for oral sex. Although Craig denied he'd ever met Jones, seven further men came forward saying Craig had not been backwards about coming forwards with them, and his protestations of innocence fell on deaf ears.

A PIG'S ORGASM LASTS FOR 30 MINUTES

REPULSION

The Roman Polanski sex scandal is perhaps one of the most legendary Hollywood misadventures. The film director's encounter with a 13-year-old model in a swimming pool led to him being charged with unlawful sex with a minor, and ultimately prevented him from ever returning to the United States. Polanski always maintained he believed the girl to be of legal age and consenting. The other party continues to claim otherwise. The scandal continues.

GOODNESS GRACIOUS, GREAT BALLS OF SCANDAL

Jerry Lee Lewis's star burned out pretty quickly in 1958 when he arrived in the UK for the start of a world tour. It wasn't that his music was criminal, but the public did get a bit put out when the press revealed that not only was his accompanying bride thirteen, but that she was his first cousin. Oh yeah, and he was still married to his second wife at the time. The scandal followed Lewis back to the States, and ended his career.

VACUUM SCHEMER

In 2005, an Utah, USA, woman came (ahem) up with the perfect solution for harried working mums with no time for sex in their lives: She invented a sex toy which they can hook up to their vacuum cleaners and which promises a climax in less than half a minute. In case you're wondering, the gadget, named Vortex Vibrations, uses the flow of air from a hoover to vibrate a lady's sex parts – without even touching them. The toy's inventor Joanne Drysdale apparently touched on the idea while cleaning her carpets.

ROCKIN' THE BOAT

The 2005 sex scandal involving 17 members of the Minnesota Vikings football team is known in the USA as the 'Love Boat Scandal' or, as USA Today called it, the 'Bawdy Boating Party.' The team were ostensibly out for a team bonding day on a boat, but many ended up indulging in various sex acts with prostitutes who were specially flown in from Mexico for the event. Most of the players were involved, but very few were charged. Those who were ended up paying only a $1,000 fine.

BELOW THE BELT

Few men have the following accomplishments to their name: a host of wrestling championship titles, 20,000 notches on their bedpost, and being elected into Government despite dropping out of high school. Atsushi Onita does. The former Japanese politician and retired professional wrestler blew his political career however, when he allegedly had a threesome with an actress and a government employee in governmental buildings.

With a career like that behind him, you can bet your life he would bounce back from his sexual misadventure. He did. In 2007 he launched his first game for the Nintendo DS. Three guesses what the content is. Atsushi Onita's Bonk-Fest Bonanza? Nope. Atsushi Onita's Raucous Wrestling Game? Nope. Atsushi Onita's Political Quiz? Yup. What a waste!

1 TO 3% OF BRITISH MALES EXPRESS THEIR SEXUAL IDENTITIES BY CROSS-DRESSING

TAPED!

In December 2005, a Hollywood star was apparently caught on tape, pleasuring a male friend orally. The 'friend' had recorded the whole incident on his mobile phone camera and it was soon all over the internet. However, the star denied everything, claiming it was a looky-likey and not her.

CATCH OF THE DAY?

A group sex romp did not open doors for four soccer players in a famous French team, but it did open the transfer window for them. Their manager, upon reading the lurid details of their taped orgy with a glamour model in a national newspaper, moved all of the players on to other clubs in the January transfer window.

OWN GOAL

Now, in putting together a book about sexual silliness, we can't very well leave out the soccer manager the British nation loves to mock. I refer of course to suave and sophisticated (cough) Swede, Sven-Göran Erikson who seemed to have more success on English soil with the ladies than his team. His affairs with weathergirl-turned-starlet Ulrika Jonsson and Football Association secretary Faria Alam are well documented.

THE SPERM COUNT OF AN AVERAGE AMERICAN MALE IS DOWN 30% COMPARED TO 30 YEARS AGO

WINDOW ON THE WORLD

In 2004, soccer ace Adrian Mutu was secretly filmed while he enjoyed a night of passion with a blonde porn star at his flat in the Romanian capital. The woman involved was in league with a national newspaper who were filming the raunchy encounter from a flat opposite. Mutu was furious, saying, "I didn't think she was that kind of girl. If I had I wouldn't have gone with her. She is a low quality woman for what she did." Um. Two words: Porn, actress...

UNHAPPY ENDING

The British press had a field day when a beautician at a luxury Dundee, Scotland, hotel claimed an actor had performed a lewd act while she was giving him a massage. The star was said to have exposed himself as he dropped a towel, no doubt hoping for a 'happy ending.' The twist in the tale came when the actor himself was exposed as Hollywood megastar Kevin Costner. The actor never denied the claims outright. The unfortunate witness to his 'disgusting act' was sacked, adding injury to insult.

NEWS OF THE SCREWS

An undercover *News of the World* reporter was offered sex and cocaine by Brit model Sophie Anderton in 2007. Claiming to be good at 'it' she was reported as saying her prowess in the bedroom had helped her to buy her house. She was dropped from an advertising campaign for a tanning product when the news got out. Never mind. I'm sure she was able to turn her hand to other things...

IMPOTENCE IS GROUNDS FOR DIVORCE IN 26 US STATES

TOP TEN BAD SEX
PASSAGES IN BOOKS

For a laugh at the worst sex scenes in literature, we need look no further than the last few winners of the annual Bad Sex Award from *The Literary Review*.

10. Sean Thomas was miffed to win the award in 2000, pointing out the passage where he compares his girlfriend to a Sony Walkman was meant to be funny, and that he intended it to be: "An insight into the lunacy that goes through men's minds when it comes to sex." Or indeed when they're writing.

9. When you compare an erotic encounter to Sir Ranulph Fiennes's exploration of the north pole, you shouldn't really be surprised to win the 2001 Bad Sex Award, as Christopher Hart did for his *Rescue Me*.

8. 2002's winner was Wendy Perriam for *Tread Softly*. The following excerpt reveals why: "Weirdly, he was clad in pin-stripes at the same time as being naked. Pin-stripes were erotic, the uniform of fathers, two-dimensional fathers. Even Mr Hughes's penis had a seductive pin-striped foreskin."

7. Aniruddha Bahal's *Bunker 13* winning passage from 2003 went thus: "She sandwiches your nozzle between her tits, massaging it with a slow rhythm. She is topping up your engine oil for the cross-country coming up." Err. I thought cross-country running did not involve petrol. Then again, I never heard of a penis described as a 'nozzle' before either.

6. Call me crazeeeee, but I kind of like my sex-talk to come without the anatomical references. In Tom Wolfe's *I Am Charlotte Simmons*, his talk of a hand having "the entire terrain of her torso

to explore and not just the otorhinolaryngological caverns," had the 2004 judges thinking like-wise.

5. When he called his first novel *Winkler*, the food critic Giles Coren might have known he'd be up for a bad sex award. He won the 2005 prize for describing his male character's bits "leaping around like a shower dropped in an empty bath."

4. The 2006 award went to Iain Hollingshead for his novel *Twenty Something*. "And then I'm inside her, and everything is pure white as we're lost in a commotion of grunts and squeaks, flashing unconnected images and explosions of a million little particles." More science experiment than sex then.

3. It's always a shame when writers receive a posthumous award. Perhaps not when it's for passages like this: "She took his old battering ram into her lips. Uncle was now as soft as a coil of excrement." Norman Mailer died before he could pick up the award for the bad sex in *The Castle in the Forest*.

2. Rachel Johnson claims to have been happy to win the 2008 award with her orgasmic 'Wagnerian crescendos' in the novel *Shire Hell*. More amusing is the line directly following the winning sex passage in the book. "I really do hope at this point that all the Spodders are, as requested, attending the meeting about slug clearance or whatever it is." So that's the kind of pillow-talk posh folk have then. Ooh. Sexy.

1. LIFETIME ACHIEVEMENT
"Do you want to see my vagina? Have you ever looked at one?" No, no. Not you. It's a line from John Updike's *Widows of Eastwick*, which helped him win the lifetime achievement award at the 2008 Bad Sex Awards for a career in erroneous eroticism.

HAVE I GOT NEWS FOR YOU?

Time to cast our spotlight of salaciousness on Angus Deayton, erstwhile presenter of the BBC's satirical news show mentioned above – until he was sacked for alleged misadventures of a sexual nature. In 2007, 'Aunty Beeb' forgave his wanton ways and he was welcomed back to present a new quiz show with open arms. Well, perhaps not that open.

LOVE LETTER TO A HOOVER HUMPER

The story of the Polish man who did unspeakable things to a hoover features elsewhere in this book. As does the foul-mouthed latter-day lothario Russell Brand. For this particular misadventure, I am pleased to combine these two carnally interesting components and come up with a brand spanking new misadventure.

Brand, having once himself been a hoover humper, wrote a letter of support to the bonkers builder early in 2008. *The Sun* revealed the content of the note: "The lure of Henry is a force I once succumbed to as a lonely youth, it was a reckless and impetuous act – I was in my teens and my options were limited. Henry was by no means my first choice." Still, at least a female was spared his advances, for once.

A VERY PECULIAR PRACTICE

Fisting. Not something everyone would discuss with their teens. Hence a scandal erupted in 2000, when presenters at a US teacher's conference tried to foster 'open discussion' on the practice, so that school children would be more aware of techniques used in gay and lesbian relationships. A representative from the Parents Rights Coalition recorded the state sponsored workshop and sent it to the

FEET ARE THE MOST COMMONLY FETISHISED BODY PART IN THE WESTERN WORLD media. In the brouhaha that ensued, the affair inevitably became known as 'Fistgate.'

THROUGH THE KEYHOLE

At the turn of the twentieth century it was not wise to be an openly gay man. It was even less wise to be openly gay if you were a public figure. Small wonder then, that Prince Francis Joseph of Braganza was forced to resign his post from the Austro-Hungarian Army in 1902 when he was spotted through a keyhole getting well acquainted with three other men. He was later rumoured to have become embroiled in further public sexploits in Hungary.

A KING'S RANSOM

In the 1930s, King Gustaf V of Sweden was held to ransom over a homosexual affair with a petty criminal. For many years the Swedish court paid Kurt Haijby 400 Kroner a month not to mouth off about his claim that he'd been having a right royal romp with the King for a 20-year period. Haijby agreed to emigrate to the States, but returned to Sweden in the 1950s, writing a roman-a-clef about the affair. The book was pulped by the court but was later reprinted, and Haijby was eventually done for blackmail.

DON'T TOUCH THAT DIAL!

Pat O'Brien is one of the USA's most famous broadcast journalists. Things went tits up for him in 2005 when he left a series of drunken, sexually offensive messages on a colleague's voicemail. He was invited to an extended stay in rehab shortly thereafter.

70% OF WOMEN WOULD RATHER EAT CHOCOLATE THAN HAVE SEX

FIFTEEN TIMES BITTEN, TWICE SHY

Marv Albert was America's golden boy of baseball broadcasting for over 30 years. The fairytale ended in 1997, when he was convicted of misdemeanour assault and battery charges. The vile voice-over artist admitted he'd repeatedly bitten his lover and forced her to engage in sexual activity graphically known as 'face-sitting.' He had also been accused of sodomy, but the charge was later dropped.

FAME, SET AND MATCH

There are times when a famous face on television has a glittering life-long career untainted by off-colour offences or salacious scandal. Britain's Frank Bough should be so lucky. Having enjoyed respect and fame as the front man for the flagship news show *Nationwide*, he became a laughing stock in the late eighties when he was unmasked as a man who liked to dabble in the odd misadventure of a sexual nature. He did not mend his ways, and was caught visiting an S&M prostitute in 1992.

MAKE MINE A PINT... SECOND THOUGHTS

There is a ridiculous sexual misadventure that is so firmly entrenched in urban legend that it is worth a mention in this book – whether it's true or not. The story goes that a star is rushed to hospital complaining of stomach pains, and immediately has their stomach pumped. Medics are then amazed to discover that the liquid content of the said star's stomach is an insanely huge amount of semen – a pint's worth in fact.

Many prominent stars have been named and shamed in this apocryphal misadventure. That it lives on with modern celebrities is testament to its enduring appeal. Or rather stomach-churning smuttiness.

PUMPKIN-ED UP

On February 5, 2002, police arrested a 22-year-old white male, resident of Dacula, GA, USA, in a pumpkin patch at 11:38 p.m. The unnamed man had been spotted by a passing police patrol car, enjoying intimate relations with the thickly-rinded fruit, in which he'd cut a one-inch hole. After his arrest the fruit fornicator gave a phone interview to local reporters from inside the Gwinett County Jail, describing the inspiration for his misadventure. "You know, a pumpkin is soft and squishy inside, and there was no one around here for miles." Then, in a moment of clarity, he added. " At least I thought there wasn't."

CROSS-DRESSED TO KILL

As sexual silliness goes, the mating habits of the octopus rank pretty high on the ridiculous scale. Finding a mate is a fiercely competitive process for this breed, so stronger males stick close to the side of females and often strangle any weaker wannabe suitors who happen to float by. To compensate, the feebler molluscs take to disguising their stripes to look more lady-like. Their randy ruse complete, they sneak past the dim-witted macho males and enjoy a little octo-pussy (sorry), often for much longer than their stronger rivals.

12% OF BRITONS HAVE TWISTED THEIR ANKLES DURING SEX

BOOB JOB

Four teenagers were charged with conspiracy to commit murder in Colorado over a sick plot to kill one of the group's mother. This was not an altruistic crime to seek vengeance on an evil or abusive parent. Rather, the breast-obsessed teen wanted to sell his dead mother's car to pay for his girlfriend's breast enlargement. The youthful assassins 'boobed' the job, and the mother escaped unharmed – well, physically anyway.

GOING APE # 2

If you're a frustrated lover and you believe in reincarnation, try not to come back as an ape. In 1986, when a sex-crazed ape went on the rampage, biting women in Indian's northern state of Haryana, locals thought the animal's unwelcome advances could only be explained by a rebirth. Nurses who'd been fondled and cuddled by the beast weren't convinced and chucked stones at him – whoever he might have been in a previous life. Eventually the ape was caught and was sent back to where he came from – that is, the jungle.

PICK UP A PENGUIN

In 2008, scientists recorded the first known case of a mammal attempting sex with another kind of vertebrate. Nico de Bruyn, of the Mammal Research Institute at the University of Pretoria, South Africa, spotted a male fur seal flattening a 15kg king penguin, the BBC reported. The penguin's ridiculous sexual misadventure lasted forty-five minutes as the seal humped and harassed to no avail. The young seal pup was apparently too much of a toy boy for the girly seals to fancy him.

BETWEEN 500 AND 740 SUICIDES A YEAR ARE THOUGHT TO ACTUALLY BE DEATHS FROM AUTOEROTIC ASPHYXIATION

WHAT A CATCH!

Ever eaten freshly-boiled lobster in a posh restaurant and felt a little guilty? Don't. Apparently the crustaceans are one of the most belligerent beasts on the planet. In fact, they're so punchy that female lobsters have to wee a sedative-like stream in the face of a male before they can perform any lobster love.

A LONG TIME 'COMING'

So, you're going through a bit of dry patch? Haven't had sex for, like, a week? Meh. Consider the microscopic species bdelloid rotifer, which scientists reported in 2007 had not had sex for... wait for it... 100 million years.

PRAWNOGRAPHY

Fish like porn. Yes, really. Porn. In 2003, researchers at the University of Fribourg discovered that male sticklebacks produce more sperm if they are shown some filthy fishy action first. We don't know the name of the film that was shown but here are a couple of educated (ahem) guesses: *Hali-butt Whores*, or *Pervy Pilchards* perhaps.

RODENT RHAPSODY

Ladies, ever had a man serenade you to seduce you into having sex? You're not the only ones. Scientists Tim Holy and Zhongsheng Guo discovered in 2005 that male mice often break into squealy song at the scent of a female mouse, and indeed that singing was an integral part of their mousy courting ritual.

A LAW IN FAIRBANKS, ALASKA, DOES NOT ALLOW MOOSE TO HAVE SEX ON CITY STREETS.

PENGUIN PROSTITUTION

Times are tough – the credit crunch is biting, so what's a lady penguin to do? Well, what else but to prostitute herself to passing males? Stones are essential for penguins to build their nests and a shortage has led standards to slip. So now female penguins, instead of collecting stones themselves for their nests, have been observed doing mating rituals in front of males and then running off with their stones. The hussies!

GOING TO THE DOGS

In 1994, Gordon Wilcox was arrested for having sex with a pit-bull terrier. The deviant act came to light when a video he'd made of the dodgy doggy doings were inadvertently shown to wedding guests expecting to see footage of a previous marriage ceremony.

NORTHERN EXPOSURE

In the northern British – and, at times, extremely cold – town of Newcastle, Jonathan Jason Harper exposed himself to women queuing to get into a night club in the December of 1986. To be fair, he wouldn't have been cold. He was wearing a full-length rubber wet-suit with a custom-made penis hole, a gas mask, and two hot water bottles hung in sinister fashion around his neck.

BAA'D NEWS FOR DUTCH SHEEP

A court in Utrecht, Holland, let a man off scot-free after he was accused of having sex with a sheep. The judge told a gob-smacked

ONE FIFTH OF MEN'S CHAT UP LINES ARE SEXUALLY EXPLICIT

court that under Dutch law bestiality is not a crime unless it can be proved the animal didn't want to have sex. And, the judge continued, it's not like they could bring in the sheep in question to testify.

DON'T STOP ME NOW # 2

An Aussie man parked in a no-stopping zone caught New South Wales police attention early in 2008 when he was seen pumping his penis into a pasta-sauce jar. They gave chase, but Kenneth Derek Battersby did not give up, continuing his 'saucy' self-pleasuring until police finally managed to bring him to a stop. Unbelievably, Australian news website news.com.au reports that the location for the pasta-jar-penetration was Nobby's Beach, on the Gold Coast.

THE WORLD'S BIGGEST GANG BANG

In 1995, Annabel Chong set a world record for the most sex acts carried out by one woman, engaging in 251 separate acts with about 70 men over a 10-hour period. The gang-bang was recorded and sold as a film imaginatively entitled *The World's Biggest Gang Bang*.

TOPPING UP THE PENSION

It's hard to get by on social security alone. What's an 80-year-old grandmother to do? Why, turn to prostitution and pimping of course. Granny Lynn Hope ran the August Playmates escort business from her two-bedroom apartment, and made $60 of every $160 she charged clients for one hour with a call girl until police caught up with her in 2001. She did not receive a custodial sentence.

STARING AT A BLUE SURFACE DURING SEX GREATLY INCREASES THE INTENSITY OF ORGASMS

SEX TRAP

Students were lured into a sex-trap in 1989, when a doctor enticed a number of young men at the University of Oregon into having sex with his wife. Colin Favour handed out leaflets asking men aged 18-23 to come forward to determine the "sexual potential of the mature female." Still, it wasn't all bad – they did offer £6 for each willing participant. It is unclear whether any of the students actually objected to the doctor's pervy plan.

FOOT FETISHIST FOILED

A Perth, Australia, man who was sexually excited by a teenager's shoe lunged at her in a busy shopping centre after "going into a trance." He was caught and placed on the sex offenders register, as well as having to wear an electronic tagging device which stopped him from going into shopping malls... Like people don't wear shoes anywhere else?

THE TRUE PATH TO PENIS EXPANSION

Arizona company CP Direct, which had sold over $74 million worth of pills that promised to enlarge penises or breasts, had its assets frozen by police in 2003. After the company went, ahem, bust, other similar outfits were forced to tone down their false promises. For instance forsize.com, which had promised "the true path to penis expansion" was forced to eat their words, admitting they could not actually "promise anything."

SPOT THE DIFFERENCE

A sexual predator got away with his crime in Hampden County, Massachusetts, in 2007 when a court ruled sex obtained through fraud is not a crime. Errol Glover had crept into his identical twin brother's bedroom and tricked his girlfriend into having sex with him. She could not tell them apart physically but he gave the game away when he forgot her name.

PRETTY MOUTHY POLLY

A British man's pet parrot let the cat out of the bag on his partner's torrid affair with a work colleague. The gob-shite parrot would squawk, "I love you Garry" as the owner, Chris, sat on the sofa with his girlfriend, Sharon. After dumping the girlfriend, the man reluctantly sold his parrot too. "I am surprised to hear he got rid of that bird," Sharon told *The Guardian* newspaper. "He spent more time talking to it than he did to me."

FOOTLOOSE FREAK

At the turn of the millennium, a phantom toe-sucker was at large in Maryland, USA. The man would approach women, and get them into conversation about their tights, saying he was looking to buy some hosiery for his wife. Having convinced them to remove their tights or stockings, he would then leap on them and suck their toes. Some 12 women were attacked over a six month period in 2001, only for the assaults to stop suddenly later that year.

ICE, ICE, BABY

Paramedics were called to the south London flat of Brixton local Damon Priestly after friends found him with his todger frozen to an ice-box. Claims that he'd only been goofing around fell on deaf ears when his flatmates discovered the kitchen area was littered with various fetish magazines. He suffered from 'burns' to his penis, but there was no lasting damage.

INTERNAL ILLUMINATIONS

A Pakistani prisoner who'd been arrested for making hooch had to be rescued by prison doctors when he woke up in his Multan prison cell with a glass light bulb in his anus. Doctors removed the bulb intact after an agonising one and a half hour operation. It remains a mystery as to how to the light-giving device ended up where the sun don't shine.

ANIMAL LOVER

Employers were quick to turn down Ralf Sweet for a job at the animal sanctuary in Barnstaple, England. Beady eyed staff recognised him from a local newspaper article which had shown Sweet's mug-shot after he'd been arrested for molesting animals while working at the local zoo.

IN THE DOG HOUSE

The Albuquerque animal shelter in New Mexico is home to animals that have been neglected or abused by their owners. Nonetheless,

Manuel Lopez Jr had no qualms about breaking in there in 2008, stealing a golden retriever and 'sodomising' it with a 'foreign object,' according to police. He had previously been arrested for allowing a Chihuahua to lick his genitals.

FULL METAL JERK-OFF

A man admitted himself to hospital in Bahrain, speechless and pointing to his stomach. However, doctors soon discovered a more acute problem, finding a two inch nail lodged in the patient's urethera. After successfully removing the nail, the man claimed robbers had attacked him and inserted the nail before stealing his wallet, the *Bahrain Gulf Daily News* reported.

CUT OFF POINT

In 2007, the *Minneapolis Star Tribune* broke the story that two men faced time in jail for trying to cut off a woman's underwear in a crowded American bar. Dominic S. Anscombe held the victim down while Anthony T. Hoban cut her knickers off with a pocket knife. Both said it was a joke. Police said they'd gone beyond the realms of anything remotely resembling humour.

ILLINOIS ENEMA BANDIT

Michael H. Kenyon was given the above moniker after terrorising women in the Illinois area in the late 60s and early 70s. He would break into homes, tie women up, and give them enemas. He ended up with 12 years in the clink, and died in 2004.

MEN WHO HAVE MULTIPLE SEX PARTNERS ARE LESS LIKELY TO BE SATISFIED WITH THEIR RELATIONSHIPS

TOP TEN PENIS MISHAPS

10. A Seattle man received 300,000 dollars in compensation after doctors were forced to remove his penis and one testicle due to a misdiagnosis in a prison hospital. A flesh-eating bacteria had worked its way from his torso to his nether regions with alarming and penis-annihilating results.

9. Fire-fighters rescued a 73-year-old man's penis with a 'wizzer' saw when he used a steel pipe as a sex-aid. Originally he had claimed the accident was a slip of the todger while he was doing DIY, but he later admitted to using the pipe as an ersatz vagina.

8. Penis envy got out of control at a urinal in Durban, South Africa, in 2008. When a man was teased over the size of his manhood in the toilets of a bar, he returned with five armed friends and opened fire. Three men died in the 'my one's bigger than yours' debacle.

7. When cannibal Armin Meiwes cut off and flambéed Bernd Jürgen Brandes' penis, ate it, and then killed him, the courts got in a tizz. The entire despicable event in the town of Rotenburg, central Germany, had taken place with Brandes' constent.

6. The *Times* of India told the story in 2006 of the 24-year-old man born with two penises who craved a normal sex life, and was undergoing surgery to have one appendage removed. The condition of Diphallus, or having two penises, affects about one in 5.5 million men world-wide. Others do it deliberately with knives, a body-modification process known as 'bifurcation.'

5. In London's busy Strand in 2007 a man ran into an Italian eatery, grabbed a kitchen knife and stabbed himself in the groin in

front of terrified customers. Surgeons were unable to reattach the penis after the self-inflicted castration.

— 4. A player for Spartak Moscow's disabled soccer team was brutally murdered by his friend's girlfriend in 2002, when he refused to have sex with her. Olga Romanov took rejection very badly during a heavy vodka session and cut off Pavel Morozov's penis, stuffed it in his mouth, and threw his profusely bleeding corpse out onto the street.

3. What's more bizarre? Cutting off your own penis? Or doing so because you think it will deter a male stalker? Over to Joey Katz who appeared on the *Jerry Springer Show* admitting he had cut off his manhood and flushed it down the toilet as a last resort to stop Ray Clemont's unwanted attentions. Next time, dial 911.

2. When Kenyan men were heard to be washing their genitals in battery acid to prevent AIDS, doctors warned them that the action could be more 'disastrous' than the syndrome itself. They might also have added. "Try using a condom..."

1. TWO PENISES TOO MUCH FOR ONE WIFE
A motorbike accident left Berni Ledochowksi one penis short of a full wedding tackle. Still, doctors in Berlin were able to build him a new one and he went on to father a child with his wife. However, all was not quite right and surgeons agreed to construct a new penis for the man – on the understanding the original replacement had to remain until they could be sure the second worked. On seeing the extra organ his wife decreed you can have too much of a good thing, packed her bags, and left him.

SELLER BEWARE

A woman selling old bras on Craigslist got a shock when 56-year-old Roland Gekko turned up to collect the items. As if seeing a man was not surprising enough, he then revealed a fake breast to the woman and forced her to touch it as he tried on one of the bras. He faced charges of battery and committing an unnatural and lascivious act.

WEE WIDDLE WINKIE

When a dishevelled young man was spotted hanging around the bras and knickers in a Madison department store, the security camera operator warned staff that a crime may be imminent. It was, but sneak-thievery was not involved. Instead, loser John Godfrey Doolan pulled out his penis and sprayed the lingerie with wee. He was immediately arrested.

ONE PENIS SHORT OF A COLLECTION

The Icelandic Phallological Museum offers visitors from around the world a close-up look at the long and the short of the male reproductive organ. Exhibits on display range from the sperm whale to the hamster – but the museum's owner Mr Hjartarson is now on the lookout for the one item missing from his collection: a human penis.

He had thought he was one step closer to his ambition when a local man offered his impressive nine incher, but the man eventually pulled out. "He has mentioned lately that his penis is shrinking as he gets older, and he is worried it might not make a proper exhibit," Hjartarson said, deflated.

THE WORLD'S MOST EXPENSIVE SEX DOLL COSTS £5,000

GET A ROOM # 2

A kinky couple who were having noisy sex in a field were arrested when a homeless woman who came across them thought the woman was being assaulted. The pair, who had met on Craigslist, looked guilty as hell, and fled the scene as police arrived – not because the sex was non-consensual but, as the man later told police, he did not want his wife to find out what he was up to.

MEMORIES ARE MADE OF THIS

Over 3,000 Canadian soldiers died at the 1917 Canadian battle at Vimy Ridge, commemorated now by a famous war memorial which has thousands of visitors a year. Hardly the setting for a ridiculous sexual misadventure. Or so you'd think. But Canadian authorities were reviewing security there when they discovered a number of swingers and doggers were persistently using the site to create memories of an altogether different nature.

PERVY POLLY

I'm no animal lover but I'd wager a parrot is easier to take care of than most other pets. That's probably why some choose to keep them, rather than a dog or cat, say. Pity then Jackie Lucking, whose pet parrot Shrek went bonkers for her feather hat and attempted to mate with the headpiece she'd been wearing at a family christening. When her hat was not up for it, the parrot had a go at Jackie's head instead.

STICK UP

Two bank-robbers indulged themselves in a 'stick-up' of a different nature during a bank job at the Credit Lyonnais bank in Rungis, Paris, in 1998. A third robber kept a gun trained on cashiers while the two accomplices had sex in full view of terrified customers and staff. The whole affair was over in minutes.

WIFE – AND HUSBAND – SWAP

Before TV's *Wife Swap* came the titillating but true tale of the Hungarian couple from Szekesfehervar (try saying that in a hurry!) who decided to swap places. In other words, they both had a sex change. Try as reporters might to interview the confused couple, neither of them were talking, Kossuth Radio reported in 1999.

FIRST KISS

A couple who taught abstinence to teenagers in Chicago married in 2008 after having had no intimate relations whatever, their first kiss being shared at the wedding altar. But Christian Agullo was lucky to get wife Melody up the aisle, never mind anywhere else. In order to marry, she had broken a seven-year vow not to date. The harlot.

RAMPY PUMPY

By way of Britain's *Daily Star*, we learn of the world's fattest man and how he was able to have marital relations with his bride on his wedding night. Friends built a 'sex ramp' which enabled Manuel

THE FIRST EVER CONDOMS WERE MADE OUT OF PIGS' INTESTINES

Uribe to consummate his marriage to Claudia Solis. The headline sizzling over this story was so apt, I've nicked it and used it above.

ANIMAL LOVER?

A 45-year-old man was uncovered by Expressen newspaper for controlling a sex ring for self-proclaimed 'zooiphiles', as well as being the 'brains' behind an internet animal sex chat room. Although the husband and dad of two admitted to sex with dogs, donkeys and goats, he was not arrested. In Sweden, it is currently not illegal to have sex with beasts.

HOW NOW DROWNED COW

When villagers from Julah on the island of Bali heard a local perv had been sleeping with cows, and one of the said cows became pregnant, they put one and one together and engaged on a ridiculous sexual misadventure. In a ceremony meant to cleanse the man of his sins, he was forced to drown the cow in the sea, flinging his clothes in the briny water at the same time in a bid to rid himself of his twisted tendencies.

SEXUAL POLITICS

A British town councillor was discovered to be a sex phone-call operator and a stripper. But Myrna Bushell told *The Sun* she wouldn't be giving up her alter-ego, "Jessica, The Devon Lady Kissogram, Strippogram & Stripper Entertainer." She resigned from her position in the town hall later in 2008, so it's probably just as well she clung on to the other job.

VIDEO NASTY

A Florida woman was so concerned about the mental state of her husband she asked for police protection in 2007. At the same time she handed police a video tape containing graphic scenes of said hubby torturing a live frog, live chameleons, and a parakeet, for alleged sexual gratification. She got police protection alright – she was thrown in the cells when police spotted her laughing in the background of the vile vid.

STOLEN GOODS

When Alan Bowers complained to police that his laptop had been stolen, things were not as they first appeared. It turned out that three hookers had taken the laptop as collateral when Bowers could not pay for a crack-cocaine-fuelled three-in-a-shower romp. For the sum of $150, he'd expected a gram of crack, the shower action, and the girls to pleasure themselves with a carrot. The skinflint.

MONEY BACK

When a major British bank put £100,000 in a Doncaster woman's account in error, she could have paid off her mortgage. Well, if she hadn't spent a third of it in sex shop chains, that is. We don't know if she was forced to return the goods when the bank asked for the money back. Let's hope not. She claimed that none were in the pristine condition she'd bought them in.

THE SEX TREE

A naturally-occurring Viagra-type substance in the Omuboro tree in Uganda gave – ahem – rise to its nickname amongst locals as the 'sex-tree.' Its aphrodisiac properties may prove its downfall yet, though. Professor Oryem-Orida was asking Ugandan men to poach their potency from elsewhere when in 2007 he announced the tree risked becoming extinct.

(MIS)ADVENTURE HOLIDAY

Airtours' website describes the Green Patch Resort hotel in Cancun as 'Strictly for grown-ups.' Unfortunately a third party bookings website for the hotel omitted this minor detail, to the shock of some Brits booking holidays there in 2005. Sex drinking games, orgies in the swimming pool and oral sex competitions were de rigeur at the Mexican hotel. Although many holiday goers complained about the hotel to Airtours, there was a silent majority who'd booked via the other site who said nothing at all. Wonder why?

TEENAGE KICKS

Women were masturbated at by hoards of marauding youngsters at markets in Greytown, South Africa, in 2002. The juvenile jerk-offs chose only women wearing revealing clothing, which is perhaps why the police refused to get involved. The women did not get much sympathy from members of the public, either. A stall holder, Mthavini Kotze told reporters she condoned the boys' action. "I wish they rape them one day so they may start respecting their bodies," she said. So much for sisterly solidarity.

NOT A DESPERATE HOUSEWIFE

When glamour-puss Eva Longoria fessed up to a love of sex toys in a magazine interview, fans sent her vibrators and dildos by the truckload. Her bosses told her to clean up her act, and she was asked, "Will you please stop saying vibrator?" Spoilsports.

TALKING DIRTY

A Long Island, NY teacher was sacked for talking dirty in his classroom when he was meant to be teaching physics. "What I say in this class better stay in this class," he told students as he boasted of his love of oral sex – both giving and receiving. Funnily enough his words leaked out of the class, and he was sacked.

WHO AM I?

Not content with assuming the identity of his ex-girlfriend, a 20-year-old Oslo man set up four profiles on a sex site based on three other women in his life. He then courted men to send in lewd messages, giving them information about where the women lived and what they liked to do in bed. He was jailed for six months for the malicious identity thievery.

MATRIMONIAL DIFFERENCES

In a fine example of stating the blindingly obvious, a Queens, New York, judge ruled in 2005 that being denied sex once by your husband is not sufficient grounds for divorce, no matter how bad the marriage is.

PRISON BREAKS

In 2005, murderer Mark Sawyer was given a sex change operation in prison at the expense of the Canadian tax payer. So far, so what, you may say. But even for liberal Canadians the information that Mark, now Celine, had been given sex toys "for medical purposes" as a form of "after care" was a human right too far.

ON THE ROAD

On the night of August 25, 2005 an unusual crime took place in Durban, South Africa. A 30-year-old man was walking along a quiet road, when he was ambushed by three women, bundled into a car, and forced to have sex with them at gunpoint. The women were never found, to the disappointment of male South African walkers everywhere.

WHILE THE CAT'S AWAY

Finding two hippies humping in your swimming pool is bad enough, but discovering they'd been using your holiday home as a porn palace must have been the last straw for Long Island, New York citizen Derek Adams. On checking his holiday home between lets in 2006, he was disgusted to uncover cigarette butts, condoms and porn accessories after chasing the horny hippies away from his garden.

ONE IN FIVE WOMEN MASTURBATE ONCE A WEEK

BALLS!

Police were able to identify a rapist by something he was missing in 2001. A 42-year-old Chicago woman told them that a truly stupid man had forced her to perform oral sex on him, so she bit off his testicles. Officers found a castrated man at a local hospital and "put two and two together," a police spokesman said.

SEX ON THE BEACH

In 2005, the Dutch Naturists Federation (NFN) tried to clarify the difference between its members and those who indulge in orgiastic displays of public slap and tickle. It asked the Dutch government for help, hoping it would set aside certain beaches for people who like to have sex in public. You can see the logic. "The police often mistake ordinary naturist walkers for a public-sex gathering. They send the naturists on their way or even issue a fine," a spokesperson for the Federation said.

BIG DEATH, LITTLE DEATH

The French call it 'la petite morte' (the small death), the melancholy moment after climax which is a mixture of joy (what fun we had) and sadness (when can we do it again?) For one woman that post-coital moment became 'la grande morte' (the big death) when her husband went at her with a claw hammer and killed her in Panama City in 2005. And why? She had asked him for a post-sex cuddle, while he wanted to watch TV.

END OF THE LINE

American bus driver Dustin Delorme ended up behind bars when he offered each of his passengers $40 to lift their shirts. Needless to say said passengers were not a coach-load of wrinklies on a sight-seeing tour, but a Pennsylvania cheer-leading team – average age 15.

FOWL MOUTHS

They must have seen it coming. Burger King launched a website in 2005 with a faux rock-band called CoqRoq, to advertise some new chicken products. The site showed photos of young women with captions saying "Groupies love the Coq." No sooner did the site go live than someone saw sense and the fast-food joint chickened out and closed it down. The fake band can still be seen on Myspace, though.

CON-TRACT

When a real estate agent received a six-page document at an open-house sale offering to buy a $100,000 house for $500,000, she could not believe her luck. Until she opened the file, that is, and found that the 'buyer' had listed six sex acts, A-F, which he expected her to carry out in return for the sale. Act B in particular catches the eye – the man suggested he would drive her to a remote location and they would then have sex. The canny agent humoured him and called the cops as soon as he had left the premises.

MAXIMUM POLITICAL CORRECTNESS

Say what you like about lads' mags (filthy, lewd, objectify women etc) but they could hardly be described as illegal. However, Stephen Short, 23, was banged up for six days by a judge when a copy of *Maxim* was found in his Florida home, along with a saucy poster and nudey calendar. As a sex offender, the judge stated that Short was committing a violation of his parole by owning "sexually stimulating" material.

PARK LIFE

A wanton workplace error led to Swansea, Wales, secretary Sarah Blackmore and partner Gwilym Isaac living in a tent in a municipal park. Blackmore lost her job when a smutty mobile phone video of her engaged in oral sex with Isaac was circulated to 300 colleagues.

PANTIE-MONIUM

Here's one way of livening up that boring supermarket shop. A 33-year-old British woman wore a pair of black leather 'Passion Pants' to her local supermarket, getting a thrill from the 2½ inch "vibrating bullet" inside them. The unnamed woman made the news when the thrill became too much: She fainted, bumped her head on a shelf, and landed a brief stint in A and E. Swansea hospital tactfully returned the vibrating pants to the unhappy shopper in a carrier bag.

THE LONG AND SHORT OF IT

Policing the police is a tricky business. Especially in sexual harassment cases, it seems. When a female Washington cop accused a colleague of rubbing his clothed, erect penis on her arm, two female investigators took matters into their own hands and measured the penis of the accused. As if that wasn't embarrassing enough, they said he did not 'measure' up, even when they added two inches to account for the erect state of the suspect male member. The male officer sued for harassment.

PUBLICITY STUNT

It took less than a day for German *Freizeit* magazine to sell out of copies when it included an ad for a free sex session at an Austrian brothel in its June 2005 issue. Anyone who snipped out a coupon from the mag was entitled to "half an hour of free sex with a lady of your choice." Ananova reported that the brothel saw a huge swelling in business following the ad.

MONUMENTAL SEX

Given their homeless status, it's not a shocker that Chris Sweet and girlfriend Tandy Taylor chose to knock their boots outdoors. But what made them climb the plinth of Baltimore's Washington monument in very broad daylight on the morning of July 7, 2003 for a very public and graphic sex display? Over to police Sergeant Harvey Gregory. "Both were naked and under the influence of a mixture of whisky, cannabis and crack cocaine."

TOP TEN NAUGHTY NUDISTS
(AND NEARLY NUDES)

10. In a bizarre twist of social mores, construction workers complained to police when in-line skater Gennifer Moss whizzed naked along the road for the city of Ashland's 2008 Fourth of July parade. She had asked for permission to streak, but police had told her to wear bikini bottoms.

9. From skates to a far less comfortable way of travelling in the altogether – cycling. In 2003, a San Marino woman was arrested – not for riding as nature intended, but because she purposefully rode to the side of the road and crashed her bike into a stationary vehicle while in the nod.

8. Naked burglars are de rigueur. There are a swag-bag full of them in this book. But burglars caught wearing not one, but two, pairs of boxer shorts are slightly less standard. A Florida man was arrested thus in 2007. His reasoning? His accomplice had inadvertently locked him in the house they were pilfering from. And that explains the two pairs of boxers how?

7. Arthur Allen was perhaps looking to reach the giddy heights of pleasure when he climbed a mobile phone mast in the nude. He spent 12 hours naked at the top of the tower in Colin County, USA, before police arrested him and charged him with criminal trespass, disorderly conduct and fleeing from police. His rap sheet did not include nudity.

6. As discussed in #8, nude burglars are a dime a dozen. Nude burglars who film themselves on a camcorder and leave the video evidence behind are worth their weight in gold. Not only did one booty-licious burglar do just that, but he forgot to wipe the

previous recording from the tape which showed all of his family members – many of whom were known to police.

5. What I love about human nature is the unfailing romanticism of some folk. Take Roger F. Watson, for instance. So proud was he of the perverted Polaroids he'd take of his missus, he plastered copies of the photos on car windshields up and down his street. Still, doesn't explain why he did his fly-posting stark-bollock-naked.

4. Drinking and driving, taking drugs and driving – both bad. But how about dangling and driving? Connecticut State Police arrested a man driving in the nude on a highway in 2002, and charged him with public indecency and breach of the peace.

3. I remember my 23rd birthday. In a club, probably got a bit messy. Not as messy as Michael P. Monn's. Breaking into a pool bar was his first mistake. Stripping naked and covering himself in nacho cheese was his second. Police said, "the nude male had a strong odour of alcohol and was semi-incoherent."

2. It's embarrassing enough to be arrested due to a squabble over your pet dog, but it's just downright ludicrous to be caught arguing over whether your dog should join you for a saucy shower. Called in by neighbours, police found one New York couple swapping blows to their cold – and totally starkers – bodies in just such a ridiculous row.

1. WHEN SADDO GOT STUCK IN THE CHIMNEY
There is such a proliferation of butt-naked burglars these days, how could we not place one in the number one slot? Garry Hoskins was arrested in Liverpool in 2002 sitting at the top of the chimney of a local supermarket, butt-naked, with a wrench half-way up his backside. Having got stuck in the chimney before he could carry out his crime, he decided to pass the time by using the tool for a different kind of breaking and entering, before the inevitable arrival of police.

JOKER JAILED

In 2005, an inebriated student got in trouble for making homophobic comments to a police horse. His quip of, "How do you feel about your horse being gay?" landed him a rather harsh night in the cells and an £80 fine.

DESPERATE MEASURES

Here's a novel get out of jail free card – a Bulgarian woman escaped a prison sentence for theft when she had a sex change operation while on bail. Bulgarian television's Nova Televizija related that a Sofia judge said she could not be charged as it was a man who had committed the crime.

KEEPY-UPPY

British researchers promised the launch of a 'condom safety device' in 2005, a chemical-impregnated contraceptive that would help men maintain an erection while wearing a sheath. Futura chief executive James Barder said about 2% of condoms slipped off during intercourse, resulting in unwanted pregnancies and increased risk of sexually transmitted infections.

ROYAL AIR FARCE

In 2005, Britain's BBC reported on a Ministry of Defence move to help ex-service personnel retrain for new careers after they've finished doing their bit for Queen and Country. The ridiculous sexual misadventure element crops up when a former RAF senior aircraftwoman was given money to train to become a pole dancer.

HELLO DOLLY (YET AGAIN)

Top tip: if you are returning a talking sex doll to the manufacturer, switch the darned thing off. So to Koblenz in 2003, when a German man caused a bomb scare at his local post office when the mannequin which he'd wrapped to look non-doll-like started to make weird ticking noises.

PREHISTORIC PENIS

Up for auction at a Beverly Hills gallery in 2007 was a rare prehistoric walrus penis. The member was 4½ feet long, and making it "the largest known mammal penis fossil," according to the I.M. Chait Gallery.

GETTING TO KNOW YOU

It's hardly surprising that a *Playboy* interview with the Russian politician Vladimir Zhirinovsky should get around to the subject of sex. However, freelance writer Jennifer Gould did not expect the interview would lead to sex itself. Urged by her subject that he would give good interview if she got to know him in bed, Gould politely declined. It's "blatant sexual harassment," the 20-year-old said.

96% OF FEMALE CELEBRITIES THINK FAME HAS IMPROVED THEIR SEX LIVES

SILVER SODOMISTS

The entire retirement community in Sun City West, Arizona, got a ticking off from officials in 2001. Maricopa County Sheriff spokesman Dick Cherry urged the elderly residents to quit their flagrant outdoor fornicating in community pools, spas and cars, on golf courses, golf carts and on park benches. Mr Cherry seemed embarrassed to have to describe the bad bonkers as both 'heterosexuals' and 'homosexuals'.

SPACE RACY

"There are millions of couples who want to try it and join the 400-mile-high club," the director of California's Space Island Group, Gene Meyers, told the *Mail on Sunday* in 2001. His plan is to take pocket rockets and eager beavers everywhere into outer-space, using specially designed love-cabins circling the earth's orbit. A quick look on the company's website eight years on reveals the plan to be lost in space.

SIX INCHES OF SEPARATION

A prudish headmaster banned his students from kissing and hugging in the street in Perth, Australia in 2001. Robert Haynes said that students of the opposite sex had to keep at least six inches between themselves on school grounds and in the local town. A good day for gays and lesbians in the school, then.

THE AVERAGE NUMBER OF SEX PARTNERS HAD BY MALE CELEBRITIES IS 82

PAYMENT IN KIND

An *Economist* report revealed that workers at the Akhtuba factory in Volgograd were paid in rubber dildos when the company ran out of cash in 1997. But sex-shops weren't interested in the merchandise, saying people were now only into electronic sex aids. The workers were left screwed.

SCREWS IN THE NEWS

In yet another example of wasteful misuse of the British television licence fee, the BBC paid London couple Tony and Wendy Duffield £12,000 to have sex for a TV documentary in 1994 with tiny cameras fitted to their respective sex organs.

The couple were in the news again in 1999 when an American magazine claimed the pair, who are both sex therapists, were called in to give advice to Tom Cruise and Nicole Kidman while filming the sex scenes in *Eyes Wide Shut*. Did a grand job, then. Not.

TROUBLE AND STRIFE

Downloading porn can hurt your marriage in more ways than one. An Athens, Greece, a man was looking at a free site with 'reader's wives' type home-made porn when he came across (not in that way) footage of his wife with another man. On confronting his wife he was relieved to hear that she did not know she was being filmed (good), but that she had been having an affair (bad). Her lover was arrested, seemingly having filmed many other young women without their knowledge.

THE AVERAGE NUMBER OF SEX PARTNERS HAD BY FEMALE CELEBRITIES IS 79

SACKED!

It doesn't take a genius to figure out that things which come in brown packages are often a wee bitty dodgy. Postman Seb Ellroy took this a step further in 1994, when he taught himself to recognise the wrappers of sex toy companies, stealing nearly eight sacks full of vibrators, condoms, and jazz mags from post he was meant to deliver. He was – appropriately enough – sacked.

FINISHED OFF

We've talked elsewhere in this book about the 'happy ending' men can receive in massage parlours of a certain ilk. 59-year-old Pradikto Suratno of Jakarta was hoping for such when he visited his regular masseuse in the summer of 1994. Unfortunately when the pummelling got a little too close to the boner, he had a heart-attack, and suffered an ending alright, albeit not a happy one: he died.

TOO COOL FOR SCHOOL

A rude but real wake-up call from our friends in the Netherlands now, where a 17-year-old boy was expelled for running a prostitution ring from his school. His expulsion was not to do with the nature of his 'business,' however – school officials took exception to his using school telephones to arrange the illegal assignations.

IT'S A DIRTY JOB

Thanks to Reuters, we learned that hard-up Romanian prostitutes were offering a personal service of a different nature in 2000.

Unable to get by on wages from living in sin alone, a Romanian escort agency put out ads suggesting that hookers could cook and clean as well. Might as well have gone the whole hog, suggest they "watch telly with you and look after your kids," and set up a marriage agency instead.

MIXED MESSAGES

"Grown men should not be having sex with prostitutes unless they are married to them." Words of wallydom from Rev. Jerry Falwell, responding to news that civil rights groups in Kansas objected to mug shots of men who'd visited prostitutes being shown on the telly. But if they were married, it is okay for the woman to be a prostitute then? Sheesh!

SMILE! YOU'RE ON CARNAL CAMERA

Let this be a warning to any wannabe sexhibitionists. Two videos appeared in the UK in the late nineties named Caught in the Act and Really Caught in the Act containing footage from insurance companies and security firms of couples caught doing the do in office cupboards, lifts and cars – or anywhere else you might find a security camera. Sequels are planned. Be warned!

REALLY BAD DAY

It's bad enough being accused of stealing another man's penis through witchcraft, but it really wasn't Baba Jallow's day when he was lynched by ten men for his ludicrous alleged hocus-pocus in the town of Serekunda in Gambia in 2003.

56% OF ADULTS HAVE NEVER HAD A ONE NIGHT-STAND

RANDY RAIDERS

If you're a sexaholic and you're going to raid a shop, it might as well be the Starship Enterprise sex shop in Stone Mountain, Atlanta, USA. And just think, with all that S&M gear around you don't even need to bring your own tools. In 2006, three masked raiders used the store's own leg irons to chain a shop assistant to a sink, while handcuffs kept the manager busy as the thieves made off with cash and a bumper hoard of sex toys.

PETRI-DISH PALAVER

Out-and-out stupidity saw a Brazilian biology teacher lose his job, as well as being sued by parents. When his Sao Paulo school told him he'd have to teach sex education, he took a practical approach, and asked three students for sperm samples so the class could study how sperm move under a microscope.

SHAFTED

A Russian woman asked for a divorce when her husband's penis extension broke off during a raucous romp. Considering they'd been married for 15 years, the sub-standard prosthetic must have been the tip of the iceberg. Doctors in Voronezh, southern Russia, had fitted the extension at her request.

BRIEFEST ENCOUNTER

A German tourist who'd just finished volunteering on a Kibbutz was arrested on the third floor of Ben-Gurion International Airport

23% OF ADULTS AROUND THE WORLD HAVE USED A SEX TOY IN PARTNER SEX

in 2001. Having some time to kill before her flight back to Munich, she'd wandered the airport car-park looking for nookie. She had one successful quickie, and was touting for another when the police car turned up and got to the bottom of what was going on with the nude blonde.

PLAN GOES WITHOUT A HITCH-HIKE

Sometimes people have real problems distinguishing between fantasy and reality. A couple had been watching a porno about a naked hitch-hiker and decided that acting out the movie could be the perfect end to a perfect night. It wasn't. Louise Malcolm was left shivering naked by the roadside for three hours before police picked her up. Her boyfriend had decided to view the film one more time and had fallen asleep.

THE PEPSI CHALLENGE

It's the old 'Thieves shoved an object up my bottom and ran away' excuse again. The location: A hospital, Pakistan. The inanimate object: A cola bottle. The theft: Two buffaloes. The diagnosis: Ridiculous Sexual Misadventure.

OH BROTHER WHERE ART THOU?

What do you do if you're worried about the size of your manhood and you plan to press the flesh for the first time with a new girlfriend? Well, if your name's Yuri Schmitt from Dresden, Germany, you ask your brother Andreas to step in. Although the siblings looked similar and the lights were out, the girlfriend rumbled the plan immediately and both men were arrested. The numpties.

THE FIRST COUPLE TO BE SHOWN IN BED TOGETHER ON PRIME TIME TELEVISION WERE FRED AND WILMA FLINTSTONE

IF THE MOUNTAIN WON'T COME
TO MOHAMMED

Prisoners in Massachusetts, USA, thanked their lucky stars in 1992 when a masculine-looking prostitute got herself put in a cell with 60 men. She managed to dole out her favours to two of the inmates before warders were tipped off. Whether she received any payment or was just looking for fun remains a mystery.

BAD BEDSIDE MANNERS

A German hospital patient got stiffed when he hired a prostitute to ease him through the long period of bed rest after an operation. The misguided guy gave the call-girl his bank card so she could get out her fee, but she withdrew more than 10 times the amount agreed, and he never saw her again.

PRICASSO

There are so many ways to make a living, it's a toughie to imagine how John Patch, otherwise known as 'Pricasso', settled on his trade. 'The World's Greatest Penile Artist' uses his penis to paint portraits, and offers his services by email or for occasions like hen nights, when he will paint portraits live... and yes, he does it in the altogether.

WHO NEEDS VIAGRA?

An energy drink gave Henry Knox more than he bargained for in 2007, when he woke with a severe case of priapism after drinking a can of health drink. Doctors were forced to drain blood from his penis to stem his erection, and Knox sued the company for the persistent woody.

ONCE BITTEN

A youngster was not taking no for an answer when he sidled up to a 39-year-old woman at the Tunnel Club in Hamburg, Germany on the night of April 3, 2007. It's a night he won't forget in a hurry. The woman undid his zip, pulled out his Johnson, and bit down hard on the shaft. She was later found to be six times over the drink-drive limit.

COOL AS CUCUMBERS

Getting frisky in the aisles of their local supermarket saw Kent, England, couple Heather Rice and Toby Dyer fined £250 by London magistrates. The cheeky pair did not show any remorse when found making love in one of the fridges in the busy supermarket. When asked by a security guard what they were up to, Rice quipped, "Chilling out."

CANNED!

Crushing beer cans between your breasts might sound like a great party trick, but not if you work in a public bar. An Australian bar-maid lost her job for the stunt, while her off-duty bar-maid friend who hung spoons off her cleavage got the can too. Amazingly the pair were also fined, for breaching hotel licensing laws.

83% OF ADULT MALES HAVE EXPERIENCED A 'WET DREAM'

INDECENT PROPOSAL

Italian porn star-turned-top politician Cicciolina did wonders for Europe's relations with Osama Bin Laden when she offered to have sex with him so he would "forget about terrorism" in 1996.

"He can have me in exchange for an end to his tyranny. My breasts have only ever helped people," she said. Which I am sure would go down well with the Muslim extremist, who believes that sex outside marriage is a sin.

ARMED TO THE TEETH

The prospective lover has all manner of weapons in his arsenal while at the local disco – cheap drinks, smooth moves, dodgy chat-up lines. One man tried a different tack when making a bid for a sexual misadventure at a German disco in 2006. He dropped his false teeth in a woman's cleavage as he made his exit. His quarry, Tina Lange, said "If he wants his teeth back, he'll have to ring me." You see – he's not so stupid after all... he ended up with her number!

DIRTY PROTEST

Considering what they get up to for a living, it's not surprising to hear that Bolivian prostitutes threatened a naked protest when officials closed all the bars and strip joints in their stomping ground. Still, they had a point. Even though locals complained that the bars and clubs were a bad influence on children, the hookers maintained they could not feed their kids without them. Conclusion: Impasse.

28% OF MEN CAUGHT MASTURBATING HAVE BEEN JOINED BY THE PERSON WHO CAUGHT THEM

A LICENCE TO LEER?

When a police officer in Fort Worth, Texas, spotted "multiple naked people" driving in a car at 2am, he immediately stopped the driver. Don't worry though. It wasn't real people. Instead Lt. Dean Sullivan found a guy who was driving under the influence of porn viewed on a ten-inch portable DVD. He was immediately arrested – not only did he not have a licence to leer, he didn't have a drivers licence at all.

SOMETHING TO CHEW OVER

A passenger on an internal flight in the USA was found to have an internal problem. Bleeping as he walked through security, he was given a body cavity search, during which security staff were stunned to find electrical wires protruding from a piece of chewing gum stuck up his fundament. The man told staff the bizarre bottom-blocker was of 'therapeutic value.' He was sent off for a psychiatric assessment.

A BUM STEER

Underwear manufacturer Sloggi made arses of themselves in 2007 when they launched a 'beautiful bum' competition. The Swedish and Danish public were invited to send in photos of their (albeit clothed) posteriors and the best one would be put to the public vote. Both campaigns were pulled when the Swedish media got their knickers in a twist over the morality of the contest.

51% OF WOMEN CAUGHT MASTURBATING HAVE BEEN JOINED BY THE PERSON WHO CAUGHT THEM

TOP TEN SEXUAL DISORDERS

10. Katoptronophilia. A mild-mannered paraphilia this one. I mean, it's not like anyone's going to get hurt masturbating or having sex in front of a mirror. Quite a few people like watching themselves and their partners getting it on. Unless of course you're one of those people who can't stand the sight of their own reflection, in which case I recommend one of the following.

9. Hybristophilia, for example, where women, generally, become sexually aroused or attracted to particularly vile criminals. Second thoughts, not sure I can guarantee your safety on that one. Next!

8. How about Salirophilia? This is the practice of making a mess of your lover via one of the following options: Mussing up their clothes or appearance by tearing them, covering your lover in mud or excrement, or bodging their hairdo or make-up.

7. Chronophilia is where folk get turned on by having a partner much older or younger than themselves – in polite circles such relationships are known as 'May to December' liaisons.

6. Fairly tame compared to Dacryphilia, where a person gets turned on by another's tears. The bigger and wetter the blubbing, the better. As such dacryphiliacs are often into S&M, relishing the moment of getting medieval on their partners and watching them squirm.

5. And now we delve into the downright weird, as we peek into the world of dendrophilia, or the sexual love of trees. And I don't mean in an eco-warrior tree-hugger type way. I mean in a god I fancy you, I'm going to ejaculate over you type-way. Bonkers.

4. Agonophiliacs get in sweat over... boxers getting into a sweat. They go all weak at the knees over combat sports of any description and often fetishize the equipment associated with such activities (ie boxing gloves/trunks, safety gear, martial arts.)

3. Abasiophilia is a psychosexual attraction to people who are less able to get around, those with crutches or in wheel chairs and the like. It is common for abasiophilia sufferers to also have an intense need to use these kind of medical aids, and even break limbs to get hold of them.

2. Chremastistophilia is a paraphilia whereby sexual arousal is obtained from being robbed, being held or alternatively from being charged. Since it's not likely you can force someone to rob you, the majority of Chremastistophiliacs just hang about in shopping malls. A lot.

1.SICKOS
There are some times in life as a hack where you come across a piece of information that you can dine out on for years, a factoid so humorous, so pants-wettingly titillating, you laugh every time you think of it. This is not one of them. Saved for last is the sexual disorder Emetophilia, or in common parlance, the sexual desire for vomit. And not just your own vomit, emetpophiliacs also enjoy making their partners vomit – a practice known as 'Roman showers'. Pass the sick bag – but not in a pervy way.

302

DOWN ON THE FARM

Move over pilots, farmers are the new sex gods! So said an Australian farm equipment manufacturer, who claimed their new hands-free tractor would be a boon for sexually frustrated farmers everywhere. "We've got the mile-high club in aeroplanes, well now we've got the auto sex club on auto-steer," a spokesman for the company said.

CONDOMS DON'T FLOAT PRIEST'S BOAT

The Rio Carnival isn't exactly known for being backwards about coming forwards. Nonetheless, the Catholic church was outraged before the 2004 parade, and not because of the gyrating hips, evocative music, or the elaborate costumes on show, but for a float that would promote condom use. "It is an incentive for sexual activity. It is propaganda and not prevention of illness," a church leader whined to media before the parade.

THE LADY VANISHES

Villagers in Yoxford, England, near the chi-chi seaside resort of Southwold, were gob-smacked in 1998 when a nude woman streaked through the town on a busy summer's day. She was spotted going into the village store, buying some pet food, and disappearing in a blur of flesh as she jumped into a parked Ferrari and whizzed off down the street.

THE AVERAGE MAN WILL EJACULATE 7,200 TIMES IN A LIFETIME

GETTING AWAY WITH IT

An anonymous letter tipped off the judiciary in Cobb County that one of their court officials was not the jobsworth he seemed. An investigation uncovered liaisons in hotels during work hours, solicitation of sex from employees, and obscene phone calls to female workers. And how long did the screwy official keep up his charade of professionalism? Twenty long, sexual misadventure-filled years.

THE DEVIL IN DISGUISE

A convicted sex offender turned up for his mug shot photo for the Illinois sex offender register wearing a wig, fake moustache and a pair of comedy spectacles. Amazingly police allowed his photo to be taken. His ruse was uncovered when a neighbour recognised him as she checked to see if any sex offenders lived in her area. When angry residents confronted police, they were blasé, saying "We photograph them the way they come in."

ALL WOMAN?

A German inventor claimed he had created a female sex robot that would out-woman any woman. Michael Harriman said, "I am still developing improvements and I will only be happy when what I have is better than the real thing." Better, how? Clue: The sex dolls don't talk and can be switched off. Let's hope he invents a male robot who can out-men men – a non-sexist sex doll inventor, for instance.

THE AVERAGE VOLUME OF SEMEN PER EJACULATION IS 2 TO 6 ML

FORGET ME NOT

If you've ever forgotten someone's name just after you've had sex, it's handy to know that scientists have come up with a convenient excuse. A 1998 *Lancet* report from Haematologists Dr Chi Van Dang and Dr Lawrence Gardner showed that tension in the abdominal muscles could make people suffer temporary amnesia after sex for up to twelve hours. Just try remembering that the next time you're caught out!

IT'S RAINING SEX TOYS

In October 2008, a Swedish ice hockey game had to be delayed several times because fans kept throwing things onto the ice. Rude things. Sex toys and dildos, actually. The bizarre deluge was meant to taunt player Jan Huokko, who had recently been caught up in a sex tape scandal. His team, Leksand, lost 3–2.

A NATION OF ANIMAL LOVERS

Being known mainly for breeding pigs is bad enough, but news reports that Danes advertize their animals for sex on the internet is even worse publicity for the country. One such animal owner told Danish newspaper 24 that his beasts were up for it, and had already had plenty of experience with humans.

FOUR HEADS ARE BETTER THAN ONE

It's every heterosexual woman's/gay man's (delete as appropriate) dream/nightmare (delete as appropriate): a four-headed penis. To the natural world again, and the amazing four-headed phallus

47% OF WOMEN DON'T BELIEVE THAT 'SIZE' MATTERS

– of the spiny anteater. Let's not be too alarmed though. When the animal has sex, only two heads swell up, to enable them to fit into the female reproductive tract. So (for the spiny anteater at least) two heads are better than four or one, after all.

DOUBLE STANDARDS # 2

Somebody had to do it. Punk musician Psichas (Psycho) and children's TV presenter Raudona were the first people to have live sex on Latvian TV in 2004. Psichas' musical career got a boost from the on-air antics; Red-haired Raudona got the boot.

HO-DOWN

Sex-workers in India perform an annual dance at a Varanasi cremation ground, to pray for better fortune in their next life. The dancers, called 'Nagar Vadhus' or 'City's Brides', are sex workers who are not allowed entry into temples, as they are considered 'impure'. "They dance and sing here so that they have a better life in their next birth and are able to be rid of this (prostitution)," said Baba Shamshannath, a priest.

NEITHER ARTHUR NOR MARTHA

Australia's *Daily Telegraph* reported in December 2008 that their official human rights watchdog has called for a third gender called "intersex" to be created for use on official documents like passports and driving licences. It would be a third legally recognised gender alongside male and female, in order to recognise the rights of transgender people and transsexuals.

MEN WILL EJACULATE 17 LITRES OF SPERM ON AVERAGE IN A LIFETIME

DOLLY BIRDS

It's an amusing, if not pretty, picture. In 2006, the Mexican government launched a TV campaign against sexual harassment in the workplace, featuring blow-up dolls dressed as secretaries and maids. The aim of the campaign was to suggest women are not sexual objects.

IF IT'S NOT ONE THING, IT'S THE MOTHER

Mothers are generally known for their unlimited selflessness. Not this one. Clare Barnes from Hull, England, was arrested for child neglect on the evening of December 3, 2005, when she turfed her sons Connor and Jaydon on the street so she could have intimate relations with her new boyfriend. The five and seven-year-old were found wandering a local park in sub-zero temperatures by a police car on patrol.

A BIT ON THE SIDE

A Chicago dentist who had rental space available in his condo let out rooms to pimps so prostitutes could do their business there, the *Chicago Sun Times* informed in 2006. If that wasn't bad enough, Harvey Pobjoy fixed the teeth of the working girls for free – those who had been battered by their pimps, that is. Weirdly Pobjoy also let the girls have use of his fleet of luxury cars. He got three years in prison for his moronic moonlighting in 2008.

STREWTH!

Magazines are known for publishing lists of 'Best Ofs'. New Zealand's *Truth* magazine is no different. In 2002, it published news of a website which had a feature on the best public toilets in New Zealand for sex encounters. Readers could not only find out what times were best for cruising, but could look forward to a weekly feature, Best Sex Toilet of the Week.

NOT AT IT LIKE RABBITS

Advertising a live sex show to promote the opening day of a new sex shop was bound to cause controversy. Women's groups and other campaigners had egg on their faces though, when they discovered Adam Bromley had planned nothing more than a publicity stunt with rabbits for his bawdy boutique's opening. The last laugh was on him: the rabbits drafted in from a local pet shop were both male and were not into gay bunny sex.

GOING OUT WITH A BANG

When you're about to pop your clogs, you might as well dream of your ideal exit strategy. A 72-year-old German man from Leipzig offered women cash if they could help him leave this world with a bang, a bonk, or a shag. This was reported in 2003, and it's not known whether the randy old sod is still knocking at heaven's door, in either way.

THE ONLY BDSM IN THE VILLAGE

A New Forest community campaigner, Thomas Craddock, was found dead at his English home wearing women's underwear and a white corset, with his hands and ankles bound together with stockings. He had been well known in his community for preserving the character of the village he lived in.

NO GANG BANGS

Outright despair at the number of killings in their city saw wives and girlfriends of gang members in Pereira, Columbia, calling a sex ban to urge their men to give up guns. The mayor of the city backed the move, which was christened 'The Strike of Crossed Legs.'

TRYING IT ON

When filling out job applications it's best to follow standard procedure. A Tallahassee, Florida, man did not, writing, 'Yes' in the slot next to 'sex'. I know, what a tool. But would you believe that the prize idiot then went on to sue the company who did not give him a job, citing discrimination as the reason. Proof, if it were needed, that schoolboy humour, sex and jobs don't mix.

EVERYTHING YOU WANT FROM A STORE

In 2002, a British supermarket chain spent over £200,000 on lighting to stop lovers getting up-close-and-personal in their wine sections. They needn't have bothered – later that year a couple chose to have sex in the loos at the shop's Basildon branch. Should have spent the money on their lavatories.

MADE TO BE BROKEN?

In 2001, the King of Swaziland fined himself a cow when he broke his own rule banning sex in his country. Angry young women protested at the violation, and 300 off them threw off their chastity tassels outside his palace, which they had been forced to wear as a warning for men not to come close.

BETTER SORRY THAN SAFE

A Milwaukee, USA, woman faced 15 years in prison and a $10,000 fine in 2001 for failing to prevent her son from being sexually abused. Her 'crime?' She gave her 13-year-old son a packet of condoms after learning the boy planned to lose his virginity with his 15-year-old girlfriend. The charges were later dropped.

FRESH FRESHERS

It was never a good idea. Authorities at an English college allowed two strip-shows, one male, one female, to take place in the 2001 fresher week, a time when new students get acquainted with their surroundings... and with one another. The strip-shows got out of hand as students joined in the act, and it was claimed that full sex took place on stage. Just another night at the students union, then!

15% OF WOMEN HAVE MULTIPLE ORGASMS

GOING FOR GOLD!

The Gold Club strip club in Atlanta, GA was closed in the late 1990s when authorities discovered the place was a glorified knocking shop. The club's owner went on trial in 2001 on racketeering charges that included prostitution, credit card fraud and money laundering. Witnesses who said they'd received oral sex from dancers at the club included many sports stars.

SPANK YOU VERY MUCH

The British press reported in 2008 on the story of Peter Jones, a London solicitor in his 50s who moonlights as one of London's most sought-after spankers. For eight years he has spent many an hour with women on his lap, spanking them with his bare hands, canes and paddles. If you're wowed and not wincing by this revelation, you'll be pleased to hear that the spank-meister has penned a book about his spanking (mis)adventures entitled, *The True Confessions Of A London Spank Daddy*.

STILL GOT IT IN 'EM

If you're sensitive about your mum and dad doing it, never mind your grandparents, I'd skip to the next misadventure. If you're slightly more thick-skinned, I can reveal that researchers from the Kansas Centre for Ageing suggested that we humans can, nay should, remain sexually active into our 80s and 90s. With this in mind, the report's authors suggested that staff in nursing homes should be better trained to cope with the sexual needs of the over-70s.

IT IS POSSIBLE FOR WOMEN TO HAVE TO UP 20 ORGASMS IN A ROW WHEN MASTURBATING

ROLL UP, ROLL UP!

A Craigslist raffle was investigated by police when it was brought to light that the main prize was an evening with a prostitute. To add to the weirdness of the ill-judged affair, the prostitute's day job was as a child sex-abuse caseworker, police said.

TAKING IT UP A GEAR

A tale abounds on the internet with such liberal enthusiasm, it'd be rude not to think it true. The story goes that a young man and his girl-friend are at a drive-in movie, when he slips her an aphrodisiacal Mickey-Finn in the form of Spanish Fly. The mischievous maiden becomes so aroused while her boyfriend nips off to buy some popcorn that she uses the gear-stick as his replacement, and impales herself upon it. Arousing? Certainly. Apocryphal? Your call.

VERY BLUE TOOTH

A new technological advancement provided a new way to arrange impromptu sex encounters with strangers. According to Reuters in 2004, users of Bluetooth phones were abusing the technology as a quick way of getting nookie on commuter trains. Instead of 'dogging', the 'craze' was known among practitioners as 'toothing.' One unnamed source said one of the best routes was the London to Brighton rail commute. It was later claimed that the whole 'phenomenon' had been dreamed up by a bored journo, although you can bet it gave some people ideas...

MEN AND WOMEN BOTH VIEW THE OPPOSITE SEX AS 50% MORE ATTRACTIVE AT CLOSING TIME IN SINGLES BARS AND CLUBS

IF AT FIRST YOU DON'T SUCCEED

Serial shagger Keir Owen slept with 100 women he'd met via the British Dating Direct website, according to the *Daily Mirror* in 2004. The 55-year-old male subscriber was dumped by the agency after a number of women complained regarding his "lack of commitment." Owen told the paper he just hadn't met the right woman.

SOUNDING OFF

Ella Ploiesti, from Prahova county, Romania was overjoyed when she got a job as a sex phone line worker (so we're told by the *Ziarul* daily paper). Joy soon turned to despair, however, when a regular client recognised her voice in a shopping centre, and beat her to a pulp when she did not look as he'd imagined.

Brave Ella said she'd carry on regardless. "As I don't look so nice and one of my legs is shorter than the other I could hardly find a job. When I finally got one it was only because I have this special voice which turns men on."

LOST AT SEA

Ralph, an Australian lad's mag, had spent over £100,000 on 130,000 inflatable boobs to give away with its January 2009 issue when they fell off a container ship travelling from Beijing to Sydney. Quick question. Just, why?

GNOME RESPECT

Romanian, Cristi Birgu, 27, came up with an unusual way of drumming up custom for his garden gnome business. He erected dummies of prostitutes on the road outside his garden centre, much to the disgust of neighbours. Mr Birgu said, "So far, my girls have attracted a lot of beeping from truck drivers but not too many customers. Sometimes I am afraid somebody might have an accident, arrested by the view, you know."

NOUGHT SO QUEER AS...

In 2001, Austrian folk pop singer Christian Anders allowed millionaire Michael Leicher, 34, to do the do with his 20-year-old girl-friend for a year for the princely sum of 500,000 marks. After initially being shocked by the agreement – made behind her back – Jenna Kartes signed a contract which included a one-year extension option, because Anders needed the money for a replacement liver. Punchline: He married someone else in 2006.

NO LAUGHING MATTER

In November 2008, a new political party gave Australian voters a wider choice in the voting stakes. The Australian Sex Party promised to "Address the sexual needs of Australia in the 21st century." It's slogan: "We're serious about sex."

LESSONS IN LUST

Who says the world is dumbing down? A university in Taiwan has opened a course, offering to teach students in the fine art of decoding and understanding one of the last subject areas to be intellectualised: porn movies. The Mass Communication Department of Providence University started the course early in 2009, and was deluged with applicants. One worried student, who did not wish to be named, commented: "If I get a very good score in this course, I don't know how I'll explain it to my parents."

YOUR EMBARRASSING SEXUAL MISADVENTURES
NOTES

YOUR EMBARRASSING SEXUAL MISADVENTURES
NOTES

YOUR EMBARRASSING SEXUAL MISADVENTURES
NOTES

YOUR EMBARRASSING SEXUAL MISADVENTURES
NOTES

YOUR EMBARRASSING SEXUAL MISADVENTURES
NOTES